FLORIDA STATE
UNIVERSITY LIBRARIES

JUN 15 1998

TALLAHASSEE, FLORIDA

KARACHI

Megacity of Our Times

KARACHI

Megacity of Our Times

Edited by
Hamida Khuhro
Anwer Mooraj

Karachi
Oxford University Press
Oxford   New York   Delhi
1997

DS
392.2
,K3
K3
1997

Oxford University Press, Walton Street, Oxford OX2 6DP

Oxford   New York
Athens   Auckland   Bangkok   Bombay
Calcutta   Cape Town   Dar es Salaam   Delhi
Florence   Hong Kong   Istanbul   Karachi
Kuala Lumpur   Madras   Madrid   Melbourne
Mexico City   Nairobi   Paris   Singapore
Taipei   Tokyo   Toronto
and associated companies in
Berlin   Ibadan

Oxford is a trade mark of Oxford University Press

© Oxford University Press, 1997

All rights reserved. No part of this publication may be reproduced,
stored in a retrieval system, or transmitted, in any form or by any means,
without the prior permission in writing of Oxford University Press.

This book is sold subject to the condition that it shall not, by way
of trade or otherwise, be lent, re-sold, hired out or otherwise circulated
without the publisher's prior consent in any form of binding or cover
other than that in which it is published and without a similar condition
including this condition being imposed on the subsequent purchaser.

ISBN   0 19 577806 5

We would like to thank Ahsan Yameen, M.A. Wali, Asif Noorani,
Rabia Zuberi, Ali Imam, Shahid Sajjad,
Mahmood Usman Khan, and Mubarak Ahmed
for their photographs.

Printed in Pakistan at
New Sketch Graphics, Karachi.
Published by
Ameena Saiyid, Oxford University Press
5-Bangalore Town, Sharae Faisal
P.O. Box 13033, Karachi-75350, Pakistan.

CONTENTS

INTRODUCTION

'You will be the glory of the East; would that I could come again to see you, Karachi, in your grandeur!'

Sir Charles Napier uttered these well-known words with an awesome perspicacity as he gazed at the congested small town perched on the edge of the Arabian sea. This was the Karachi, the fledgling sea port of Sindh that he had captured for the British in 1843 and which had existed precariously for several centuries before. It had never until then had much of a purpose: hardly relating or connecting to its massively important hinterland where the river Indus had for a millennia produced a prosperous and settled civilization of great renown.

It is hardly likely that Napier envisaged the thundering great megacity which is Karachi today, but he imaginatively realized that it would play a hugely important role in the global world which the industrial and social revolutions and upheavals of the nineteenth century were bringing about.

During a hundred years the British fashioned Karachi into a successful commercial city. It was well planned, well run, with wide streets, open spaces, a sufficiency of public buildings, and most of the conveniences that a thriving merchant class required. During that time, the foundations were laid for a growing economy based on the commercial activities of Karachi's port which the British quickly exploited and encouraged.

In 1936 the city became the provincial capital of Sindh, when that province was separated from the Bombay Presidency. This gave the city a focal point for the political activities and acumen of a generation of local Sindhi politicians who had worked and argued with their imperial masters. Soon the arguments were to dissolve into a bitter fight to remove the British altogether, and when they finally departed with the creation of Pakistan on 14 August 1947, Karachi was suddenly catapulted into becoming the capital city of the newly made state of Pakistan. From that moment its fate was sealed. From a city of 450,000 people, with a reputation for being one of the best maintained cities of South Asia, it helter skeltered in a demographic onslaught which only a few cities in the world have matched. Now in the mid-nineties, even though it ceased to be Pakistan's capital in the early sixties, it is likely that the population of Karachi could be somewhere in the region of eight million.

The city's headlong unbalanced growth has resulted in an unprecedented, unplanned urban sprawl, covering over fifty square miles where woeful under-funding and a total lack of managerial capacity have resulted in pitiful living conditions for a majority of the city's residents. But still the newcomers, the migrants pour into the city. So much so that the United Nations, in a recent report on the world's population, estimates that Karachi by the year 2015 will be one of only five cities in the world to have populations of over twenty million. That hardly seems credible. Growth of such dimensions are just not sustainable. The city cannot possibly sustain the continuous impoverishment that has occurred in the last fifty years of its explosive growth.

Karachi today is a relatively unsung, unromantic city, raw, new, turbulent, post modern. Most cities have a weight of writings, literature and poetry telling their story, but Karachi has inspired very little in that quarter. The editors and contributors are thus keenly aware that they have had a difficult task in delineating the story and the present position of this lightly documented city, and very sensible that in their undertakings they have often moved in uncharted and unfamiliar territory. If our work inspires readers to look with more favour and fondness on Pakistan's own megacity, to enquire further about its state, and maybe to improve its lot, then our labours will have been worthwhile.

This book about Karachi, the only 'city' of Pakistan and its first capital, is an offering in the golden jubilee year of Pakistan. It covers most aspects of life in the city, but cannot claim to be a comprehensive encyclopaedia by any means.

We have not, for instance, given any account of the different historic communities that live in Karachi: the ancient coastal people of Lyari—the irrepressible

Makranis—who take their name from the Makran coast of Sindh and Balochistan and indicate a common history of the two provinces; the Mir Bahar of the sea coast, include the Bhattis who live on the islands of Bhabha and Bhit and other coastal areas of Karachi; the Numrias, a major tribe of the area, the Burfats; the Jam of the Jokhias with his headquarters in Malir who used to provide safe passage for caravans from the eastern borders of lower Sindh to the Lakki mountains of Sehwan and Dadu; the Palaris who live in the area through which the new 'Super Highway' passes; the Hindu communities the Amils and the Bhaibund, who dominated the administration and the business of the city respectively. It was the Bhaibund merchants who came to Karachi from the interior who brought the initial prosperity to the city through their trade. Very few of this community have remained in the city after 1947, but Karachi owes them a debt of gratitude for their public works and philanthropy, the signs of which remain visible to this day.

The town of Karachi was a conglomeration of neighbourhoods or 'villages' that included not only the ancient villages of Jokhias, Memons and Mir Bahars on the fringes of the old town, but the picturesque and characteristic neighbourhoods of Silawats who live in the central areas of the city. They immigrated centuries ago from Rajasthan as stone workers to live in the capital of Sindh: first Hyderabad where they made their unique contribution to that city, and then to Karachi when this city was being built in the nineteenth century. Khojas, as the Ismaili followers of the Aga Khan are known, live in communities around their Jamaat Khanas on Britto Road, and in the old town near Khadda. The small Jewish community with their synagogue on Lawrence Road lived around it and on the edges of the Government (or Gandhi) Garden. This and the Bahai community, that had come as refugees from Iran, were among the more prosperous communities of the town. The Bahais owned the inexpensive but excellent cafes, the Irani restaurants, in the city. The Christian Goan community of Karachi lived around St. Patrick's Church in Saddar and in the Catholic Colony on Bunder Road. Here also was the upper middle class Parsi Colony, with its well built and good looking houses, bordering on Amil Colony and the minuscule upper middle class Muslim Colony. The Bohra community that came to Karachi in the nineteenth century and was mainly a trading community, lived in the city around the Civil Hospital, where it had its beautifully built mosque and in spacious apartments around Bunder Road and Burns Road. These neighbourhoods of the city, unlike the new 'colonies' of Bunder Road Extension, were not exclusive and the Bohras, Khojas, Memons, and Hindus lived cheek by jowl, as near as possible to their places of business. There were also the itinerant migratory groups, the Brahuis, Bhils and Kolhis, the permanent 'scheduled' caste communities, and so many others who came to this city to make their lives and their fortunes.

The history of these communities, their customs and cultural activities would make very interesting study, but falls outside the limited scope of this book as does any detailed history of the post independence immigrant groups. There is certainly scope for a social and anthropological study, or studies, of the communities of Karachi that could form an endless supply for academic studies. Karachi has a large number of satellite *abadis* of immigrant groups from up country, such as Pathans and Punjabis, for instance who have played a very positive role in the development of Karachi: the former in physically building it and the latter in adding to the prosperity of the city through trade, industry as well as in crafts such as wood work. The foreign migrants, mainly illegal, such as Bengalis, and innumerable other nationalities have also provided services to the rapidly growing city and although resented for taking away jobs from the locals are in the process of being assimilated. To deal adequately with these new additions to Karachi's population would be an immense task requiring a different kind of book.

Karachi is above all a city of opportunity as generations of migrants have found. The immigrant either makes good as an entrepreneur in the city, or he tries to use it as a conduit to greener pastures in the Gulf or the West. The population of Karachi is upwardly mobile, at least in its aspirations. The middle class life of 'English Medium' schools for their children, a flat in a high rise building or a small independent 'bungalow' is the aim of the majority of Karachi citizens.

No story about Karachi would be complete without an account of the pioneers of trade and industry in the city. Chapter five includes profiles of some of the early traders of the colonial period who used a part of their wealth to benefit the city. Haridas Lalji was an entrepreneur who organized the Buyers and Shippers Chamber for which he built the handsome building (opened by M.K. Gandhi in 1933) which is now the Chamber of Commerce building.

There was hardly any industry in the area which is now Pakistan and therefore hardly any industrialists to speak of. The owner of the Dalmia cement plant was not a resident of Karachi and the only local magnates were Nusserwanji with Sind Patent tiles and sundry other interests and Mohatta with Herman Mohatta Iron works— although of course smaller industries such as leather work, aerated waters etc. abounded. The decision to make Karachi, seriously, the home of industry came in the post war world of 1946. Plans for an industrial estate were approved and investment in industry was encouraged. The Government of Sindh funded the first industrial unit to be set up in Karachi, the Valika textile mill. This was followed quickly by the Bawany textile mill set up in 1948 and the path was clear for the city to become the biggest industrial city of Pakistan which paid seventy per cent of the revenue of the country in its heydey and still continues to be responsible for a large chunk of the national income. The majority of the industrial pioneers were Memons and these included some very distinguished names such as Adamjee, Ahmed Dawood, Rangoonwalla and others. Karachi's position as the finance centre was established by the pioneering banks such as Adamjee's Muslim Commercial Bank set up at the initiative of the Quaid-i-Azam and the Habib family's Habib Bank.

Two hundred years from its founding as the port of Sindh, and fifty years from its position as the only port of Pakistan, Karachi has an undisputed place in the economy of the country and in the affection of its citizens. This glowing capital of Sindh is loved in spite of its glaring shortcomings. In the imagination of the people it stands for a lifestyle that is at once modern and yet more leisured than the frenetic megacities elsewhere. At the heart of the city is nostalgia for a calm oasis of a fifties Saddar, and a tram journey from Keamari to Soldier Bazar. Karachi is above all a cosmopolitan city which demands civilized attitudes from its most unruly citizens. It is this mainstream Karachi that this book is about.

The first four chapters of the book cover the history of the city from its early barren beginnings to the middle of the twentieth century when it became the capital of Pakistan. In the fifth chapter profiles of some of the founding fathers of Karachi have been given. This is, of course, an arbitrary selection to the extent that the limitation of space has restricted the number of the major Karachi personalities that could be included. The economy and the expansion of the city in the last half century have been covered in chapters six and seven. The next three chapters give an account of the contribution of Karachi to the literature of English, Urdu and Sindhi. The chapter on Saddar describes the centre of colonial Karachi.

The world's largest cities in the twenty-first century.

Population, millions
— 2015 (projected)
— 1994*

* 1995 figures for Delhi, Dhaka, Lagos, London, Karachi and Manila

No increase projected for London and Osaka

Population living in urban areas

%
90
80
70
60
50
40
30
20
10
0

1950 1970 1995 2025

Entire world
☐ Less-developed regions
■ More developed regions

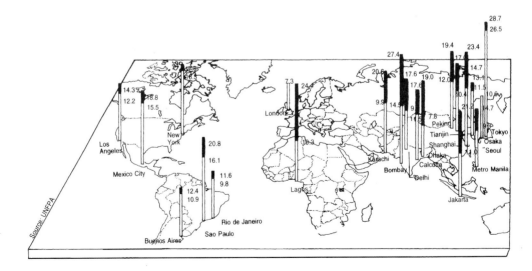

Source: UNFPA

Karachi has often been accused of philistinism—of indifference to culture. In addition to the literature and poetry, we have gathered up the admittedly fragile strands of culture and entertainment in the chapters on art, entertainment, theatre and cinema which include both the elite and popular culture of the city. A notable omission is the popular culture of Lyari and the Makrani community that includes wonderful dances, games, and donkey races. Also, unfortunately, it was not possible to have a chapter on sports activities in Karachi. That would appear to be a glaring omission for which the editors apologize. It is to be hoped that this omission will be filled in the next edition of the book. We have tried to capture the contrasting mood of the city over the last fifty years by giving two personal accounts: that of being young in the fifties by Anwer Mooraj and of being young in the nineties by Ayela Khuhro.

The humour of the book is optimistic. We feel that the citizens of this megacity are capable of dealing with their problems. Karachi is a new city but it is old in its wisdom and tolerance. It is the capital of a supremely tolerant land— the land of sufi saints. Before it ever became a city it was a land of shrines. Pilgrims came to Rambagh—a stage in the journey of Rama and Sita,* as well as to old saints like Mangho Pir. They would then continue on the journey to legendary shrines like Hinglaj. The legacy of the saints must prevail. Akbar Zaidi's article on the future prospects of Karachi details the problems that Karachi faces today, but he points a way out of the quagmire of administrative failure, and complex and destructive politics. These or other solutions cannot be out of the competence of Karachi citizens, and indeed of the country, for all of whom the city is their gateway to the twenty-first century.

---

* *Rambagh, now called Arambagh, is in the heart of the city near Burns Road.*

ACKNOWLEDGEMENTS

We would like to thank the contributors for their ready co-operation, their willingness to meet deadlines and above all for their excellent articles on which depends the quality of this book.

We would also like to thank the individuals who contributed the illustrations and photographs from valuable collections. Among those we would particularly like to thank are: S.M. Shahid, Syed Hussain Razi of Razi Photographers, the Haroon family and Herald Publications, Dr Durreshahwar Syed, Arif Hasan, Hamid Zaman, Noman Ahmed, Asif Noorani, the Mooraj family and the Khuhro family. Our particular thanks to Shamyl Khuhro for his drawings of the forts of Karachi and Manora island from Charles Masson's original sketches. Thanks are also due to Mr Wali for his excellent photography.

We would like to thank Dr N.A. Baloch for the material and help in filling in the historical blanks about the origins of Karachi, and Khadija Baloch for the material on Sindhi literature. Our thanks also to Mr Ardeshir Cowasji for turning up trumps with a write up and photographs of his two grandfathers. Mr G.M. Adamjee and Mr A. Karim, Mr M. Yahya Bawany and Mr Ismail Bawany for information on the early years of post-independence industrialization of Karachi. Mr P.K. Shahani has been, as ever, a valuable source person for information on the city and its history.

Thanks are due to Mahesh for his hard work on the computer and other secretarial work in connection with the preparation of the book. Thanks also to Mr Mohammed

Ijaz Hussain and Mr Amjad Ali for their data collection and compilation.

Grateful acknowledgement is also made to Mrs Rita de-Souza for her invaluable background information on the Karachi Goan Association, to A.K. Siddiqui, and Tariq Mahmood of the Railway Hall Institute for allowing Ms Shahbano Alvi of the Oxford University Press, to photograph the club premises, to Muzaffar Hussain, a former Secretary to the Government of Pakistan, for his valuable comments on night life in the fifties, and to Fakir Mohammad and Shafiullah, music teachers at the PAAC for checking that the section on native style entertainment does not contain any inaccuracies.

Our grateful thanks to Elisabeth Davies for her ideas and her help in planning the book in the early stages and her weeding out of the more extravagant notions.

Shah Abdul Latif, the eighteenth century sufi poet reciting his verses to a disciple in a cave near Karachi.

Chapter 1

HOW IT ALL BEGAN

Hamida Khuhro

Although Alexander himself did not set foot in Karachi or any of its ancestral townships, and Krokala cannot be identified with Karachi, it is a historical fact that the commander of his fleet, Admiral Nearchus, anchored very close to the harbour of what is now Karachi. We know that Alexander explored the Indus delta and chose a river on the eastern side for Nearchus to sail down to the ocean with his fleet[1]. Thus Nearchus set out from Patala, some distance north east of present day Nasarpur and sailed down the Indus (Sinthus or Sindhu) to Barbaricum, a harbour at the mouth of one of the eastern branches of the Indus, and then went on to the island of Krokala in the Gulf of Eirinon. The Gulf of Eirinon is identified as 'some portion of the mangrove swamps extending along the delta coast from some spot to the east of Barbaricum up to the eastern Indus branch or even beyond'.[2] It is mentioned by Arrianus as 'Crocala, the promontory called Eiron and Alexander's Haven.' About Alexander's Haven, a recent historian of Alexander's campaign in India says

> In the course of time Nearchus' choice of Alexander's Harbour proved to have been a good one. Its star rose high in the history of commerce. It lost, though, its original name which was replaced by the name of the island which lay at the heads of the harbour. By popular etymology the name of Bibacta or Bibaga changed into Barbaricum....[3]

and further that

> The Gulf of Barace represented only a small portion of the wide bay of the Arabian sea between the island of Cutch and

the Indus delta. The Gulf of Eirinon was situated along the delta coast adjacent to the Gulf of Barace, and it derived its name from the dangerous mangrove swamps. As to the chain of hills, which rose high above the coast and both the Gulfs, its fame was perpetuated throughout Antiquity by the Altars of Alexander, which were erected, most probably, on top of the promontory near the northern entrance to the Gulf of Barace.[4]

After a prolonged stay at Alexander's Haven, Nearchus sailed along the Sindh coast and reached a place near the Hub (*Arabis*) river. He anchored in a delightful harbour which he calls 'the ladies pool'. Arrianus describes the position

Then making their way through two rocks, so close together that the oarblades of the ships touched the rocks to ports and starboard, they moored at Morontobara, after sailing some 300 stades. The harbour is spacious, circular, deep and calm, but its entrance is narrow. They called it in the natives's language 'the ladies' pool', since a lady was the first sovereign of this district. When they had got safe through the rocks, they met great waves, and the sea running strong; and, moreover, it seemed very hazardous to sail seaward of the cliffs. For the next day, however, they sailed with an island on their port beam, so as to break the sea, so close indeed to the beach that one would have conjectured that it was a channel cut between the island and the coast. The entire passage was of some 70 stades. On the beach were many thick trees, and the island was covered with shady forests. About dawn, they sailed outside the island, by a narrow and turbulent passage; for the tide was still falling. And when they had sailed some 120 stades they anchored in the mouth of the river Arabis. There was a fine large harbour by its mouth; but there was no drinking water; for the mouths of Arabis were mixed with sea water. However, after penetrating 40 stades inland they found a water-hole, and after drawing water thence, they returned back again. By the harbour was a high island, desert, and round it one could get oysters and all kinds of fish. Up to this the country of the Arabeans extends; they are the last Indians settled in this direction; from here on the territory of the Oreitans begins.[5]

Ladies Harbour has been identified as being near Manora and this brings Nearchus' fleet very close to the present day Karachi harbour. The river *Arabis* has been identified as the Hub river by Tomaschek and this has been supported by Sir

Aurel Stein and confirmed by the twentieth century scholar Dr Eggermont. The 'high and desert island' has been identified as Churna situated about $4^1/_2$ miles off the coast at Cape Monze (*Ras Muar*) later called '*Ylha de Camelo*' by the Portuguese. The coastal area between the eastern and western branches of the Indus and the territory beyond the delta up to the Hub river was called *Aberia*, and its inhabitants a people called *Aberians* by Ptolemaeus in his description of Indo Scythia. The *Aberians* of Ptolemaeus have been identified with the *Arabeans* of Arrianus. The Hub river was known as *Arabis* after the *Arabean* tribe which occupied the coast of the Indus delta and its neighbouring area of Karachi at the time of Alexander's invasion in 325 BC. The coastal region of Sindh and Balochistan has had connections with the Arab regions of Arabia proper and the Persian Gulf and has shared common characteristics of race and close economic ties of

Indo Scythia and neighbouring countries. Map by Mercator Ptolmey, 1584.

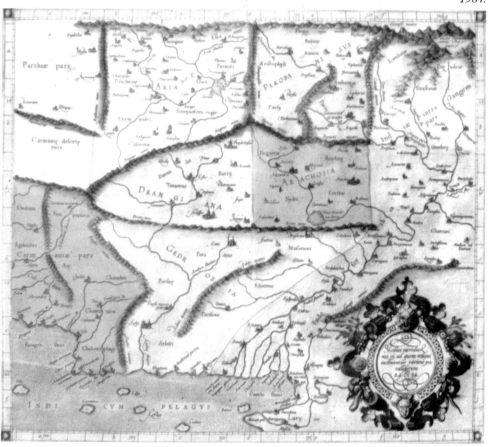

trade since times immemorial. Indeed the coastal people of Sindh could well be the *Arabeans* found in the text of Arrianus. So although Alexander himself did not step into Karachi and did not found an Alexandria on the site of the city, it is certain that the commander of his fleet, Nearchus, did sail near by and that he anchored close to the present day Karachi harbour. He certainly knew the Hub river and that the name of the residents of the area was Arabeans.

In a paper on the origins of Karachi, the noted scholar Dr N.A. Baloch has used Arab authorities to prove that the earliest mention of a name on the Sindh coastline which resembles that of Karachi is in an early literary work in Arabic by Al Hasan bin Muhammad bin Al Hasan Al Saghani written in the thirteenth century. Probably settled in Lahore, he visited Baghdad twice, in AD 1220 and AD 1227

> On both these occasions, on his way back, he acted as the emissary of the contemporary Abbasid Caliphs Al Nasir B'illah (AD 1180-1225) and Al Mustansir B'illah (AD 1226-1242) respectively, to the Sultans of Delhi. During these journeys, he not only happened to pass through Yaman four times, he also stayed there, mainly in Adan for three years (AD 1213-1216). The direction of his journeys would indicate that most probably he travelled by sea to Yaman from the coastline of Sindh. His sojourns in Sindh are also on record and he himself confirms that he stayed in Sindh for 'some years'.[6]

Dr Baloch quotes as evidence the description Al Saghani gives of the delta of the Indus from the knowledge he gained of the area from his journeys there. The great Arab navigator Ibn Majid who died *circa* 1500 refers to *Karazi* in his work *Al Fawaid*. The next reference to the early existence of the port of Karachi comes from the work of a celebrated Arab navigator Sulayman al Mahri's *Umdah* (AD 1511). In this book he mentions *Ras al Karazi* and also *Ras Karachi*. Al Mahri gives the route to be followed from Pasni to *Ras Karashi*. On reaching the latter place, he advises, 'There cast your anchor, and the *doongis* and the fishermen (in their boats or *doongies*) will come to you.'

He also gives the formula of the *quadima* (i.e., the ancients or the navigators of previous ages) how to circumnavigate *Ras Karashi* but his own advice is that, 'It is better to halt at *Ras Karashi*'.[7]

Indus and the Indian Ocean. Map by Mercator Ptolmey.

Based on his work as well as that of Ibn Majid, the Turkish Captain Sidi Ali Reis in his famous work *Muhit* (*circa* 1553-1554 AD) which was a compendium of sailing directions for a voyage from Diu, formerly a Portuguese island south of Kathiawar, to Hormuz in the Persian Gulf, mentions *Kaurashi* which indicates that a harbour with a name closely resembling Karachi was familiar to navigators of the sixteenth century and even an earlier period

> What is said of Indian whirlpools is all a tale except the whirlpool in the gulph of Jaked, and in the Barbarian channel near Kardafun, where ships falling in are unavoidably lost. If you guess that you may be drifting to Jaked you must take before your precautions, and endeavour to reach from the coast of Makran, either the port of Kalmata or Kawader, or Kapchi Makran; Bandar Kawander (one of the three Bunders on the coast of Gujerat) is the place where coconuts grow; or you must try to get to Kaurashi, or to enter Khur-diul Sind, that is to say the Port of Lahore, to get rid of the fear of Jaked. In Sind are a great number of liver-eaters, against whom you must be on your care; because if they meet a man who eats his dinner in public, they have the talent of eating up his liver with their eyes, and so kill him. This is not to be slighted.[8]

Capudan mentions a whirlpool which is indicated also in the Greek texts with reference to the Gulf of Barace, which says,

A promontory stands out from this gulf, curving around from Eirinon towards the East, then South, then West, and enclosing the gulf called Barace, which contains seven islands. Those who come to the entrance of this bay escape it by putting about a little and standing further out to sea; but those who are drawn inside into the gulf of Barace are lost; for the waves are high and very violent, and the sea is tumultuous and foul, and has eddies and rushing whirlpools.[9]

According to a comparatively recent writer

Karachi was an important rendezvous of the Arab navigators in Sindh. It was written *Karashi* and was according to Sulayman, a cape of the bay of Diul al Sindh. Apart from this sentence, no exact relationship between the two places is given. Sometimes *Karashi* is mentioned and sometimes *Diul al Sind* but never together...Portuguese and early European maps and charts never refer to Karachi but only to *Diulsinde* or Diulcinde, etc. The position given by them to the place would seem to indicate that this was the same as Karachi. Perhaps 'Diul al-Sind' was the bay which was in actual fact an estuary of the Indus delta, and Karachi the town on the estuary—nothing is certain.[10]

The conclusion that Dr Baloch comes to prove is that by the early sixteenth century and possibly even earlier in the fifteenth century, Ras Karashi was well known to navigators of the Indian ocean as an anchorage. It was variously known as Karashi or Karazi or even Kaurashi.

Locally the name which seems to be longest in use is *Kalachi* which is the name used in the ancient Sindhi legend of *Morriro and Mangar Machh* or the story of a fisherman Morriro and the whale. According to this legend, a ferocious whale had swallowed up six brave brothers of *Kalachi jo kun* (the whirlpool of Kalachi) who were the most daring fishermen of the day. Eventually their youngest brother Morriro avenged them by killing the whale. The story puts the event in the days of King Dalura (*circa* AD twelfth century) one of the earlier rulers of the Sumra dynasty. This legend has been used by the sufi poets of Sindh, notably Sindhi *zakirs* in the *sama* performance before Saint

Shaykh Abdu Jalil Chuhar Bandagi (AD 1504) who use the name Kalach, by Shah Abdul Karim who writes of the *Kun of Kalachi* (*circa* 1560-1634) and by Shah Abdul Latif in his *Risalo* (*Sur Ghatu*) where he talks of *Kalachi* or *Kun Kalachi*.

Karachi lies in the foothills of the Khirthar range of hills and is not part of the Indus delta. It has formed part of the territories of the chieftains who have controlled the Hub Malir region and the Makran coast, which, though part of Balochistan, has been a Sindhi speaking area right up to the 'Jam-dom' of Lasbella, the most important chiefdom of the region. In the seventeenth century, the region was in the control of the Kalmati Maliks who had dominated the area perhaps since the thirteenth century.[11] The spectacular tomb sculpture of the region bears witness to the domination of the Kalmatis and the later Jokhias in the region right up to the Indus delta.

The Indus Delta at the time of Alexander's invasion, circa 325 BC.

*Carved stone tomb,
(probably Kalmati),
Karachi area.*

Karachi was an important centre and route for pilgrims who not only came to the ancient shrines in and around the town, but it was also used as a route for the journey to the ancient shrine of Hinglaj in the Baloch mountains just beyond Karachi. Shah Abdul Latif, the eighteenth century sufi saint and the premier poet of the Sindhi language, made a pilgrimage there in the company of *jogis* and *sanyasis*. The oldest Muslim shrine in the subcontinent was the tomb of Abdullah Shah Ghazi who came with one of the invading Arab forces, earlier than the successful one led by Muhammed bin Qasim in AD 711. He was martyred here and buried on a promontory which was some way into the sea off the coast of Karachi. As the sea recedes from the coast line of Karachi the shrine is now on the mainland in the Clifton area still high on its hill but with no other sign of its ancient heredity. An ancient Hindu pilgrimage site which is reputed to be mentioned in the *Mahabharata* is situated below the Kothari Parade at Clifton and was perhaps on an island cave centuries ago when the ancient Hindus built it.[12]

There are ancient Muslim and Hindu shrines as well as those belonging to both the communities, such as Hinglaj

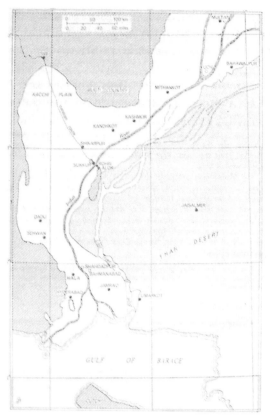

The lower Indus valley,
circa 325 BC.

Crocodile pond at
Mangho Pir.

and Mangho Pir. The shrine of Mangho Pir is on a rock in a hot spring oasis about ten miles north of Karachi. Its most well known feature is a crocodile pond where the oldest crocodile is reputed to be six hundred years old and is known as *Mor Sain* or Mr Peacock. Both Hindus and Muslims traditionally sacrificed goats at the shrine and fed them to the crocodiles which were considered to have holy status. The springs and the pond are at present surrounded by shanty towns. But even in the mid fifties the area was as it had been for thousands of years

> Mr Peacock lives some ten miles north of Karachi, in the foot-hills. It is arid, unrelenting country, but he has the best of it. He lives in an oasis, with a pool of dark water surrounded by rocks and palm trees...
> Crocodiles like to lie about in heaps, as if they were spillikins

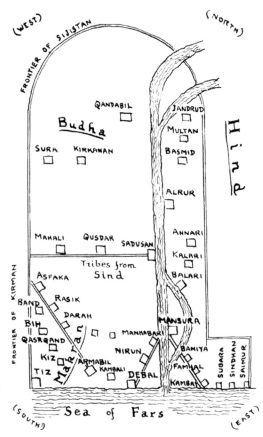

Ashk-ul Bilad
(circa AD *1100)*
Sindh and the
adjoining countries.

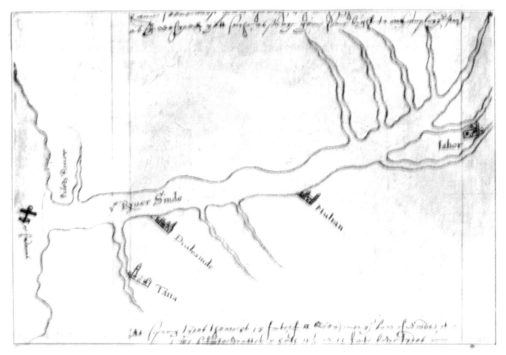

*Diul Sinde
mid-seventeenth
century.*

but heavier and less innocent...Mister Peacock... is famous in the neighbourhood. He is the biggest and most splendid crocodile here, and some people consider him sacred... [He is] six hundred and something years old, for it is claimed that he arrived here in the thirteenth century with the intention of serving the saint whose tomb stands high on a rocky eminence above the pool enclosure. The saint's name is Mangho Pir. The hot springs which gush out of the rocks under the shrine are popular with pilgrims who hope for a cure for all kinds of illnesses.[13]

The Karachi area was until the eighteenth century, controlled by the chieftains who ruled the coast and hilly region of the Sindh and Makran coast. In the eighteenth century it was part of the chiefdom of the Kalmati Maliks. The rise of the Kalhoras from Larkana district in the early eighteenth century and the unification of Sindh, under their rule, saw the control of Karachi passing to them in this period. There is evidence to suggest that at some point the Karachi region passed back into the hands of the local chieftains, but by the third quarter of the eighteenth century, when Lieutenant John Porter visited it in 1774-5, it was definitely in the hands of the rulers of Sindh. Porter gives what is perhaps the earliest description of Karachi, the small town which has developed into the modern metropolis

> Crotchey Town is situated about five or six miles from where the vessels lay, and about a mile from the side of a creek which has not water in it for anything else than small boats. It is fortified by a slight mud wall and flanked with round towers, and has only two cannons mounted in all, and those so old, and their carriages so crazy, as would render the firing of them unsafe.[14]

Porter also mentions the fact that it formerly 'belonged to the Bloachees' and then says that the 'Prince of Scindy, finding it better situated than any part of his sea coast for the caravans from the Inland Countries; made an exchange with some other place for it.'[15] It is therefore certain that at least from the time of Mian Ghulam Shah Kalhoro, who died in AD 1772, Karachi was the major port of Sindh.

Karachi is the first port of Sindh which is situated directly on the sea coast. Historically the ports of Sindh, as befits the land of the Indus, have been river ports situated just above the delta proper. The earliest recorded river port is Patala where Alexander's fleet started its homeward journey. The port at the time of the Arab conquest is generally given the name of *Daibul* (or Dabul) as the port of Sindh which was conquered by the Ommayed General Mohammed bin Qasim in AD 711.[16] This was the first time in the written history of the subcontinent that a successful invasion of an Indian region had been mounted from the sea. Most of the conquerors earlier, and for a thousand years subsequently, came from the passes of the northern mountains. Daibul continued to be an important and commercial centre for many centuries. The Arab geographers and travellers who journeyed throughout Asia, particularly during the pax Islamica from eighth century AD onwards used the port of Daibul and mention it frequently. The commercial revival of the region from the tenth to the thirteenth century when the Mongol invasions destroyed the Abbasid empire,

> received its impetus from two centres, one located in the north, that is Kabul, and the other in the south, that is Kandahar and Daibul. The contact with foreign trade, maintained at these

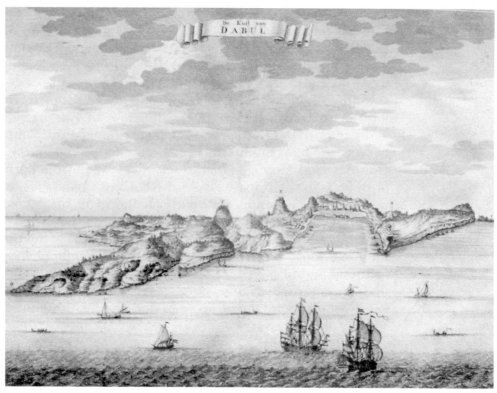

*A Dutch print
of Daibul.*

points continued unabated and the routes converging to or
forking from these places became much frequented tracks
henceforth.[17]

The most likely site for Daibul of AD 711, complete with
the first mosque in the subcontinent, is that of Bhanbhore
about forty miles north east of Karachi. The commercial
traffic which was carried on from Baghdad and Basra and
went throughout Asia, came to the Indian subcontinent,
either to the mouth of the Indus (i.e., to Daibul) through
Balochistan or to the Punjab through Kabul and Ghazni.
The ports of Sindh were changeable however

on the Indus, from times immemorial, new riverine ports have
been utilized; have had a certain period of existence; have died
a natural death; generally because the waters deserted them;[18]

Diul Sinde (or *Daibul*) appears to be the generic name for
the major port of Sindh and in many accounts *Diul Sinde*

has been used to describe Thatta as the port of Sindh. But at some point this port became difficult of access and a number of other ports became the *Diul Sinde* in succession. The first of these is Lahri Bandar which is first mentioned by Al Beruni in the early eleventh century AD. In the early seventeenth century it was approximately three days journey away from Karachi. At the time of Aurangzeb another port Dera Jam was renamed Aurangbandar and became the most important river port of Sindh. When the river deserted Aurangbandar, it was succeeded by the port of Dharaja in the principality of the Rana of Dharaja. This principality was conquered by the Kalhoras in the latter part of the eighteenth century. Shahbandar on the eastern bank of the river also remained an important port of Sindh for some time. The river ports of Sindh throughout the medieval period served Sindh and the regions around but they were particularly the ports of Thatta, the capital of lower Sindh from the Samma period in the thirteenth century.

Thatta suffered a terrible fate when the Portuguese, coming in at the request of a 'King of Sind' in 1555 AD ravaged, looted and destroyed this highly civilized city of 400 colleges and started the decline of the region. This infamous act of the Portuguese clearly indicated the future of the history of the Indian subcontinent where a highly developed civilzation would be a helpless prey to the naval powers of Europe. The decline of the Mughal power in the eighteenth century and the rising importance of trade with the Europeans who came to Indian ports by sea, made a more permanent sea port necessary for Sindh. The eighteenth century Kalhora and Talpur rulers of Sindh decided to develop Karachi, a suitable natural harbour, as the port of Sindh.

In 1799 Nathan Crowe of the Bombay Civil Service landed in Karachi and proceeded inland to set up his factory. He was, however, not allowed to live in Karachi, he believed because of the jealousy of the merchants of Karachi but possibly because the Amirs of Sindh were well aware of the track record of the East India Company and the ports of the subcontinent. It was after all several decades since they had used the Calcutta and Madras settlements to establish their dominion over sizeable portions of India. Crowe gives a description of Karachi at the end of the eighteenth century which clearly indicates the intentions of the British towards the city

> Currachee is fortified with a thick mud wall upon which some guns are planted. No vessel can batter it from the sea as they are obliged to be at a distance of at least three miles from it but their guns could cover the landing of the troops abreast of the place of anchorage. A vessel of more than two hundred tons could not safely cross Currachee bar and if she entered in a hostile manner, she might expect to find herself surrounded by all the dinghies then lying there and they would often be more than a dozen, carrying guns, some of them as heavy as her own and each of perhaps more men, for such an occasion of attack there would be no scarcity of volunteers.[19]

In 1830 the deserting soldier, inveterate traveller, and possible spy, Charles Masson, visited the town of Karachi and left behind a description

> Karachee, although not a large town has much trade; it is surrounded by dilapidated mud walls, provided with towers, on which a few crazy guns are mounted. The suburbs, extensive, and generally comprising huts, are inhabited by fishermen and mariners. The port has one hundred vessels, of all sizes and

Maggar Tallao (Alligator Tank)at Mangho Pir, said to have been miraculously created by Lal Shahbaz Qalandar, the mystic saint of Sindh.

The town walls of Karachi, nineteenth century, adapted from Masson by Shamyl Khuhro.

descriptions, belonging to it, and its dunghies venture to Daman, Bombay, and Calicat, also to Gwadar and Maskat. The harbour is commodious for small craft, and is spacious, extending about two miles inwards, at which distance from its mouth, the town is seated.[20]

The importance of the island of Manora as the strategic point guarding the harbour of Karachi was realised by Mir Fatehali Talpur who became the ruler of Sindh in 1797. He fortified the island and appointed a separate governor for it. About the island of Manora, Masson says

On a high hill, or eminence, overlooking the entrance to the harbour on the left hand, as it is approached from the sea, is the fort or castle of Manorah, garrisoned by a small party of Jukias; it is said there are many guns in it, but it is unexplained who are to work them. The eminence slopes to the beach, on the town side, where there is a circular tower, on which four guns are said, whether true or not, to be placed. These constitute the defences of the harbour, whose entrance is well defined, having, opposite to the hill Manaroh, five detached rocks and a sandbank exposed at low water. Karachee has a cool climate.[21]

To Masson also is attributed a description of the town of Karachi itself at this time

The town is enclosed by a low mud wall strengthened by unshapely circular towers on many of which a piece or two of unserviceable ordnance is mounted. It has two gates on the opposite sides of east and west. [Masson is obviously referring to the two gates of the town Mithadar (sweet water gate) and Kharadar(salt water gate) which faced the green belt and wells and the sea respectively.] The principal street or bazaar extending from one to the other. Within the walls are wells but the water is too saline in taste to be available as beverage and the inhabitants get supply themselves from pools of water without the town. There is a large tank always abounding with water near the gardens on Tatta road, but the liquid is reputed "sungheen" or heavy, and is seldom used. The bazaar of Karachee is narrow and in many places covered to exclude heat. It is fairly supplied with shops, and in it are several respectable merchants and bankers.[22]

Commander Carless who was deputed with the task of surveying the coast of Karachi also wrote an informative description about the town at this time

The population of Karachi consists of seamen and fishermen, and their total number is nearly 14000... The Hindu merchants and traders of Karachi are wealthy and resourceful. Their trade offices are doing roaring business as far away as Multan, Hirat, Kabul, Qandhar and Muscat.... Mohana clan is very brave and hard working and is settled in Karachi in large numbers. Mirs of Sind have appointed two governors in Karachi, one is Hasan bin Bachho Khan Sobedar and the other one is Khair Muhammad who is the Commander of the Manora fort.[23]

By the last quarter of the eighteenth century Karachi thus had been established as the main port of Sindh which the

Manora Island and the Talpur Fort adapted from Masson by Shamyl Khuhro.

caravans from the north used as the port of their sea borne trade. The Talpur rulers were well aware of the rising importance of Karachi. They had appointed a governor for the town and a separate governor for Manora island.

The development of Karachi as the port of Sindh coincided with the rise of British imperial interest in the area. By the second and third decades of the nineteenth century the British had become the 'paramount power' in India. Sindh and the Punjab were the only important states outside British control. Ranjit Singh had established his powerful Sikh kingdom in the Punjab taking his control right up to Peshawar. The British were anxious to maintain friendly relations with him and did not expect to use his state for the passage for their army whenever the need arose. The alternative route was obviously Sindh and the Indus. The rulers of Sindh were less militarily powerful than Ranjit Singh, although they had successfully maintained their independence and even added to their territories in the face of the Sikh threat. Well aware of the expanding British power they, nevertheless, hoped to maintain their independence and neutrality through a mixture of diplomacy and avoidance of direct involvement in British Indian affairs. In the face of the realities of the politics in the subcontinent this was to prove a vain hope. Already Nathan Crowe had hinted at the use Sindh could be put to for the British in the developing 'great game' in Central Asia

It would make Sindian help likely if attack on Afghanistan became necessary; it would make it possible for the British to foment a revolution against Kabul, if this proved necessary or desirable; it would preclude the entry of the

H.H. Mir Muhammad Nasir Khan Talpur with his sons.

French, Afghans, or Marathas; it would be an excellent centre from which to spy on Afghanistan.[24]

Crowe thus pointed out the importance of Sindh in the interests of British imperial strategy in India and the countries to the north west. At the time of Crowe's mission, the expanding power of the French under Napoleon was felt to be the greatest danger to the British interest in India and this threat grew even greater after the Franco-Russian alliance (Treaty of Tilsit) of 1807. Persia and Afghanistan were seen to be vulnerable to the expanding northern powers and Sindh was the key factor in the security of the Indian subcontinent. After the defeat of Napoleon at Waterloo in 1815 and in view of the subsequent predominance and expansion of Russia in Central Asia, British fears about the security of north western India increased. The disintegration of the Durrani empire and its collapse in 1818 had left a power vacuum in the region and it was only after some time that Dost Mohammed was able to establish his control over Kabul. By this time there was little left of Ahmed Shah Durrani's kingdom and the Kingdom of Kabul extended barely a hundred miles around the capital. This weakness of the Afghan kingdom and the defeat of the Persians at the hands of the Russians in 1813 rang the alarm bells for the British in India and Lord Ellenborough, the Chairman of the Board of Directors of the East India Company, expressed these fears: 'The Directors are much afraid of the Russians, so am I...I feel confident we shall have to fight the Russains on the Indus,[25]

H.H. Mir Sobdar Khan Talpur with his sons.

H.H. Mir Muhammad Khan Talpur and Princes.

British policy makers including the Duke of Wellington, the victor of Waterloo, were convinced that Russia had its eye on India and that this drive south could only be pre-empted by controlling the Indus. This conviction would provide the motive force for British policy towards Sindh for the next few decades.

In 1830 Alexander Burnes asked for permission from the rulers of Sindh to sail up the Indus to the Punjab, ostensibly with a gift of horses for Ranjit Singh. The real purpose of this journey was to survey the Indus and to get a report on its potential as the 'frontier' for British India. At the same time the East India Company sought to make treaties with the Amirs to open the region to British traders. Dr James Burnes, Alexander's brother, had come to Sindh just a couple of years earlier to treat one of the Amirs and had given a glowing account of the commercial possibilities and the wealth of Sindh.

Between the years 1830 and 1839 several British officials and travellers visited Karachi and reported on its particulars, such as the town and the facilities it provided, its climate, and its trade potential. They commented on its defences and pronounced their opinion that it was a weakly defended town and harbour, and the British would have very little trouble taking it. The climate of opinion in the Imperial corridors was definitely moving in the direction of the conquest of Sindh. Lord Auckland, the Governor-General, was dreaming of immense wealth

If I can open channels of commerce to Central Asia and if I can make the Indus the thoroughfare for navigation, that gold and silver road…which it ought to be, I shall not care much else.[26]

The British negotiated a number of treaties with the Amirs 'opening the Indus' to their commercial activity, but very soon there were differences over the question of the charging of tolls at Karachi. The British insisted that merchants under their protection should not have to pay taxes even when they were natives of Sindh. The Amirs pointed out that quite apart from the amount of revenues they would lose, the treaties with the British had specified that there would be no interference with the internal affairs of the state. Lord Bentinck had given

> The Ameers every assurance that the internal trade of their country would not be interfered with. Nevertheless the amirs agreed to remove their most recent taxes but claimed that they (especially Nasir Khan) thus would lose a considerable amount annually.[27]

Mir Yar Muhammad Khan Talpur and Mir Muhammad Khan Talpur.

The British were determined however that the Indus should be free of tolls and Auckland wrote optimistically, 'I look upon the Indus as the high road from London to Delhi and it requires but good arrangements to make the travelling easy.'[28]

This dream was never to be realized however, as the navigation of the Indus was to prove too difficult and camel caravans would continue to carry the trade to Karachi rather than sail down the Indus like Nearchus, through the delta to the sea.

The cat and mouse game with the rulers of Sindh would not continue long and soon an opportunity arose to give the British an excuse to annex Sindh to their dominion. The occasion was provided by the need for the Bombay army to be sent up to Afghanistan. The Amirs reluctantly gave permission for the army to proceed through Sindh and the Bolan pass. The Army of

A Talpur soldier and a bania.

Wagheries *or*
crocodile hunters
of Sindh.

A fakir *of Sindh.*

the Indus made its way through Sindh to Afghanistan in 1838 in aid of Shah Shuja as the British candidate for the throne of Afghanistan. The incumbent ruler Dost Mohammed was removed and Shah Shuja, a far less competent man, was put in his place. Predictably, the volatile Afghans did not tolerate this situation for long and the British found themselves in a far more complicated situation than they had bargained for. Their strategic needs now required that the 'line of communications be fully secured'. This policy meant that the British were now ready to establish their direct control of Sindh. The first practical step in this direction was taken by the occupation of Karachi in 1839, a clear example of *force majeure*.

In February 1839 Admiral Frederick Maitland, while transporting the Bombay reserve force under Brigadier Valiant, claimed he was fired upon from the Fort of Manora. He immediately bombarded the fort and captured the town. Pottinger, the British Resident, reported that the only shot fired was probably 'the salute customary when a square rigged vessel came in sight or approached the place.' The Amirs even insisted that there had been no shot in the cannon at the time. Pottinger later investigated the matter and found that

There was not a single ball in the fort that would fit any of the guns and that the whole supply of gunpowder amounted to six

Sir Charles Napier on horseback.

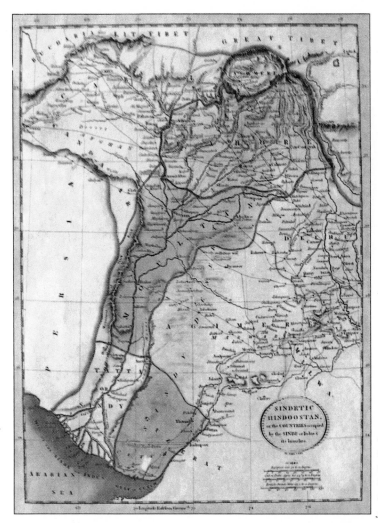

Sindetic Hindoostan, or the countries occupied by Scinde or the Indus and its branches. Map by John Cary, 1813.

pounds which was kept in an earthen pot. The entire garrison consisting of sixteen men, many of whom were armed only with swords, were standing outside the fort admiring the *Wellesley* when the firing began. The Governor of Karachi informed Pottinger that the landing was not to be resisted and that he had orders from the Amirs to co-operate with the British in every way.[29]

The Amirs continued to demand that Karachi be returned to their control but it was too late. Just three years later the rest of Sindh was to be annexed to the British Empire.

*Manora Church
and lighthouse.*

Chapter 2

THE MAKING OF A COLONIAL PORT

Hamida Khuhro

The conquest of Sindh in 1843 saw the establishment of Karachi as the administrative capital of the province. Hyderabad, so closely associated with the Kalhoras and the Talpurs, although a working capital at this time, was considered too insecure. Karachi was also the most convenient location for a maritime colonial power. The city was to be developed to serve as 'the port nearest to Europe' —a military necessity, the importance of which was particularly emphasized by the 1857 Indian War of Independence which put communications from the north of India with the ports of Calcutta and Bombay in jeopardy. Karachi was also seen as the port that would open up not only the hinterland of Sindh itself, but the entire north western areas of the subcontinent and also be the port of areas to the north west, which could thus be safeguarded from the embrace of the Russian bear.

The colonial city of Karachi developed quite distinctly from the old native city with its twin quarters of Kharadar and Mithadar. The old city lived alongside the new one and was the heart of the native business life. It had housed the rich 'banias' who had had their worldwide trade based on the *hundie* which could provide easy credit to the merchant or traveller anywhere in the world. The traditional trade had its own caravan routes and its links with Iran, Afghanistan and Central Asia. These links reached out all the way to central Asian cities and went as far as Moscow. The caravans went to a chain of legendary cities which were strung together by centuries old trading ties—Karachi, Hyderabad, Shikarpur, Kandahar, Herat, and the cities of

A nineteenth century photograph of the Karachi Harbour.

Persia. There was also the northern route of Kabul, Khiva, Yarkand, Samarkand, Bukhara and north to Russia, and east to Sinkiang and China. Fairs played a great part in the promotion of this trade and were held in these great cities where merchants from all over the area flocked.

The acquisition of Karachi by the British in 1839 and of the rest of Sindh in 1843 changed the direction of the trade from the traditional land routes to the north and south east, to sea borne trade south to Asian ports and west to Europe. Shikarpur had lost its importance by the collapse of the Durrani empire and the rise of the Sikh kingdom. The commerce of Multan and Amritsar was already flourishing at its expense. Now the sea emporium Karachi took pride of place as the trading city of the region and the rapidly developing administrative capital of the new colonial regime.

Brought up on the classics, for quite a long time the British were under the impression that the Indus river would be the key to the commerce and the defence of the north west of India and beyond. To gain control of the Indus had been one of the main planks of their policy for some decades and this had now been achieved. But they soon found that they had been labouring under a misapprehension of the role of the Indus in the life of the region. It was true that Alexander had explored the delta of the Indus and had sent his fleet down the river to the sea, and the belief that the Indus would be the main means of commercial transport died hard. Even in the 1850s English entrepreneurs were writing of the past history and future potential of the great river

> When the rapid progress of Mohammedan arms had wrested Egypt from the Byzantine power, and thus closed the overland route of Suez to the Greek merchants, they forthwith turned to other means and sought out a new channel, by which the productions of the East might be transmitted to the great emporium of the West. The route thus discovered was that by the Indus.[1]

But the British found through experience that the Indus was not a suitable river for navigation with its seasonal variations and uncertainties. Boats found the delta difficult to negotiate and the port of Karachi was inconveniently placed for the river traffic. Gradually they discovered that the romantic hopes of successive governor-generals who had expected the Indus to be 'a highway of commerce' could not be realised and alternative arrangements had to be made to carry the trade up country. The alternative arrangements, a combination of rail and river transport, would make Karachi the true gateway of the north west.

But before Karachi could take its place as the pearl of the east it had to go some way. The old town of Karachi, with its narrow streets and 'oriental squalor', was not to the taste of the incoming rulers who set about building their own Karachi as soon as it was possible. Sir Charles Napier, the conqueror of Sindh, became the first governor of the province. He established himself in Karachi and began laying the plans which would bring Karachi into the front ranks of the British cities of the subcontinent. He set up a rudimentary administration dividing Sindh into three 'Collectorates', Karachi, Hyderabad, and Shikarpur and placed his army officers at the head of each collectorate. Colonel Keith Young, who was appointed Judge Advocate

The Trinity Church,
Karachi, 1855.

General to be in charge of dispensing justice in the
province, was sanguine in his remarks on his arrival in the
province: 'Here I am at last in the promised land of Scinde,
and not a bad place does it appear to be.'[2] But though the
weather in September seemed to him to be quite pleasant
he was not so pleased with the town

> A dirty-looking, mud built, walled town, with low, dirty, swampy
> ground about it. The cantonments, about two miles, like so
> many tents on a bare plain: not a tree to be seen; ; low hills are
> in the distance, and to the northward of the entrance to the
> harbour.[3]

Apart from the 'ragged, sandy, barren appearance of the
place generally...' Keith Young noticed that the style of
houses and the number of donkeys were very similar to
those in Egypt.

The new Judge Advocate General went to call on Napier
who had not been too well: 'I found him in bed, looking, I
thought, very wild and haggard, and certainly most
particularly uncomfortable, with a dirty blanket over him.'[4]
It was this highly eccentric Napier who had a vision of
Karachi as the great commercial entrepot and important

not only as the gateway to the north west of India, but the port nearest to Europe. He was now ensconced in his Governor's House, a basic structure with a few rooms and deep verandahs with extensive grounds. It was to be the spot to be marked out for future governors' houses.

But apart from a scattering of colonial bungalows and offices, a club or two, and the barracks, there was little to attract the newcomer in the brown vistas of colonial Karachi. Colonel Young was reminded of a verse of Sir Walter Scott written to describe the Scottish scene but which he found applicable to Karachi

Far as the eye could reach no tree was seen,
Earth clad in russet scorned the lively green
No birds except as birds of passage flew,
No bee was heard to hum, no dove to coo,
No streams as amber smooth, as amber clear,
Were seen to glide, or heard to warble here.

But in spite of this desolate scene Colonel Young managed to be entertained royally

Had a grand dinner at the Persian prince's last night. Aga Khan is his name. He married a sister of the late King of Persia, and came to this part of the country via Kurrachee. He is a great knave, but he has an excellent cook. The dinner was to the General, and there were about a dozen of us. Such pillaus and stews and things of all kinds to drink as well as eat, champagne and beer included. I preferred the sherbets, but they were rather sweet. The feast was held in a summer-house in a garden near the town, and commenced with a profusion of sweets and fruits. There being no knives, one of our hosts peeled an apple with a pocket-knife, and cut bits off which they handed to us. This of course was little touched, the sweets being principally compositions of ghee and sugar. The pillaus, etc., followed and were heaped on the table till there was not a vacant inch of table-cloth to be seen, and indeed the dishes were piled one over the other. Dishes, however, and plates were rather scarce, and large chuppaties served their place. I ate of several things, and much approved of pillaus, a kind of minced collop, some stuff like pish-pash served in bowls, and the common little kabobs which were brought in on small spits, and pulled off in the most primitive style by one of our hosts, using a chapatee to hold them with. A nautch finished the entertainment...[5]

The conqueror of Sindh, Napier, had the ear of the Governor-General Lord Ellenborough who shared his dreams of a great future for the province

> ...in Sind we must do all for futurity, we have to create an Egypt, and we must not allow little views of present advantage to interfere with the realization of the greatest future objects. We must redeem the character we have lost in India, on this new field for the exercise of the European mind in the administration of an Asiatic Province.[6]

The Government of India, sitting in the opposite corner of India in Calcutta, gave a free hand to Napier to make his plans for Sindh. Eccentric and with delusions of grandeur, Napier set about to exercise his mind in the administration of this Asiatic province. Many of the ideas developed by Napier and his administration were very progressive. He realised that this Young Egypt was, like the old one, dependent on the river for its life. So one of his earliest acts was to set up an Irrigation Department. The head of this department was Colonel Walter Scott, a nephew of the great nineteenth century novelist Sir Walter Scott, and as his assistant he appointed Lieutenant Richard Burton, who would later acquire fame as a traveller and orientalist. Burton spent more time observing life in Sindh and studying the language rather than working on the canals. Richard Burton made a scholarly study of the Sindhi language and his report on the language would eventually persuade the government to make Sindhi with its Arabic script, as against the advocates of the Devanagiri script, the official language of the province. Making a survey of the irrigation the engineers of the Canal Department produced a report which recommended a barrage on the river at Sukkur which would allow a perennial supply of water to the canals of Sindh, a proposal which was implemented in the next century. The other task that was assigned to Burton by Napier was to report on the brothels of Karachi. The report that he gave to the governor was quite unique in the annals of colonial literature and

Richard Burton in Sindh.

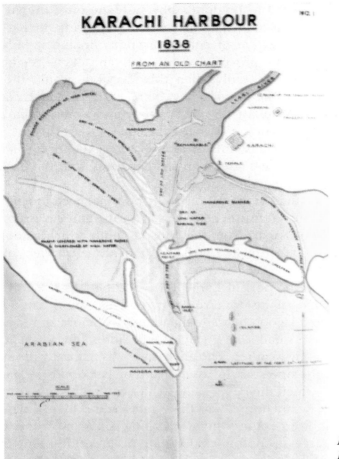

*Map of the
Harbour (1838).*

although some brief glimpses of it are available to the
diligent reader of colonial record, this report from the
translator of *A Thousand and One Nights,* appears to be lost
and its discovery continues to be a challenge to the historian
and to the collector of curious literary pieces.

Much of Napier's attention was given to the progress of
Karachi, particularly to the improvement of the harbour
which was central to any well laid plans for the growth of
the city. The potential for the port was great. The harbour
of Karachi was well sheltered from the monsoons and could
be used at any time of the year, and served vast areas of the
north west of India as well as the countries beyond. But

much needed to be done. Obviously the most urgent task therefore was to take up the work of improving the harbour and of the system of communications linking it with the interior of the province, the Punjab, and of the regions of the north west. Only when this was done would the full potential of the Karachi port be realized. Although Napier laid out the plans for the harbour and some preliminary work was done, it was not as speedy or efficient; and although fair amounts of money were expended, it would not be until well after Napier's departure that the harbour would be adequately organized.

At the time of the conquest the port had been functioning for about a hundred years. Its annual revenue was Rs 2,00,000 apart from the duty on opium which amounted to Rs 1,00,000 to Rs 1,50,000. About three quarters of the income was from imports.

When the port of Karachi was occupied by the British it consisted of just one anchorage. This was situated in a sheltered lagoon between the island of Manora and Keamari and here small sailing ships could ride safely at anchor in almost any weather. The anchorage was naturally protected from the open sea by a sandbank or bar opposite Manora point, which the larger sailing ships could only cross at high tide. The anchorage was three miles from the mainland by the shortest route, which was along a narrow channel not navigable even for small boats at low tide. The other approach to the town was by the Chinna Creek, three miles to the east of Keamari, which was wider and deeper but involved a circuitous route of over seven miles. Whatever the approach used, the passengers and goods had to be transported to the mainland by shallow draft 'bunder' boats. This was the experience of Keith Young on his arrival in Sindh

> We anchored soon after eight some two miles or so from the shore, but a considerable distance from the place of disembarkation.... A little steamer came off to us, the *Auckland*, drawing too much water to go over the bar that crosses the harbour. After running about four miles, we got into smaller boats, which took us within a few yards of the pier, and canoes put us on shore. It was near high water, for when the tide is out, you cannot get within some hundred yards of the shore.[7]

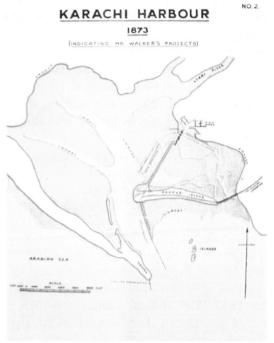

Map of the Harbour (1873).

The picture would change out of recognition in the next century. The first phase of necessary improvements took about thirty years to complete. The first important project initiated by Napier was the joining of the Keamari island with the mainland by a causeway or 'mole' which was completed in 1854.

This enabled wheeled traffic to approach within a few hundred yards of the anchorage and provided great convenience, not only for merchandise but also for people who no longer had to travel in a variety of boats to get to the ships. At the same time, the anchorage was deepened and extended and improvements made so that ocean-going ships could enter in almost any conditions of weather.

In 1847 Sir Charles Napier left Sindh which was joined with the Bombay Presidency for administrative purposes. The province was now in charge of a senior official who was designated Commissioner-in-Sindh. Sindh was a 'Non-

Regulation' province and the Commissioner-in-Sindh was a very powerful officer who was practically a master of all he surveyed. In 1847 a remarkable man, Sir Bartle Frere, came to Sindh to occupy this post. Frere proved to be the most imaginative and energetic administrator of Sindh. The period of Frere's commissionership which lasted from 1851 to 1859 saw the plans for the development of the harbour, as well as other schemes for the improvement of communications and of the province in general. Frere initiated major engineering schemes and got the support of Lord Dalhousie, the Governor-General, who fully supported Frere's schemes

> Without a good harbour at Karachi I think you would never have really good trade by the way of Sind. But with a good harbour there, I know not why it should be very far behind Bombay.[8]

Frere had already undertaken the removal of the sandbar at the mouth of the harbour which prevented the entry of bigger ships and also the completion of the Napier Mole Bridge. The 1857 War of Independence which enveloped the whole of northern India· and even interrupted communication with the capital Calcutta, dramatically emphasized the importance of Karachi as an alternative port for northern India

Sir Bartle Frere.

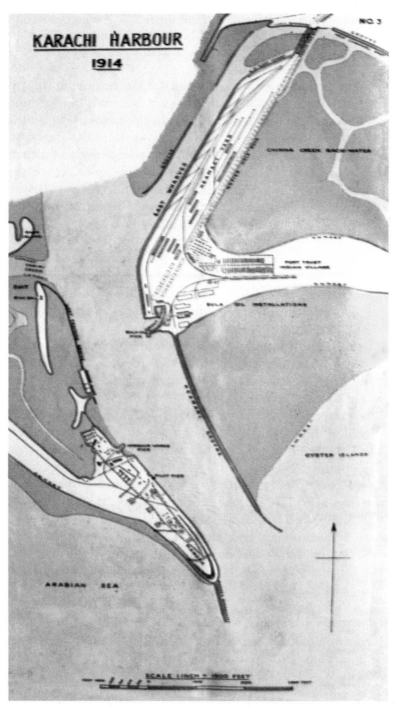

*Map of the
Harbour (1914).*

The best possible port at Karachi would be needed because of its importance for the defence of the north west border against some outside invader, but it is even more important for the import and deployment of troops in this part of India.[9]

When the crisis occurred in 1857, requiring highly increased activity at the Karachi port, the existing facilities could not cope and demonstrated to the administration the urgency of completing the work at Karachi harbour. Strategically, Karachi had become an alternative to Calcutta for the internal security of the Indian Empire. Once the events of 1857 had emphasized the importance of British sea power in her ability to hold India, Sindh at once fell into place as a 'bastion of Imperial defence'.

As soon as it was decided that improvements of the harbour be undertaken seriously, the best advice possible at the time was taken. The Court of Directors asked James Walker, the President of the Institute of Civil Engineers in England and highly experienced in the matter of harbour works, to design the improvements at Karachi. His proposals to some extent modified by discussion and by engineers on the spot were accepted by the government.

By 1873 major preliminary work was completed which resulted in the adequate deepening of the entrance channel. The other improvements that were completed by 1873 included the cutting of an opening in the Napier Mole near the Karachi end and the construction of the bridge across the opening; closing of the former entrance to the Chinna Creek backwaters from the sea; construction of the Keamari Groyne and lastly, the construction of the Manora breakwater. The funding of the projects and their completion owed a great deal to Frere who, as Governor of Bombay in the 1860s, pursued the matter vigorously with the Government of India which was pleading poverty in the wake of the 1857 operations.

In 1886 Karachi Port Trust was constituted and in 1909 a full time chairman was appointed. Karachi was now given the status of one of the four major ports of India. In the second phase of development, from 1873 to the outbreak of World War I in 1914, the projects that were undertaken were those of constructing wharves and jetties which had not been done in the first phase. The Napier Mole was widened by reclamation to accommodate railway sidings and

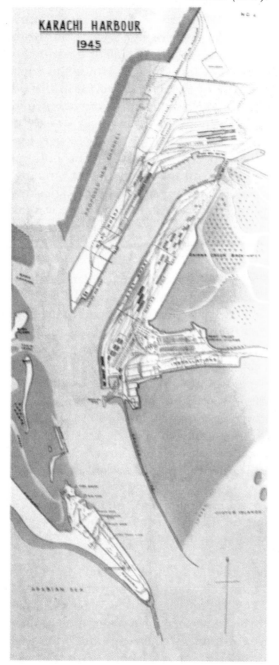

Map of the Harbour (1945).

became known as the Keamari Yard. The new wharves were built not only to accommodate the existing trade but to anticipate its expansion. The bulk of this trade was the export of wheat. By the beginning of World War I, Karachi was the largest wheat exporting port of the British empire with a record shipment of 1,380,000 tons in the financial year 1912-13.[10] The Manora Light House was constructed in 1909 and was one of the most powerful in the world at the time, the light being visible up to eighteen miles in clear weather 'and the loom anything up to seventy miles.'[11] At the same time, a number of wharves were constructed increasing the capacity of the port. The bulk oil pier was completed in 1909 and the Burmah Oil Company, as well as the Standard Oil Company set up their establishments there. In the same year, 177 acres of tidal swamp was taken by the port authorities from the municipal authorities for land reclamation. On this reclaimed land Thole Produce Yard was constructed.

By 1914 over 350 acres of valuable land had been added to the port area. Thus by the outbreak of World War I, the Karachi port was well enough equipped to become the main base for Britain and its allies' operations in Iraq. By now it had climbed in the order of importance to becoming the third most important port in India.

It was not, however, sufficient just to improve the harbour and the port of Karachi in order to make it the port of this region of the subcontinent and beyond. By the time Frere became Commissioner-in-Sindh it had become clear that the Indus was not suitable for large scale and all weather commercial traffic. By 1862 it was still possible to say

> ...although steamers have been running between Karachi and Mithunkote for the last twenty years, by far the greater amount of goods still goes on camels.[12]

The alternative was either to fall back on the time honoured camel caravans, or find other efficient means of transport. Two options appeared to be available to Frere. One was to build a canal to connect the Karachi harbour with the river at Kotri or Gharo and the other was to build a railway connecting the harbour with the river. Some differences of opinion occurred between Frere, 'a man of transcendent ability' and John Jacob, the innovative and energetic tamer of Sindh's northern frontiers who had 'clear and decided opinions'. To begin with, Jacob strongly advocated the construction of a navigable canal to link Karachi with the Indus which would ensure safe and direct communication by water between the Indus and the sea port at all seasons. It would also afford an ample supply of fresh water to the city of Karachi for its needs well into the future. 'Cultivation along banks of the proposed canal would also provide it with fresh supplies which had to be brought in from some distance in the interior.'[13]

John Jacob.

The relative merits of a canal and the railway were discussed to bypass the delta and link Karachi with the river. The report by a Lieutenant Chapman suggested that the canal would reduce the distance of the water route considerably. He suggested Jherruk as the point at which the head of a link canal should be constructed as it was the nearest permanent river bank and was also conveniently near a large town. An earlier suggestion that Kalri canal be used as the link canal was rejected by Chapman as it would reduce the usefulness of the canal as an irrigation channel, and also as it would stop fifty miles short of Karachi, and another canal would have to be projected. But attractive though this option was there was still the question of difficulties of navigating the river in some areas, particularly above Multan which was 'shallow and tortuous and almost impossible to navigate.' Also by the fifties when the canal was being discussed railways had been introduced into India and had enough capital available to make the railway alternative more feasible. So although Jacob's arguments for a canal make sense even today, and the best solution would have been to have both the canal and the railway, the contemporary case for railways was more powerful. As Frere put it

...of the two projects I prefer the railway as being more the means of attaining the desired object, as regards the position of the river terminus, speed and cheapness, as the more profitable; the less liable to mishaps from unforeseen accidents, and caprices of the river; the more comprehensive as regards the classes of traffic it will accommodate; but more especially because there is no rival or alternative means of ensuring the speedy rivalry of a railway.[14]

Frere also pointed out the all important consideration of finance, Moreover a railway would meet the ready support from capitalists at a distance, who would be less likely to view a canal as a favourable investment.[15]

The problem with the canal was of course that it had been left too late and railways had displaced canals in England itself. The investors were now firmly behind the railways as the more profitable alternative.

...the traffic would probably be sixty or eighty percent greater than at present before the line can possibly be opened, however speedily it may be commenced; and the making and still more the opening of the line, will give it a vast impetus.[16]

The solution that was eventually found was to build the railway from Karachi to Kotri on the Indus on the opposite

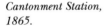

Cantonment Station, 1865.

bank from Hyderabad. Kotri was also the depot of the Indus Flotilla, the company which carried the commercial traffic on the Indus. From Kotri the Indus Flotilla boats would carry the goods and the traffic to Multan from where the Punjab Railway would take them on to Lahore. In addition to the Indus Flotilla, Kotri was also a convenient spot for the trade which converged on Hyderabad from Rajputana, Cutch, upper and lower Sindh.

Jacob, with his Balochistan and Jacobabad orientation, could see no merit in taking the train to Hyderabad at all. He preferred that the railway be built towards the northwest, rather than go on the Left Bank and the Punjab. He could not succeed in convincing the investors or the government, and in the first phase the railway was built up to Kotri thus combining the rail and river transport from Karachi up to the Punjab.

A Sinde Railway Company was formed in 1854 which undertook to build the Sindh railway and was also responsible for the construction of the Punjab Railway from Multan to Lahore and Amritsar. This company also owned the flotilla of steam boats which plied on the Indus between Kotri and Multan, thus completing the system of transport between Karachi and Lahore. The Sind-Punjab Railway was seen by its promoters as part of an ambitious scheme. It was to be part of a new short cut from India to England through the Euphrates valley. Karachi, as the nearest port to the Persian Gulf, was to be an integral part of the scheme. The enthusiasm with which it was taken up by administrators as well as investors in England gives an indication of the spirit of enterprise and optimism which characterized the British imperial mind in the nineteenth century.

On 29 April 1858 work was begun on the Sindh section of the railway. The distance was to be just over 108 miles and one line was opened for traffic on 11 May 1861. The Multan-Lahore section was completed by 1865, thus establishing a rail and river link from Karachi to Lahore. The railway line came in for a good deal of criticism notably from that old Sindh hand, Richard Burton who, revisiting Sindh in 1876 called it the 'the very worst chosen line in the British dominions.' Burton made his criticism on the grounds that the railway avoided the established towns of Jherruk, Thatta and Gharra 'the only places deserving mention in the Trans Indine valley'. Burton condemned the compromise which had been made as having

*Edulji Dinshaw
Dispensary, Saddar,
1882.*

succeeded admirably in avoiding the merits, and in combining the defects of both projects... This iron road runs through a howling wilderness, which for one 'spell' of twenty miles, cannot supply even a drop of water. There is no hope for this desert: the Cairo-Suez line has restored prosperity to ancient 'Goshen', but there the rail runs along a sweet water canal.[17]

The fact was that by taking the shortest route to Kotri the railway avoided the most important towns between Karachi and Kotri which were the ones mentioned by Burton— Jherruk, Thatta and Gharra. By diverting traffic from these ancient towns the railway would accelerate their decline. The alternate line which was proposed by Jacob, going up the right bank of the river to Jacobabad and Balochistan would be built by the end of the century and so would a line from Hyderabad east to Jodhpur and Marwar in Rajputana, linking Karachi with Delhi to the north and Bombay to the south. The building of this network of railways by the last quarter of the nineteenth century gave Karachi a chance to realize its potential as the sea port for the whole of north west India.

In spite of its shortcomings and the drawbacks of the river link which would take until 1878 before it was replaced with a through railway line all the way to Lahore, the railway gave a great boost to the trade of Karachi and, although the Euphrates valley link did not come to anything, Karachi did serve the strategic needs of the empire as the Indian port nearest to Europe.

Karachi was also the obvious port from which British goods could be sent up to the Central Asian markets. The conquest of these markets and even those of areas under British control was not automatic, and Frere spared no efforts to win these markets for British goods. In the 1850s Russian 'chintzes' were reported to be selling better than British goods in the bazaars of 'Cabul, Kandahar and Karachi'. Although this could have been due to the fact that their pattern and colour were more suited to the local taste, the government felt that it had to meet the challenge. Frere came up with the idea of using traditional means of a fair to popularize British goods with the local merchants, as well as those from Central Asia and Russia. Karachi was the most suitable place for holding such a fair as merchants from Bombay could easily send their goods here. It was convenient too for merchants from the north to come on their traditional caravan routes to buy these goods

City Courts on M.A. Jinnah Road, 1868.

The fair is intended to be to traders between Central Asia and Bombay what a 'clearing house' is to bankers, or an exchange or bazaar to merchants in general, a place where people who have wants, which they can mutually supply for each other, may meet and save time, trouble and money which would be otherwise expended by each individual going round to the others individually.[18]

An annual fair was thus established in Karachi which did play its part, not only in sending British goods to Central Asia but also in adding to the prosperity of the city. In addition to the fair the government had to improve the roads in the British territories, ensure peaceful transition for caravans through Balochistan which Jacob suggested was best done by paying a subsidy to the Khan of Kalat. This ploy proved as successful as Jacob had predicted and by 1852 Frere was able to report success to Lord Falkland, the Governor of Bombay Presidency.

The trade of Karachi which was calculated as being worth Rs 1,221,500 in 1847-8 rose steadily and stood at Rs 8,000,000 in 1858 and went up to the enormous total of Rs 21,000,592 in 1863-4. This last figure was largely due to

The Victoria Museum, later the Supreme Court building, 1887-92.

*The Sind Club,
1883.*

the American Civil War which caused a boom in the cotton exports of India. This figure was to fall sharply with the return of peace in the United States. The trade would not reach such heady figures again until the railway line was completed till Lahore in the late seventies.

The improvement of the harbour and the construction of the railway brought Karachi more than anything else into the industrial age. The pace of life changed. The railway served the harbour where it had railway sidings and lifted goods for up country. The town itself was served by two railway stations, one of which was McLeod Road Station at the financial hub of Karachi and the other, Frere Street Station, to serve the new colonial town and the military cantonment.

The city of Karachi had already begun to take shape by this time. The old town situated on the banks of the seasonal Lyari river, and with its river gate and sea gate at either end, continued to be the heart of traditional and 'native' trade.

The old Town of Karachi deprived of its wall and much changed by sanitation and other innovations, but still retaining many of the old alleys to which Sir Richard Burton alluded.[19]

The trading bazaars flourished here and it would continue to be the centre of the business community well into the twentieth century, these bazaars flourish even now particularly the areas surrounding Kharadar and Mithadar such as Jodia Bazaar.

The colonial administration laid out plans for a new Karachi, adjacent to the old one extending from its edges, fanning from the coast on the south all the way to the north. The Napier Mole Bridge linked the Keamari island harbour with the mainland and then bifurcated into two major arteries, Bunder Road on the left and McLeod Road on the right, with the Merewether tower marking the divide. McLeod Road was the new business quarter of the town

> Between the Bunder and McLeod Roads, about half a mile behind the Clock Tower, was the old Kafila Serai, now absorbed into the Sind Madressah, where the camel caravans from Khorassan used to put up out side the city walls. On and between Bunder Road and McLeod Road beats the commercial heart of Karachi. Here all the leading firms have their places of business.[20]

Here was located the handsome Bank of Bombay designed by Strachan, the Judicial Commissioner's Court, the National Bank, and the offices of the commercial firms that had started business in Karachi. The railway station was conveniently situated in this business centre of colonial Karachi.

The Sind Madressah at the site of the old Kafila Serai opened its doors in 1885 and was to prove a key institution in providing the 'new education' not just to the Sindhi children of Karachi, but was to be the alma mater to students coming from the entire province. Although a number of other schools had been established in Karachi, and indeed in other towns of Sindh under the Grants-in-Aid scheme established by Frere in the 1850s, Muslims had been slow in taking advantage of these 'secular' schools. The Muslim community had suffered with the decline of the traditional schools which had been run by Sayed families and had been dependent on endowments and jagirs given for this purpose by the successive governments including the Sultans, the Mughals and their successors. These grants had been withdrawn by the British rulers with the result that the traditional system declined rapidly after the British conquest. Although 'Mulla schools' would continue to exist, teaching the holy scriptures and the 'three Rs' and would have their students mostly in rural neighbourhoods, slowly and rather reluctantly Muslims turned to the new education introduced by the British.

The Sind Madressah with its acceptable name and Islam as part of the curriculum, played a major role in overcoming the prejudices of the Muslim elite in sending their children to English teaching schools. The Sind Madressah owed its existence to the efforts of Hassanally Bey Effendi, a member of an important family of religious preceptors under the Amirs. Effendi was thirteen years old at the time of the British conquest and was among the earliest Sindhis to learn the English language. He realised the importance of English in the advancement of the Muslim community. Effendi rose to distinction in government service and was appointed Public Prosecutor. After retirement he made great efforts to collect funds from all over the province and with additional government help, started the Sind Madressah.

The first government school established in Karachi was Narayan Jagannath High School in 1855. It was right in the heart of the town at the junction of Bunder Road and Mission Road, and was named after a Maratha teacher and education officer who had come from the Presidency to establish the 'new education' in Sindh. He was one of a long line of Maratha teachers who would serve the cause of education in Sindh with dedication, and would leave behind generations of well taught and grateful students. Karachi was adequately served in terms of the new education with a number of schools opening particularly under the Grants-in-Aid scheme. The Catholic and Protestant missionaries also opened a number of schools in Sindh. In Karachi the premier Catholic school was St. Patrick's School for boys, with its sister St. Joseph's Convent for girls. To begin with both St. Patrick's School and St. Joseph's School were co-educational, founded by a Reverend J. Willy in 1861, but were separated as boys and girls schools very shortly thereafter, the latter housed in a handsome building by Strachan. Although missionary schools would play an important role in educating the elite of India, without distinction of religion or even any overt missionary zeal, at this period these schools were attended on the whole by native Christians with a special section for European children. The children of European Protestant officials and civilians in Karachi attended Karachi Grammar School which had been started by Frere in 1854.

For a long time Sindh sent its students on the arduous journey, either by train or boat, to Bombay to sit in the matriculation examination. The first batch which journeyed to Bombay to matriculate consisted of three Amil boys from Hyderabad, Dayaram Jethmull, Navalrai and Chuhar Mall. Writing about them the Educational Inspector said

> They are all three natives of Sind, intelligent and willing to undergo any ordeal that may be required of them, before entering upon a course of instruction at the presidency.[21]

The education of the province suffered from not having the right to hold the matriculation examination and also from not having a degree college. In 1882 a Memorandum was addressed to the Education Commission by public men from Sindh headed by Dayaram Gidumal Shahani, offering a contribution of Rs 30,000 and asking for permission to establish a college in Sindh. The Commission turned down the proposal as it felt that the amount offered was too small. By 1884 subscriptions reached the figure of Rs 90,000 and the Local Bodies offered an annual grant of Rs 10,850. In 1886 the Sind College Association was formed and in January 1887 finally an 'aided' college was founded. This college was named after one of the first graduates, Dayaram Jethmull, by his disciple and friend Dayaram Gidumal, who was also the moving spirit behind the college. The building of the college was designed in the classical style by Strachan and was to be one of the most graceful buildings in Karachi. The Shahani family also donated the Metharam hostel which stood directly opposite the college.

The D.J. College was to be the first of a number of institutions of higher education which would be built in this area of Karachi, near Burns Garden and on Kutchery Road. Cutting across Kutchery Road, McLeod Road became Ingle Road and led to the heart of official Karachi with its 'Camp Bazaar' or Saddar, its official buildings, churches, clubs, and barracks, bounded by the railway line to the south ending at Frere Street or Cantonment Station.

The heart of colonial Karachi was the area described as Saddar. This well laid out area with its geometrically straight streets intersecting each other had as its north west boundary the major artery of Karachi, Bunder Road. It had on its left right angle, St. Patrick's Cathedral, the Catholic church with the largest following in the Christian community. Next to it was the St. Joseph's Convent School, and in the well arranged neighbourhood streets the Goan Christian community congregated in the apartment blocks that were so new to Karachi. Clerk Street leading from St. Patrick's Cathedral, cut across the centre of Saddar Bazaar, Frere Street, Somerset Street, Elphinstone Street, and Victoria Road and ended at the 'artillery maidan'. Here in due course the handsome building of Sindh High Court would be built making a grand avenue. At right angle to the Cathedral and parallel to Bunder Road was the Empress Market, another handsome structure which would continue to serve its original purpose through the next century. Elphinstone street was the fashionable shopping centre with smart shops stocking the latest goods for the Imperial market from 'home'. Memsahibs in their Victoria carriages and protected from the sun by their umbrellas and sunshades shopped for gewgaws from the Army and Navy Store in London, that lifeline of Englishmen serving the Empire. The advertisements for the latest imports of goods from fashionable clothes for the tropics to mosquito nets, goods which could carry the 'civilian' or army family from the cradle to the grave, were advertised in the *Sind Kossid*, the newspaper which served the English reading public of Karachi. Englishwomen were very evident in Karachi, the men on duty in the interior usually leaving them behind in the milder climate of Karachi.

At the bottom end of Saddar and the streets cutting Clerk Street was the residential area where low one storied bungalows had been built for the military officers in the Staff Lines, the engineers in E.I. Lines, and so on. Official Karachi revolved around the Governor's House which had been built by Napier. The Government House, as it was known, stood in forty acres of ground and was a plain one storied building. After Napier left it was bought by the Government as residence for the Commissioner-in-Sindh. John Jacob, when he was Acting Commissioner in 1856, added an upper storey to the main block of the house, similar to his famous residence in Jacobabad. In anticipation of the visit of the Prince and Princess of Wales electric lights and fans were installed. The house had five entrances, three of them facing the official Anglican Trinity Church.

*The Sind Madressah,
1885.*

Kutchery Road, going along the railway line enclosed official Karachi on the southern side. Here were government offices, the houses of the officials, the churches, the clubs, the Cantonment with its well laid out barracks, some of them, such as the Napier Barracks elegantly built from Karachi's native sandstone. In between, some areas were marked out for civilians and were appropriately called 'Civil Lines'. Here the wealthier citizens, such as Parsi and Hindu businessmen and very rarely a Muslim, bought the acre or two they were allotted for their houses. Inducements had to be offered to the Indians to build their houses here in unfamiliar open ground when they would rather have lived in their familiar intimate neighbourhoods. The barracks marked the outer limit of the colonial town on the north with a road leading to Malir, Thatta and beyond. On this road to Malir flanked by low hills, a couple of miles from Napier Barracks, was the latest European graveyard, an oasis of greenery on the arid road, which had replaced the older cemeteries which were now in the middle of the expanding town.

The most handsome building nineteenth century Karachi produced was Frere Hall, built to commemorate the Commissionership of Sir Bartle Frere and his elevation to the Viceroy's Council in 1859. It was funded by the Karachi Municipal Corporation and by public subscription with a small contribution from the government. Frere Hall was completed in 1865 and served admirably as the Town Hall of Karachi with ample room for 'public meeting, lectures, balls, concerts and dramatic performances.' It also accommodated a fine public library. The hall was surrounded by a garden on both sides with a splendid marble statue of Queen Victoria on the Queen's Lawn and, on the opposite side, King Edward VII's statue on the King's Lawn. The opening was performed by the Prince of Wales who was later to be King George V

Merewether Tower, 1892.

The Queen's Statue, which is by Sir Hamco Thorneycroft, R.A., was unveiled by His Royal Highness the Prince of Wales in March 1906. The monument consists of a classically treated architectural pedestal with statues of bronze around the base, and crowned with a colossal white marble Statue of the Queen Empress, wearing a widow's veil and the imperial crown and robes of state, and holding in her hand the sceptre and the orb. The principal group at the foot of the pedestal represents India approaching Justice and Peace. On one side is a lion, and on the other a tiger, with heads erect, guarding the monument. At the rear the river Indus is symbolized by a woman carrying an urn and pouring water on the thirsty soil.[22]

Water was indeed the most pressing problem for thirsty Karachi. The population of Karachi was growing fast and was estimated at 80,000 by the 1860s. It desperately needed potable water. So far Karachi had subsisted on well water drawn from the banks of the seasonal Lyari river and this, according to Frere, tasted like a weak solution of Epsom

The newly built Frere Hall, 1865 (nineteenth century photograph).

St. Andrew's Church, 1868.

Salts. Even this was no longer adequate. In 1868 Colonel C.J. Merriman, who discovered reserves of water beneath the seasonal Malir river, proposed a scheme which would supply water at the rate of twenty-two gallons per person every day. In spite of its essential nature the proposal was

D.J. Science College, 1887.

turned down by the Government of Bombay on grounds of expense. The scheme was taken up again by James Strachan, engineer and secretary to the Karachi Municipality. Strachan modified the scheme to replace the expensive iron pipes with masonry ones but even then the scheme was not found acceptable. Finally, the scheme was cut down from the original Rs 1,859,000 to a mere, Rs 850,000 which would provide eight gallons per head of population instead of twenty-two gallons. This modificiation was accepted and by 1883 the Dumlotee water supply was completed, thus bringing the much needed water supply to Karachi.

The credit for the successful completion of this scheme, under the restraint of limited money and difficult circumstances, goes entirely to the efforts of Strachan. He should also be given credit for this as well as the excellent planning of the new Karachi town being laid out, and for the admirable public buildings that were built by him to give Karachi its pleasant and interesting character. Strachan, a native of Aberdeen, the northernmost town of Scotland. was the Divisional Engineer on the Great Indian Peninsular and Bombay and Baroda Railways and was appointed Engineer and Secretary to the Karachi Municipality in 1873.[23] Strachan was just what fledgling Karachi needed. He provided the infrastructure needed by the city and the elegant buildings to give it character. Not only did he work out the way to provide a plentiful

Nineteenth century commercial buildings on Bunder Road.

water supply for the city but also planned its public transport. He promoted a tramway as the backbone of this public transport. The tramway system was opened in 1885 by the East India Tramway Company. The lines extended from Keamari to Cantonment (Frere Street) Railway Station, with one branch via the Napier and Lawrence

Nineteenth century
Karachi flats.

Roads to the Zoological Gardens and one to Soldier Bazaar. The tramway was to serve Karachi till the middle of the twentieth century. It was originally driven by steam but curiously 'subsequently horse traction was substituted, and at a later date motor traction.'[24]

Bunder Road was the link between the old city and the new. Along it were built all the amenities needed by a rapidly growing capital of the province: the Civil Hospital and the Lady Dufferin Hospital for women; markets such as Boulton Market, a classical building which like the Empress Market, was designed by Strachan although in a completely different style of architecture and replaced an old market on the same site; the Mission school and the Mission Church built by Karachi's first Collector, the evangelizing Major Preedy; the Small Causes Court and 'the travellers bungalow'; the tramway stables, the headquarters of the Municipal Corporation and the jail were all along this road. The road petered out into barracks and the parade ground of the Native Infantry regiments. The nineteenth century Bunder Road extended up to Garden Road.

Turning left on Garden Road, a few furlongs ahead was the oldest garden laid out by the British, initially for the purpose of supplying the troops with fresh vegetables. This garden even made a profit selling vegetables and fruits and fodder to the army

In 1847 Major W. Blenkins, Assistant Commissary-General and Superintendent of Gardens was able to report that he had discontinued drawing [the sum of Rs100 for the support of the Garden] that for two years and during that period had made a profit for Government of Rs17,032. This was by issue of vegetables to the troops and fodder to Government cattle, the sale of vegetables and forage to private persons and the supply of pigeons, rabbits and leeches to the hospital. He appended three medical certificates to the effect that the leeches bred by Major Blenkins were infinitely superior to those formerly obtained by contract.[25]

The Government Garden, which was popularly known as Rani Bagh after Queen Victoria, was eventually handed over to the Municipality. On over forty acres of ground 'probably a part of the ground surrounding the old Factory', the Government Garden was given a good deal of care and planned anew by municipal officers including Strachan. It

Empress Market, 1889.

59

*Lord Curzon
in Karachi, 1901.*

was 'laid out with trees, shrubs and even fountains'. Sir
Evan James who was Commissioner-in-Sindh in 1890-9 and
who took a great interest in the flora and fauna of the
province, introduced California grapes which flourished and
for which the garden became famous for well over half a
century. These grapes which were also grown in Burns
Gardens eventually disappeared after independence,
presumably from neglect. A small zoo was also started in
this garden which continues to exist to this day.

The Government Garden was bound by Lawrence Road,
and just a little further ahead on this road was another
garden. Recreation and refreshment was also provided for
the citizens of Karachi by Dr Burns' Garden laid out in just
over twenty-six acres near the D.J.College and the Victoria
Museum. This garden included a vineyard which also grew
the California grapes introduced by Sir Evan James well
into the twentieth century. The other notable garden in the
Cantonment area was the Frere Hall garden It was expected
that the water supply ensured by Dumlotee wells would allow
the Karachi Municipality to extend its gardening activities,
but the fact was that a century and a half has not added
greatly to the gardens laid out in the initial years of British
rule.

By the end of the nineteenth century Karachi had been provided with a modern infrastructure. Water supply was ensured, railways had put the city in touch with the rest of British India. Karachi port was the third most important port in India and the nearest to Europe. Entrepreneurs from Bombay and elsewhere were immigrating to Karachi to set up their commercial houses. Karachi was attracting Gujerati businessmen of all varieties, Parsi, Hindu and Memon. It had Marwaris and Marathas, many of the latter as dedicated teachers in its new schools. Sindhi business houses were moving up from Shikarpur and Hyderabad. Rural Sindhis were gradually becoming aware of this cool new capital and gradually taking up residence there; shopping at Elphinstone Street, at Haji Dossul's arms shops and department stores. Karachi's population was multi ethnic and its tastes eclectic. It was poised, unencumbered by historical baggage, on the point of take off as a twentieth century city.

Strachan's map of nineteenth century Karachi.

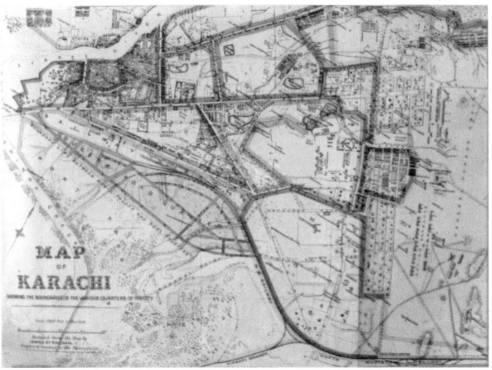

The Karachi Municipal
Corporation Building,
1931.

Chapter 3

THE HALCYON YEARS

Hamida Khuhro

The outbreak of World War I in 1914 reinforced the strategic importance of Karachi for the defence of the subcontinent. It became the headquarters of Allied operations in the Middle East. The port came under pressure from heavy war traffic while Karachi itself saw huge army encampments of soldiers from the Punjab on their way to fight Turkish armies in campaigns in Iraq and German armies in France. T.E. Lawrence was seen striding down Bunder Road in his Arab robes in between his spectacular achievements in Arabia.

Within the first few months of the war 80,000 British troops and 200,000 Indian troops were despatched, many of them from Karachi, to France, East Africa, Egypt as well as the Persian Gulf. In France the Indian soldiers fought in circumstances which were in great contrast with the desert conditions of the Middle East. Here they spent agonizing years in the cold and the misery of trench warfare.

The Middle Eastern Arab countries were part of the Ottoman Empire at this time and the British Indian troops left from Karachi to arrive at Basra which they captured from the Turks. But it was a long and bloody war and disastrous for the Indian troops who suffered heavy casualties and the 'medical and commissariat arrangements collapsed in a manner reminiscent of the Afghan wars.'[1] The Indians under General Townsend, were pushed back from their drive on Baghdad by superior forces and besieged at Kut el Amara where on 29 April 1916 they were forced by starvation to surrender after a siege of 150 days. Fresh troops were sent out from Karachi and eventually succeeded at the

*The Sindh
High Court,
1929.*

second battle of Kut el Amara. They were able to push on
to Baghdad which they finally took in March 1917. Although
the Indian troops which fought in Iraq included many
Muslims and they fought loyally for the British, the war
against fellow Muslims was to bring a revulsion of feeling
which would lead to the emotional and political upheaval
of the Khilafat movement.

In January 1919 the prisoners of Kut came back to India
to be greeted at Karachi port with due ceremony and amidst
touching scenes

> The whole scene was blinded with light, fluttering with flags
> and pennants, blazing with red carpets and bunting...Words of
> command, troops, crowds, winking of brass instruments of the
> band, boat sirens, all making up a jig-saw puzzle of brilliant
> sight and sound. Out thundered the salute, and *H.M.S.
> Elephanta*, both fluttering with flags and pennants in the stiff
> breeze and incandescent sunshine.[2]

The message from the Commander in Chief was read out
and the Commissioner-in-Sindh made a welcoming speech
praising the courage of the returning men. Lady Lawrence

garlanded the officers with roses and they were 'cinematographed'

After all kinds of food, gifts and entertaining of various kinds, they went off in a decorated train with garlands round the engine's necks, and the coal whitewashed, to the Rest Camp where they will spend some days. There each man receives a large card designed by me and printed. On a jet black background, surrounded by a wreath of bright red roses and bright green leaves, two white horses. On one an Indian woman in a sari, on the other Britannia. Both hold spears which are united over their heads by a banner on which is printed in English and in Urdu 'India proudly welcomes her returning heroes'.[3]

This war saw the first involvement of aeroplanes in combat. Handley Page had developed a plane intended for bombing Berlin but before it could be sent on its intended mission Armistice had been declared. It was then sent on the very first flight to the subcontinent. It started its flight on 13 December 1918 from Ipswich in England and was expected to arrive in Karachi only weeks later. But it ran into trouble on the way because of too much weight and not enough horse power. The story of its landing in Karachi on 15 January 1919, a month later is narrated by Lady Lawrence.

For the past three days the big Handley Page biplane, the very first to attempt to fly to India, has been expected here. The landing place is prepared in the desert on the Magar Pir Road. It is all marked out with white stones. There is a hut and shamiana erected for addresses and welcomes and so forth, from the Army and Municipality. But after three days of alternate expectation and disappointment the news comes through that the arrival is indefinitely postponed. One of the four cylinders had blown off and the machine was forced to land at Ormara on the Persian Gulf.

General MacEwan decided she would have to be dismantled. Dreadfully disappointed...

At the Gymkhana an ADC hurried past me, and muttered between his closed teeth, not looking at me, 'Don't let it out. But she is coming. *Now.* You may just get there in time'.

What a temptation to leap into the car, and go straight away to the landing place!...but I overcome it and hurry off to look for Henry. Find him in his office, still in his tussore suit.

*The boundary wall
of the Mohatta Palace,
1933.*

No time to change into anything warmer. We dash into the
Fiat and tear away in clouds of dust down the Magar Pir Road.

Sunset when we arrive. She has not yet come! Just General
Fowler and Henry and a few officers and myself waiting. We
get out and stand there on the sand, shivering with cold and
excitement. The sand was a curious dark purple. A full moon
was rising at our backs swimming into a violet East, whilst in
the West a daffodil band of sky shone behind the black craggy
line of low hills over which the 'the old Carthusian', as she is
called, must come. A tiny hum. One didn't know whether it
was a loud sound a long way off, or a tiny sound inside one's
own ears...but now it was getting louder, and louder...*it was
she*! A tiny speck against that still faintly bright West...and
here she came flying terribly, oh! so terribly low over those
cruel peaks, the engines thumping hard. Our hearts were in
our mouths. The merest novice could tell she was in great
distress. It was moonlight now. Rockets soared into the
zenith.They dropped a Verey light, green as *creme de menthe*.
Another. She was looming enormous up there, the noise
tremendous. She dropped down a light before her as she
alighted. The moon cast her gigantic shadow across the desert
as she feebly taxied a very few yards, and then abruptly came
to a standstill. Out of her tottered Major Maclaren, Captain

Halley, Sergeant Smith, and a very small fox terrier, and stood there in the moonlight motionless. All were dead beat, and frozen stiff. They were in their shirt sleeves. To get over those jagged peaks they had been forced to throw out maps, instruments, glasses, even their clothing as ballast. They were almost speechless with cold and fatigue.[4]

On board was the very first 'aerial' letter to India. It was a communication from Lord Willingdon at the India Office in London for Sir Henry Lawrence, the Commissioner-in-Sindh. From this hesitant beginning Karachi would go on to become 'the premier airport and international air junction of the subcontinent'. In 1920 a regular air mail service was started between Karachi and Bombay. In the same year the British Government presented one hundred aeroplanes to the Indian Government in order to encourage civil aviation and Handley Page wrote to the Karachi Chamber of Commerce 'on the subject of providing landing grounds and other facilities in the subcontinent and also on the necessity for reducing customs duties on aircraft and aircraft accessories.'[5]

The Indian Chamber of Commerce, 1923.

The age of air travel definitely made an early mark in Karachi. The city was strategically and climatically well situated for air travel. To begin with, the Drigh Road area was developed as a landing ground for the use of the Royal Indian Air Force as well as civilian air traffic. As the need for airfields grew dramatically with World War II, Mauripur Airport was also developed to serve as a military air base and Drigh Road became an important base for the American air force. After the war the Drigh Road airport was given over to civilian use.

The twenties and thirties were the period when airships or 'Dirigible Balloons', self propelled 'lighter than air' craft were being promoted as the air transport of the future and the 'Zeppelin' was a household word in Europe and America. In 1925 Group Captain Fellowes, Director of Airship Construction in the UK, selected Karachi as a base in India for experimental airship flying. It was selected because of its favourable climate and because it was the obvious stepping stone to Calcutta. The aircraft scheme would bring Karachi within eight days of London for passengers and mails.[6]

A huge hangar was built at Drigh Road to house the R101 airship which was expected to start the passenger service from Europe to the east. In October 1930 the R101 started its journey from Paris but, unfortunately, before the ship reached Karachi it crashed south of Beauvais in France. A few years later the famous airship, the Hindenburg, met with a disastrous accident in 1936 in the US, giving a death blow to this form of transport. The huge black R101 hangar at Drigh Road known as *kala chapra* remained till well after Partition as a famous landmark of Karachi and was eventually dismantled and sold to 'gain space' which had been occupied by the hangar. Thus although airships failed, heavier than air aeroplanes did prove to have a future and Karachi found its place as the major Indian airport for this form of transport. In 1927 a contract was signed with Imperial Airways to establish a weekly service between England and Karachi. This did not however come into effect till 1930 as it had to wait till local links with Bombay and Delhi could be established. Karachi was also an important stop for sea planes which landed at Korangi. The landing area for these sea planes is now part of the Pakistan Air Force Base at

*The Masonic
Lodge Building.*

Korangi. Sea planes continued to land here till late in the
forties. The age of the airmail and air travel had arrived in
the subcontinent by the early thirties.

The end of World War I saw the rise of political activity
in India and Sindh, this once 'backwater' also felt the shock
waves. The Montagu-Chelmsford Reforms of 1919 had
proved a disappointment, particularly as they fell short of
expectations of Home Rule and also lagged behind the
concessions given to the 'White colonies' of the Empire
such as Canada, Australia and New Zealand. To add insult
to injury, repressive laws were passed affecting political and
press activity which sent the message to the Indian people
that all the support that they had given in the war effort
had been in vain. The Non Co-operation Movement
launched by Gandhi and simultaneously the Khilafat
Movement started by Muslims, and also supported by
Gandhi, put tremendous pressure on the British in India.
Karachi fully participated in this national struggle. The
atmosphere in Government House echoed the earlier
tension of Revolt of 1857

These are horrible days. For the past week Henry has ordered
that Owen is not to leave the compound. Indeed he has to play
immediately in front of the sentry under the palms and the

amaltas. It is difficult to explain to Nanny, as the civil population knows nothing and is to be kept unsuspecting. We are on the edge of a volcano. There is dissatisfaction amongst the British troops also, as leave is cancelled.[7]

Nationalist politicians, including, Rais Ghulam Mohammed Bhurgri and Harchandrai Vishindas, were to be arrested but managed to escape to Bombay and then to England putting Sir Henry Lawrence in a very awkward position, and eventually forcing his departure from the province. This was in itself an unfortunate development as Lawrence was highly sympathetic to the Muslims of the province who he felt were suffering from unnecessary disadvantages in a province of their majority, and who had tried his best to improve their position. Lady Lawrence had put his policy in her own inimitable style 'Henry championed the Muhammadan, who by reason of being generally less educated, got pushed and shouldered aside from any appointment carrying responsibility.'[8]

Lawrence was quite unique among the officers who ruled Sindh. He worked hard to get the plans for the Sukkur Barrage approved and he strongly supported the idea of separating Sindh from the Bombay Presidency. Later when

The Khaliqdina Hall.

he was Finance Member of the Governor's Council at Bombay and Acting Governor himself, he would continue his support for the advancement of Sindh and Sindhi Muslims. It was ironic that this was the Commissioner who had to confront the nationalists who wanted to restore autonomy to Sindh. It was at the annual session of the All India Congress Party at Karachi in 1913 that a resolution was tabled by the Sindh delegation for the separation of the province.

Karachi had its share of excitement in the political ferment of the twenties and thirties. This included such spectacular events as the trial of the Ali brothers for sedition in Khaliqdina Hall in 1921

On 14 November 1921, Mohammed Ali was arrested at Waltair railway station while he was travelling with Gandhi to Madras. All those who had supported the resolution at the Karachi session of All India Khilafat Conference (July 1921), against service in the army were picked up from their respective provinces and brought to Karachi. These included Maulana Shaukat Ali hauled out of his bed at his Bombay residence at midnight and taken by ship to Karachi; Saifuddin Kitchlew from Lahore, Maulana Madni and Maulana Nisar Ahmed of UP, and Bharati Krishna of Gujerat.

The case was remitted by the trying magistrate at Karachi to the Sessions Judge. The trial had an element of high drama- and even melodrama. The crowds anxious to see the trial were so large that it had to be held, not in a court room but in a public auditorium, which gave the Ali brothers an excellent opportunity to display their polemical skill. They waved gaily to the crowds waiting outside the building. And inside the hall they refused to rise when the magistrate arrived. Why, they asked, should non-co-operators honour a judge of the British Government? When their chairs were removed to oblige them to stand, they took off their long cloaks, spread them on the floor and sat down. Though Mohammed Ali asserted that he did not recognize the jurisdiction of the court, his address to the jury ran to more than 20,000 words.[9]

But these spectacles notwithstanding, on the whole Karachi did not lose its cool. On one occasion Gandhi had to denounce an act of indiscipline of a Karachi crowd which had reportedly 'run amuck in July 1921 on the conviction of Swami Krishnanand, a popular preacher and a local leader'.[10] Karachi played host to conferences and

*The Sukkur Barrage
Dinner which was held
at the Karachi
Gymkhana, 1932.*

courteously welcomed the national leaders but tended to stay out of the heat of the battle. The city was too much of an ethnic mix, too busy with business in Kharadar and Mithadar, too prosperous, too modern, spread out with straight avenues and the wide brown vistas, straight roads with the stately camel sailing down them, and the occasional tram ringing its bell, or the Victoria carriage carrying a prosperous Parsi family down to Clifton, or even the happy Makrani driving his donkey cart furiously to Keamari, oblivious of the political dramas being played out in the overcrowded cities of the subcontinent. They may have heard of Jallianwalla Bagh and of Chauri Chaura but these were problems for *babus* to worry about, and not for the doughty fishermen of Lyari.

Karachi matured intellectually and physically in the two decades between the world wars in spite of the great depression and political unrest. It had grown into a prosperous town with a population of about 400,000. It boasted two major English language newspapers, *The Daily*

A garden party held at the Karachi Club in honour of the Governor of Bombay in 1933.

Gazette which was started by Sir Montagu de P. Webb, an English businessman who had adopted Karachi and became one of its most active citizens, and the Indian owned *Sind Observer*. There were also the two important Sindhi language newspapers, *Al Wahid* the famous Khilafat newspaper, and *Sansar Samachar,* as well as a host of smaller Sindhi and Urdu publications. This was a period of intellectual ferment with journals expressing all points of view despite the notorious Vernacular Press Act and the repressive laws which had been enacted during and after the War. Its educational establishments increased with the establishment of the Nadirshaw Edulji Dinshaw Engineering College, and later the addition of the S.C. Shahani Law College bringing the number of major colleges to three. These educational institutions were clustered around the area near the end of Kutchery Road (now known as Ziauddin Road) and Pakistan Chowk. In the early thirties this was still a fish market which did not fit in with the development plans the city fathers had for Karachi. The area was bought by Kewalram Shahani, the son of Dayaram Gidumal, and donated to the city to be kept as an open space. This was the educational heart of Karachi with the N.E.D Engineering College, D.J. College, S.M. Law College, the Metharam Hostel which had also been donated by the Shahani family.

Physically the city grew apace. The extension of the city was made into well appointed squares and streets with public parks and recreational facilities. The city was well integrated with its charming residential areas spreading now nearly as far as the central jail marking its northern boundary. The tramway did not come up quite all the way to the jail but stopped at Soldier Bazaar which served the new residential areas or 'colonies'. From Soldier Bazaar the tram took its passengers for two annas to Saddar with its fashionable shopping in Elphinstone Street or to the Empress Market. Or one could take the tram all the way to the crowded and busy Boulton Market on Bunder Road from where one could walk or take a tonga to Kharadar. This was not entirely devoted to wholesale trading and women still came shopping here for silks and cottons, and for embroidery and *zari* work.

Lady Haroon gives a ladies lunch at her home in the 1930s.

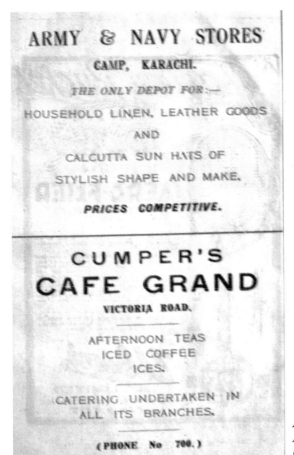

An advertisement for the Army and Navy Stores and Cumper's Cafe Grand.

This end of Bunder Road and across to McLeod Road was the business and trading centre of the city, its 'city' area. From here down to Keamari, the area was full of ware houses and grain and cotton sheds. But the ordinary citizen, intent on a weekend pleasure trip, could also go down to Keamari and take a sail boat, or a launch for a couple of hours sailing, or go to Manora for a walk and a picnic. Nearer in, at the corner of Queens Road and the Napier Mole Bridge, was the Native Jetty and the temple where the annual Hindu religious festivals terminated, as did the Moharram processions.

Karachi was well served with clubs, that British institution for the upper classes, to spend their leisure hours. The Sind Club was the favoured haunt of the British officials, both civilian and military, as well as the businessman. Sunday was

An early twentieth century commercial building on Karachi's Wall Street.

invariably spent with a game of golf in the sand—'with a heavy luncheon at the Sind Club afterwards.' Lady Lawrence comments 'The bar at the Sind Club plays an important part in Karachi society. There business, war, scandal is discussed over whiskies and milk punch...'[11]

There was the Ladies Club which then became the Gymkhana when that term was invented. This stood on Scandal Point Road, its wall adjoining the Government House. Indians were of course excluded from these clubs where the rulers took their ease but just round the corner on Kutchery Road was the Karachi Club where the rich Indian businessmen and the occasional politician spent their evenings. The leading Sindh politicians entertained the visiting Governor of Bombay to garden parties here at the Karachi Club or at public receptions in Frere Hall Gardens. The *Daily Gazette* of 16 January 1933 reported the activities of the Governor of Bombay, Sir Frederick and Lady Sykes in Karachi for a winter tour of Sindh. The Sindh Muhammadan Association gave a reception for him at Frere Hall where he was informed of the conditions of agriculture and the plight of the agriculturists of Sindh. He met the British community at the Sind Club where he made a speech telling his audience of the future plans of the British Government with regard to constitutional reforms for India, as well as the development schemes the government had in mind for the province of Sindh as a whole and for the city of Karachi. Then he and Lady Sykes met the politicians and the cream of Karachi society at a Garden Party hosted by M.A. Khuhro at the Karachi Club. The description of the event in the newspaper gives a unique flavour of the British Raj acting out its role in India

> Whilst in Karachi His Excellency the Governor of Bombay and Lady Sykes were entertained at a Garden Party given by Khan Bahadur M.A. Khuhro, M.L.C. of Larkana on the beautiful and shady lawns of Karachi Club on Sunday.
>
> Hundreds of leading citizens of all communities had been invited to do honour to the Governor by Khan Bahadur Khuhro and the lawn presented an animated appearance, ladies' bright saries and gay afternoon frocks being set off by the more sober colours of lounge suits and male costumes.
>
> All rose as His Excellency the Governor and Lady Sykes arrived and were greeted by the host Khan Bahadur Khuhro who escorted them to seats at one of the tables.
>
> A pleasant hour was spent in this fashion, the Governor and Lady Sykes proceeding from table to table chatting with all the guests, who were presented to them, before they departed to the accompaniment of three cheers.[12]

The club scene would be enhanced later by the Boat Club on Chinna Creek with its European clientele and the Karachi Club Annexe for the 'natives'. But the family man could take his children to the newly built Kothari Parade at New Clifton and walk down the pier to the sea or walk at the promontory at Old Clifton with the waves dashing against the rocks below. A real treat for the citizens was the delightful Cumper's Cafe Grand run by a German couple which was situated on Victoria Road just across from Sind Club, where real home-made ice cream was served in heavy silver plated dishes and wonderful pastries in bone china plates. This was a real European style cafe with its wicker chairs and marble topped tables reminiscent of old Vienna. Life was unrushed in Karachi of the inter-war period. There was time to take a Victoria carriage to Clifton and to sit in

Kothari Parade, Clifton, 1920.

An outing at Clifton Pier.
Note the snake charmer in
the foreground.

Cafe Grand or in the many 'Irani' restaurants in Saddar with their bentwood chairs and again marble topped tables and have *chai*. It was a clean, well kept city where the citizens were secure in the knowledge that the city fathers were doing their very best.

This was mainly because of the practical sense and the vision of one man above all—Jamshed Nusserwanji Mehta. In 1920 Jamshed Nusserwanji became a councillor of Karachi Municipality. He became President of Karachi Municipal Corporation in 1921 and remained so for over a decade. In 1934 he was elected the first mayor of the city of Karachi. It was an immense stroke of luck for Karachi that such a selfless and dedicated man, was also imaginative and realized that the city needed the infrastructure and planning for the inevitable growth that would and was taking place. Nusserwanji explained how he saw the function of a municipality

Taking the air at Kothari
Parade, Clifton.

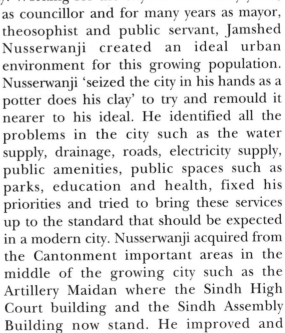

In fact anything and everything that inspires, that brings joy, removes sorrow and makes each one draw towards the other and towards Nature, is the work of a Municipality entrusted with this department of building, engineering, garden, recreation and other subdepartments.[13]

The population of the city was growing at an immense rate largely by immigration from the interior as well as from other provinces. The growing commercial importance of the city was attracting businessmen from Bombay and the Punjab. Empress Market had shopkeepers from as far away as Iran and Afghanistan, trading in their traditional goods of dry fruits. Karachi was taking shape as a multi ethnic, multi cultural, urbane and tolerant city. Working for the city for over thirty years, as councillor and for many years as mayor, theosophist and public servant, Jamshed Nusserwanji created an ideal urban environment for this growing population. Nusserwanji 'seized the city in his hands as a potter does his clay' to try and remould it nearer to his ideal. He identified all the problems in the city such as the water supply, drainage, roads, electricity supply, public amenities, public spaces such as parks, education and health, fixed his priorities and tried to bring these services up to the standard that should be expected in a modern city. Nusserwanji acquired from the Cantonment important areas in the middle of the growing city such as the Artillery Maidan where the Sindh High Court building and the Sindh Assembly Building now stand. He improved and

Clifton beach in the thirties.

A residence in Civil Lines.

extended the drainage system to areas of the city where the waste was still removed every morning by a bullock driven sewage cart. Karachi became one of the few cities in the subcontinent with a complete underground drainage system.

Many of Nusserwanji's plans could not be implemented because of the miserliness of the Bombay Government which would not release adequate amounts for the needs of the city and the province. It was obvious that water could only be supplied adequately for the needs of the city if the supply connection from the Indus was established but the cost of such a project would not be countenanced by Bombay. As it happened, with the advent of World War II and the stationing of large numbers of air force personnel and other troops the need for adequate water supplies became imperative. Consequently, money was found and the Haleji Lake water supply was established. This source of water would carry Karachi just adequately through the sudden huge demand created by the refugee influx of 1947 and the needs of the capital of Pakistan until a regular supply was assured from the Indus when the lower Sindh Barrage at Jamshoro was completed in the mid fifties. Nusserwanji increased the road mileage of Karachi from fourteen miles to seventy-two miles of well engineered asphalted roads. Most notably he extended Bunder Road into Bunder Road Extension and kept it wide enough for the needs of a city far bigger than Karachi was in the thirties and forties. It was characteristic of Nusserwanji's attention to the detail of cleanliness in the city that the roads of Karachi were washed regularly every night.

Nusserwanji initiated co-operative housing societies to help develop Karachi and saw to it that well planned areas with open spaces and squares with gardens were built giving Karachi wonderfully planned housing with all possible amenities, including gardens, in every quarter. The Parsi

Plan of the Indus water supply scheme from Kalri canal (Keenjhar lake) and Haleji lake.

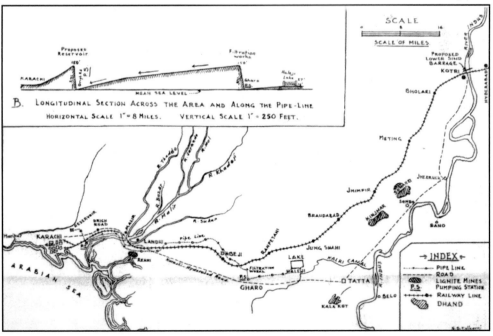

Colony with its charming villas, the Amil Colony, the Catholic Colony and the Muslim Colony looking on to Patel Park (now known as Nishtar Park), Jamshed Quarters and the entire Bunder Road Extension area with its well made roads, well lit streets, well looked after gardens and the Exhibition grounds on a rising (the Quaid-i-Azam monument area) bore testimony to the way in which Jamshed Nusserwanji saw the development of Karachi. The splendid Karachi Municipal Corporation building was also the realization of his vision.

Nusserwanji's Karachi was the health resort of the subcontinent. Here people came to rest and recuperate. The health of the city was jealously guarded and it was kept scrupulously clean. It was in a position to take its place first as the capital of its own province and then would become the capital of a new state.

This was also the period in which Sindh fought in an organized and single minded way for restoring its separate and autonomous status which it had enjoyed even in the first few years after the British conquest. The anomaly of Sindh being ruled from distant Bombay, which could only be reached by a two day journey by train or a sea voyage, was obvious. Although a modicum of autonomy and representative government had been introduced in 1919 which allowed Council members to be elected and represent their constituencies in the Bombay Legislative Council, Sindh was very much the fief of officialdom under the extra-ordinary powers of the Commissioner-in-Sindh. The demand grew in the province for autonomy and an accessible and non bureaucratic government.

The demand for autonomy for Sindh had been put on the platform of the All India Congress by the Sindh leadership in 1913. It had been again put to the visiting Secretary of State for India, Sir Edwin Montagu in 1917, and although Montagu had seen justice in the Sindh demand, no concession had been made in the subsequent constitutional reforms. In the twenties the demand gathered strength. It was put by Sindhi leaders on the Congress and Muslim League platforms. It was one of the points in Jinnah's Fourteen Points which he put at the Delhi Muslim Conference in 1929. But the demand was taken seriously by the British Government only when Sindhis organized themselves and lobbied strongly, both in India and England.

A remarkable unity of purpose was seen in the Sindh leadership at this time. The leadership which would dominate the next few decades of Sindh politics and lead the province into Pakistan emerged into prominence at this time. Sir Abdullah Haroon, Shaikh Abdul Majid, Mohammed Ayub Khuhro, G.M Syed, Allahbaksh Soomro, Syed Miran Mohammed Shah, Pir Ali Mohammed Rashdi, were among the most active of the leadership associated with the struggle of the separation of Sindh.

The Sindh Mohammedan Association revived by Khuhro took up the cause. In 1928 Sir John Simon brought the British Parliamentary Commission to India to examine the working of the 1919 reforms and suggest a further tranche of reforms. The Simon Commission came to Karachi to hear the Sindh case. It sat in the newly built Sindh Chief Court building where the pro separationists led by Khuhro and anti separationists led by Professor Chablani presented their cases. Arguing for separation Khuhro pointed out that geographically, historically and economically, Sindh was quite distinct from the presidency and was suffering also because of the distance from the presidency headquarters. The bureaucracy ruling the province was unresponsive or too dilatory and consequently public work suffered. The Presidency officials were strongly against the separation as they were reluctant to give up what they felt was a wonderful perquisite. They argued that a separate Sindh would not be financially viable. The Simon Commission decided against the separation on financial grounds. But the Sindh leadership did not give up. They renewed their efforts and made out a strong case based on facts and figures that Sindh would be financially self supporting, particularly with the construction of the Sukkur Barrage which was due to be completed in 1932. Even though Sindh was to pay back the loan which had been given to it to build the Barrage it was expected that the prosperity of the province would increase enough to support an autonomous government. Eventually in the Government of India Act of 1935 Sindh was constituted into a separate autonomous province and Karachi became the capital of the new province.

A year earlier the government constituted an administrative committee to set up the administration and the infrastructure for the new province and its capital. This committee was headed by Hugh Dow, an officer who had

*Flats on
Burns Road.*

served long in Sindh and was familiar with its administration
and had also been involved with the finances of the Sukkur
Barrage. The committee, which had Muslim and Hindu
legislators and officials went into the question of preparing
Karachi to function as the capital of the new administration.
The construction of an Assembly Hall and the secretariat to
house the Government of Sindh was authorized. A
questionnaire was circulated to elicit opinion on organizing
separate service cadres for Sindh and for setting up a
separate university, as well as other administrative problems.
It was decided that although it would be desirable to have
separate service cadres, for the time being Sindh would
remain joined with Bombay for this purpose and that
Sindh's educational institutions would remain affiliated to
Bombay until such time as Sindh could have its own
university. A committee was set up to work out the details of
the university. The site for it was selected but World War II
intervened and it was not until 1946 that the new Sind
University came into being.

By the time Sindh became autonomous on 1 April 1936,
the infrastructure for Karachi as a modern city was already

Flats in downtown Karachi.

in place, thanks to the efforts of the Karachi Municipality under Nusserwanji. The Sindh Government with the advice of the Sindh Administrative Committee, worked out plans and developed the framework for the orderly development of Karachi as the capital of Sindh. An impressive, if not very elegant, building was constructed to house the Secretariat and the Sindh Provincial Assembly, and plans were made to

A welcome procession for Mr Mohammad Ali Jinnah (Muslim League Session 1938).

house the staff and ministers in Karachi. Unfortunately, during the war years of 1938 to 1945 practically all development work was at a standstill and the only notable improvement that was made was the increase in the supply of water, made necessary by the presence of a large number of military personnel in the town.

During the war years, Karachi felt as if it was the hub of the war effort. It had the American air force base at Drigh Road and the RAF base at Mauripur. Its harbour was busy with troop ships and war supplies. The city was full of soldiers walking down its streets, bargaining with shop keepers and filling its restaurants and cinemas. Far away from the scene of war, unlike Calcutta, Karachi experienced the excitement of war without its hazards and gained prosperity from the price rises of these years. The war came to an end in August 1945 and the reality of the freedom struggle and the withdrawal of the colonial power had to be faced again.

In 1946, however, the Government of India recommended to the provincial governments that plans should go ahead for post war development. The Government of Sindh created the portfolio of Post War Development which was given to Khuhro who was also the Minister for Public Works. Khuhro was aware that Karachi would have to play its role in the post colonial world and would have to put in industries which were practically non existent so far. It was also necessary that the further expansion of Karachi be planned so that the city should continue to have a proper modern infrastructure and not grow in a haphazard manner. Khuhro acquired the services of town planners from England to make plans for an industrial site for Karachi, as well as for housing areas. Colonel Swayne Thomas was employed by the government

Governor's House, Karachi (Governor-General's House after 1947).

as Town Planner. The demarcation and development of the industrial area was a priority and during this time Sindh Industrial Trading Estate was set up with the requisite infrastructure to encourage industries. The Government of Sindh offered concessions to entrepreneurs to set up industries and a beginning was made. The SITE would take off with the advent of freedom and make Karachi the biggest industrial area in the country.

For the next ten years Karachi made its mark as one of the most important cities in the struggle for the freedom of the subcontinent and for the creation of the new state of Pakistan. Autonomous Sindh was the cornerstone of the demand put by the Muslims for a separate state

The separation of Sind from Bombay Presidency and its constitution as a fully fledged autonomous province...was the most significant event in the process that led to the creation of Pakistan. If there had been no autonomous Sind with its 75% Muslim population, if Sind had continued as part of the

Jehangir Kothari Hall on Victoria Road.

Sarnagati Building, Pakistan Chowk.

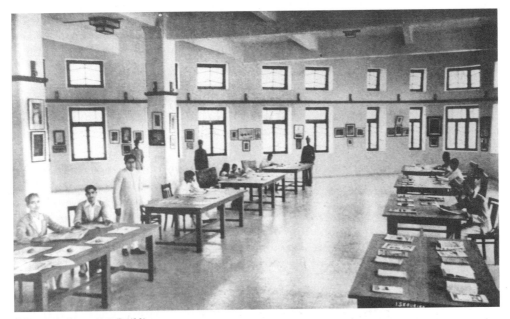

Library at Sarnagati Building.

huge Bombay Presidency with its multi racial, multi linguistic and multi religious population, the case for Partition would have been considerably weaker. Punjab and Bengal had bare Muslim majorities, Baluchistan was sparsely populated and subject to Frontier Regulations. The North West Frontier Province('s)... politics were ambiguous from the Muslim League point of view. From 1937 to 1946 therefore the mainstay of the Pakistan demand was the existence of autonomous Sind.[14]

The key role Sindh played in the struggle for Pakistan was marked first by the gaining of autonomy and then underlined by the historic session of Sindh Muslim League held in Karachi in October 1938. Mohammad Ali Jinnah, President of All India Muslim League presided. All the major Muslim political leaders in India had been invited to the conference

On 7 October Jinnah arrived by special train at Karachi and received a right royal welcome. From the railway station he was taken on a specially bedecked camel cart at the head of a three mile long procession along the major roads of Karachi accompanied by bands playing suitably rousing music. An aeroplane was hired to shower flower petals on the procession. Vast crowds turned out to welcome the visitors. The conference started the next day at 8 in the evening and continued till 2'o'clock in the morning. ...for its grandeur, majesty and attendance (this conference) was never equalled in the history of the movement.[15]

A resolution was passed at this session which was to prove the precursor of the Lahore Resolution of 1940 which was to become the charter for Pakistan

This conference considers it absolutely essential in the interests of an abiding peace of the vast Indian subcontinent and in the interests of unhampered cultural development, the economic and social betterment, the political self determination of the two nations known as Hindus and Muslims to recommend to the All India Muslim League to review and revise the entire question of what should be the suitable constitution for India.[16]

In 1942 the first Muslim League Ministry was formed in Sindh. In March 1943 the Sind Legislative Assembly passed a

Resolution in favour of the formation of Pakistan which had been introduced by G.M.Syed, thus scoring a historic first.

The constitutional situation was immensely complicated with the minority rights and the demand for Pakistan still unsettled. The Muslim League Party under Jinnah was willing to compromise all through 1946 if it could get adequate guarantees for the Muslim community. In January 1946 a parliamentary delegation, arrived in India to assess the situation. The first stop for this delegation, as for others that would come to India or depart from there, was Karachi. A few months later the Cabinet Mission came with its historic proposals suggesting groupings of provinces which would have conceded the substance of Pakistan and which was rejected by the All India Congress Party. This turned out to be the last chance for a compromise solution and after its rejection partition became inevitable.

An event occurred in February 1946 which would serve to expedite the British departure from India. On 19 February a naval mutiny broke out in Bombay. For three days there was serious rioting in the city and the Indian naval ratings took over the ships in the harbour. Their example was followed by the naval ratings in Karachi. This naval mutiny

Art School at
Sarnagati Building.

Max Denso Hall.

in Bombay and Karachi, although it did not get support
from the Congress Party, whose leaders advised the
mutineers to cool down, strengthened the resolve of the
British to leave as early as possible because they could no
longer rely on the loyalty of the armed forces.

In 1946, the decisive year for the history of the
subcontinent, the fate of the country hung in the balance
as the elections took place in the early months of the year.
Of the Muslim majority provinces on whose votes Pakistan
was expected to come into being, Punjab was still in the
hands of the Unionists, North West Frontier Province had a
Khudai Khidmatgar government which was pro-Congress
and in the Bengal Legislature Muslims had a bare majority
which could go either way. If Sindh were to give a decisive
vote for Pakistan it would tilt the balance and without Sindh
and without Karachi, Pakistan would never be feasible. The
first elections of 1946 gave a majority to Muslim League but
not decisive enough and G.M. Syed, the mover of the 1943
Pakistan Resolution, had abandoned the cause. It was up to
Khuhro now as the only major Muslim League leader, to
win the second election of 1946 for Muslim League and for

*Art deco house on
Bunder Road extension.*

Pakistan. This he was able to do with some help from his friends. It was this second Sindh Assembly of 1946 that voted in Pakistan in 1947.

The Quaid-i-Azam Mohammad Ali Jinnah had already made the decision that the city of his birth Karachi, which was also the capital of Sindh, that secure bastion of Pakistan, would be the first capital of the new state of Pakistan.

Chapter 4

THE CAPITAL OF PAKISTAN

Hamida Khuhro

On 3 June 1947 Lord Mountbatten announced his plan for the withdrawal of the British and the creation of the two states in the Indian subcontinent, Bharat and Pakistan. The date he gave for this momentous event was 15 August 1947, a mere nine weeks from the date of the announcement and nine months earlier than the previously announced date of withdrawal, June 1948. In these two months two new states were to emerge, one of which had to set up its entire structure from scratch. This would complete the entire transfer of power and the establishment of the two new states, including the division of assets and the division of the armed forces. The officials of the government were to exercise their options and then to set about organizing the administration. The two major provinces of Bengal and Punjab were to be divided and, at the same time, would face unprecedented communal violence and the biggest cross migration history had as yet witnessed. The states would start functioning even before it was known what their boundaries were to be. There was no clear idea of what the parameters of territory or powers the new states were to have. The new state of Pakistan had also to find a capital.

The Quaid-i-Azam faced with these problems turned to Sindh. He told the Premier, Sir Ghulam Hussain Hidayatullah, that Karachi had to be the temporary capital of the new state. The reasons for the selection of Karachi, were as a senior civil servant of Pakistan, wrote

> In West Pakistan the only province which had a Muslim League ministry was Sind....Karachi is a clean modern town with a mild

Quaid-i-Azam, Miss Jinnah and Lord and Lady Mountbatten outside the Sindh Assembly Building.

climate; it has a fine harbour and an airport which provided ready means of communications with East Pakistan and the outside world. It was also the birthplace of the Quaid-i-Azam though this was not the reason for the selection of Karachi.[1]

Karachi had thus to be ready to receive the Government of Pakistan, its officers including 'four thousand clerks' and its paraphernalia most of which would have to be provided by the Government of Sindh. The task of preparing Karachi as capital was formidable. It was a small town of four or five lakhs of people which had grown at a leisurely pace, and was now a charming well kept city with a flourishing port. It had never imagined itself as another Calcutta or Delhi, especially when called upon to function as such a capital at eight weeks notice. Fortunately, Karachi had the open spaces which would have to be sacrificed for the 'temporary' housing of the Central Secretariat. Mohammed Ayub Khuhro was the Minister for Public Works and Post War Development and was now entrusted with the job of getting Karachi ready for the influx. For him the next two months were to be the most demanding he had faced in his career of hard work. He decided that the open spaces of Artillery Maidan around the Sindh Chief Court building and the Sindh Assembly building would be filled with 'barracks' to house the offices of the central government. Work was started and went on round the clock. Madras tiles were imported to build the roofs and building materials requisitioned in the province to complete the job. The expenditure on all this building was borne by the Government of Sindh. The Government of Sindh vacated its own secretariat and gave it for the use of the central government, itself moving to Napier Barracks and the newly completed building for N.J.V High School on Bunder Road. The barracks on Bunder Road Extension and in the Lines area were given to the incoming officers of the government and to the office staff as were any empty houses in the city. Even Khuhro as minister shared his house with the officers because of the shortage of space, and when Begum Liaquat Ali Khan could not find another suitable house for the use of the Prime Minister, Khuhro vacated his house and moved into a smaller house on Khuhro Road. The Government House was vacated for use by the Governor General of Pakistan and the Sindh Legislative Assembly Chamber was to be given over to the Pakistan Constituent Assembly, with the Sindh Legislature sitting when it was not required by the Pakistan Assembly.

Miraculously the city was ready for the arrival of the Pakistan government officials in the middle of August. Khuhro was thankful that ministers had been accommodated and offices completed

> By August 15, somehow or other, shelter had been found for the thousands of families that poured into Karachi, and office accommodation for every ministry and department had been found or hastily constructed.[2]

Quaid-i-Azam had arrived in Karachi on 7 August to an enthusiastic welcome. On 11 August the Constituent Assembly of Pakistan met for the first time in the semicircular chamber of the Sindh Assembly. The chamber was filled to capacity with the sixty nine members occupying their seats, guests and the press filling the galleries to overflowing. Miss Jinnah and other notables sat in the

The Quaid-i-Azam taking the oath as Governor-General.

Distinguished Visitors Gallery along with such diplomats as had already arrived in Karachi. The Quaid-i-Azam was in the Speaker's chair and the first task of the Assembly was to elect him its President.

On the afternoon of 13 August, Lord and Lady Mountbatten flew in from New Delhi to perform the formal ceremony of handing over power. They were received by the Sindh cabinet at the airport and driven to the Governor-General's House where the Quaid-i-Azam and Miss Jinnah greeted them. The next morning, 14 August, the simple but impressive ceremony of handing over power took place in the Sindh Assembly Chamber. The ceremony was over in an hour and Pakistan emerged as an independent state. The Mountbattens did not stay for any of the celebrations and flew back immediately for the Delhi transfer of power ceremony which was to be held the next day.

Karachi went ahead with the independence day celebrations, which were of necessity somewhat subdued

Prime Minister Feroze Khan Noon addressing the Constituent Assembly of Pakistan in 1958.

because of the bloodshed, particularly in the Punjab and Bengal. The Government of Sindh was also faced with the serious problem of sheltering and feeding the thousands of refugees who were pouring into Karachi and Hyderabad. Refugee camps were built on all available space to house them till more permanent housing and occupation could

Quaid-i-Azam's mazar.

be found for them. It was a huge challenge for the quiet and orderly city of 400,000 that Karachi was in 1947.

The Quaid-i-Azam, now Governor-General of Pakistan, was deeply worried about the situation. He had not anticipated the serious communal problems and the massive transfer of population which was taking place and which had been unprecedented in history till that date. He was in close consultation with the Government of Sindh about the way in which it was coping with that situation, and also keeping the minorities re-assured about their safety. Karachi was to be kept free of the communal troubles which were sweeping the northern Indian plains.

For several months the Government of Sindh kept Karachi and Hyderabad peaceful. But unfortunately, on 6 January 1948 riots broke out in Karachi as a mob attacked a Sikh *gurduwara*. The riots were controlled very quickly. The Premier of Sindh, M.A. Khuhro, took immediate firm action and himself supervised the restoration of law and order and called in the army to help the civilian administration. Within two days peace was restored and the Quaid-i-Azam who had been extremely worried about the situation, was taken round Karachi by the Premier of Sindh and shown that complete peace had been restored. The Quaid-i-Azam publicly expressed his satisfaction with the situation and his confidence in the Government of Sindh at the session of the Pakistan Muslim League at the Khaliqdina Hall in February 1948. It was particularly to the credit of the Sindh administration that Sindh remained peaceful when the rest of the subcontinent was going through massive disruption and bloodshed.

Although the administration of Karachi by the Government of Sindh could not be faulted even by the Quaid-i-Azam, the central government decided to take over the control of the city from the Government of Sindh and to cut off the 'federal capital area' administratively from Sindh. It seemed that the central government was not satisfied. There was a strong protest from the government, the legislature and the people of Sindh at this proposal. The Government of Sindh took the stand that Karachi had been well administered by it and that provincial governments administering the capital of a country was not unprecedented. For over a hundred years Calcutta, the capital of British, India was administered by the Government of Bengal which shared the capital. Similarly Simla, the summer capital of India, was administered by the Government of the Punjab. It was therefore right and proper that the administration of Karachi remain with the Government of Sindh which had made every effort to make the central government welcome, giving up its own buildings, secretariat and houses to the centre, not counting the cost to itself and also helping the centre out financially when it was not in a position to pay the salaries to its staff. The central government was adamant. Karachi would not only be the capital of Pakistan, it would have to be administered by the centre and the Government of Sindh could make its own arrangements.

As the news spread of this decision of the centre, feelings in Sindh ran high. The Sindh Assembly as well as the Sindh Muslim League Council passed strong resolutions against the proposal. The Council in a meeting on 2 February passed a strongly worded statement

The Sindh Assembly building (1941) used as the National Assembly building of Pakistan.

Residence of the Premier
of Sindh after 1947.

This Council of the Sindh Provincial Muslim League while placing on record its amazement and alarm at persistent reports that Karachi city and its surrounding areas are to be taken away from Sind Province to form a separate area to be centrally administered by the Pakistan Government, deems its sacred duty as the accredited mouthpiece of Sind Muslims and also a well wisher of Pakistan, to place on record its emphatic protest against such a move, and in view of the following reasons and facts, earnestly urges upon Quaid-i-Azam Mohammad Ali Jinnah, both as the constitutional Head of the State and as the chosen head of the Muslim League organization to be pleased in the best interests of all concerned to disapprove such a move, for the following reasons:

Firstly, Karachi has been a natural and a corporate part of Sind since centuries and is now nerve centre entity of economic, commercial, industrial, educational and cultural entity of the Province and any attempt to deprive the Province of its nerve centre will completely strangle the life and growth of the Province.

Secondly, such a move will not only be a flagrant violation of the express provisions of the Pakistan Resolution passed by the All India Muslim League at its Lahore Session in 1940, according to which the territorial integrity of every unit constituting Pakistan is guaranteed but it will constitute a serious breach of faith with the people of the Province but for whose unequivocal and clear lead, the ideal of Pakistan would have remained an empty dream.

Thirdly, such a move is fraught with grave consequences inasmuch as, on the one hand, it will be an ill recompense for the spirit of Islamic brotherhood and generous hospitality shown by Sindhi people in welcoming Pakistan Government and doing everything possible in the cause of those lakhs of their Muslim brethren who have migrated to Sind not only from various areas of the Indian Dominion but also from several areas of Pakistan itself.

Fourthly, such a move is likely to prove a grave menace to the growing spirit of unity among Pakistan Muslims, as the natural and legitimate urge of the people of the Province to safeguard their vital interests will be exploited by those anti Pakistan forces which have lain low on account of the sincere and solid support that Sind Muslims have hitherto unreservedly given to the cause of the Muslim unity above everything else.

This Council further calls upon all its accredited representatives and constituents especially the Sind members of the Pakistan Constituent Assembly, the Sind Ministers and Members of the

Flagstaff House, E.I. Lines, Miss Jinnah's residence after 1948.

The Metropole Hotel.

*An elegant dinner party
at a Karachi hotel.*

Sind Legislative Assembly, the district and primary branches of the Muslim League and indeed every well wisher of Sind and of Pakistan to do everything in their power, to resist this unjust, impolitic and unwise move.[3]

A few days later on 10 February, the Sindh Legislative Assembly passed a Resolution on the issue

This Assembly records its apprehension and alarm at the contemplated move of the Pakistan Government to remove the city of Karachi from the control of Sind administration and to place it under its own immediate jurisdiction as a centrally administered area. This House, therefore, resolves that Karachi must not be handed over to the Central Administration at any cost and further to call upon the Leader of the House and his Cabinet colleagues to bring home to the Government of Pakistan that such a step would not only cripple Sind economically and politically, but would also constitute a flagrant contravention of the Pakistan Resolution at Lahore in 1940 which emphasizes the sovereignty and the territorial integrity of the autonomous units constituting Pakistan, not to speak of the violence which it would inflict upon the loyal and patriotic sentiments of the people of the Province towards their own independent State of Pakistan.[4]

The Beach Luxury Hotel

The Assembly included the 'Pakistan Resolution' with its Resolution to remind the public and the central authorities of the basic commitments that had been made to the provinces to win their support for Pakistan

It is the considered view of this Session of All India Muslim League that no constitutional plan would be workable for this country or acceptable to the Muslims unless it is designed on the following basic principle, viz., that geographically contiguous units are demarcated into regions which should be so constituted, with such territorial re-adjustments as may be necessary, that the areas in which Muslims are in majority, as in the North Western and Eastern zones of India, should be grouped together to constitute 'Independent States' in which the constituent units shall be autonomous and sovereign.

But in spite of these strong protests and the display of public opposition to the idea, the centre went ahead with its plans to take over the city. The struggle of the elected representatives, the Muslim League Party and the people of Sindh proved of little avail against the determination of the centre to carry through its will with regard to Karachi. This was to be the first demonstration of the problem that would bedevil Pakistan's subsequent history, the centre's determination to impose its will in the face of the provinces' desire to observe the democratic norms and ensure autonomy.

In April 1948 M.A.Khuhro, the Premier of Sindh was dismissed and a few weeks later on 22 May, a Resolution was introduced in the Constituent Assembly on the afternoon of the last day of its sitting, about the take over of Karachi. Due to the very short notice only two Sindh members out of four could be present. Khwaja Shahabuddin, the Minister of Interior moved the Resolution

(a) that the capital of Pakistan shall be located at Karachi;
(b) that all executive and administrative authority in respect of Karachi and such neighbouring areas which in the opinion of the Central Government may be required for purposes of the capital of Pakistan shall vest in and or shall be exercised by or on behalf of the Government of Pakistan and the legislative power shall vest in the Federal Legislature; and
(c) that notwithstanding anything in law for the time being in force, the Government of Pakistan shall proceed forthwith to

Karachi Municipal Corporation Building.

take such steps and adopt such measures as may be necessary to give effect to the purposes of this motion.[5]

The debate lasted for four hours. Hashim Gazdar, the Sindhi member from Karachi made a speech against the Resolution and read out the Resolution passed in the Sindh Assembly on the issue

This Assembly records its apprehension and alarm... that such a step would constitute a flagrant contravention of the Pakistan Resolution passed in 1940 which emphasizes the sovereignty and the territorial integrity of the autonomous units constituting Pakistan.

Gazdar said prophetically, 'Sir, if you do not want to make democracy a farce, if you do not want tracking towards absolute dictatorship, you should have respect for the people of Sind... we do not want to give up Karachi.'[6] But in spite of these speeches and resolutions in the elected Assemblies and public protests the centre went ahead and annexed Karachi.

On 23 July 1948 the Governor-General exercising his powers under sub section (1) of Section 290 A amended the Constitution (Indian Independence Act of 1947) and made a law to be known as Pakistan (Establishment of the Federal Capital) Order 1948. It was now proved that the Resolution of the Constituent Assembly was gilding the lily since the take over of Karachi was to be effected through the Governor General, exercising his viceregal powers. The question that now remained was how much Sindh area was to be taken over for the Federal capital of Karachi?

The town planners had given their opinion that the total requirement of the federal capital was about 800 acres which would include the assembly, secretariat and other government buildings; residential buildings for ministers and other officials and employees, foreign embassies etc., all of which would amount to about a sixth of a square mile. The area which was actually taken over by the federal government was 566.81 square miles. It included fifty-four registered villages stretching from Bund Murad and Hub on the west to as far as Dabeji in the East.

Lakshmi Building,
Bunder Road

Bunder Road in the late forties with Max Denso Hall in the background.

Karachi which had so far been regarded as the 'provisional capital' of Pakistan was now termed the 'permanent' capital of Pakistan. This was a clear usurpation of the prerogative of the future elected Assembly of Pakistan to make a decision about the permanent capital of the country. As it happened Karachi remained the capital of Pakistan for about fourteen years and was federal territory for a few years more. During this period the population of the city increased dramatically through migration from other provinces as well as from other countries. But the growth of the city was haphazard and the immigrant population settled largely in *katchi abadis* or shanty towns which grew uncontrolled around the city, and even in the middle of it on any vacant land. It would take many years and a lot of effort to clear the city of the most blatant encroachments. The centre of the city and its offices were not much better cared for. The Government of Pakistan continued to work from the emergency barracks built by the Government of Sindh in 1947 and its secretariat continued to be the vacated Sindh buildings. In the two decades that the federal government was in Karachi the only building it built was the nondescript utilitarian Tughlaq House, taking up an open space near the Sindh High Court building. The federal government was eventually to build the new city of Islamabad and the many impressive structures in its new capital. Karachi was finally returned to Sindh in 1968 on the break up of the One Unit in West Pakistan.

In the four decades plus after 1948, Karachi expanded enormously. As there was no shortage of space, its expansion was outwards to the north and north west, swallowing up ancient villages and grazing grounds. The sacred crocodiles of Manghopir and the hot springs there became a suburb of Karachi, as did the villages of Landhi at the other end, and the numerous old settlements in between. The population of Karachi stood at 5,437,984 at the census of 1981 and went on increasing at a rapid rate, mainly through migration from up country and through illegal immigration from abroad. The infrastructure of the city could not keep pace with its increase of population and encroachment of

Qamar House

*Women mourners at
the grave site of
Prime Minister
Liaquat Ali Khan.*

space. The construction of the lower Sindh Barrage by the Government of Sindh in the 1950s solved the problem of the water supply almost permanently. Now it was the efficiency of distribution, and not the lack of supply, which became the problem for the citizens. Other civic amenities did not keep pace with the expansion of Karachi and problems of sewerage disposal, adequate transport, electricity, and above all of unauthorized settlements. Most of Karachi's problems arose from the lack of foresight in planning. There was no Nusserwanji to build roads for the twenty-first century and look after the health of the city. The wonderful advantage of space that Karachi enjoys has offset the problems to some extent but if the city is not to turn into a vast slum integrated planning will have to be done and, at the same time, the much abused environment of the city will have to be cleaned and refreshed.

*Napier: who had great
visions for Karachi as
a major city and port.*

Chapter 5

THE FOUNDING FATHERS OF MODERN KARACHI

Muneeza Shamsie

SIR CHARLES JAMES NAPIER
1782-1853

The first governor of Sindh from 1843-7, Sir Charles Napier belonged to an eminent British family, descended from the medieval Earls of Lanais.[1] He was born in London, but grew up in Ireland where his military father, the sixth son of the sixth Lord Napier, was garrisoned. He became a gazetted ensign at eleven, took part in the Peninsular War against Napoleon, where he was badly wounded twice, captured once and freed. He greatly impressed the Duke of Wellington with his intelligence, as did his brothers, one of whom, William, became a military historian and wrote *The War in the Peninsula* and *The Conquest of Scinde*. In 1812, Lt. Col. Charles Napier took part in the war against the United States in Bermuda. He later carried out assignments in Greece and Cephalonia. In 1838, he was promoted to general and given command of northern England which seethed with political unrest, bordering on open rebellion. He controlled this so successfully within two years, that he was sent to India at Wellington's suggestion.

The Russian expansion in Central Asia and turmoil in Afghanistan had made the British anxious to secure their frontier defenses in India, to which Sindh, its river and coastline were very important. By 1839, the British virtually controlled the province by imposing harsh treaties on its Talpur rulers which included the garrisoning of British troops. Napier came to India in 1841 and was appointed commander-in-chief with wide military and civilian powers in Sindh. He came with a view 'to finding or provoking hostility'. He made territorial demands on the Talpurs, involved himself in a dispute between two members of the Talpur family and having precipitated a crisis, he defeated the Talpurs at the decisive battles of Meani and Dubba in 1843 and is reputed to have sent his famous message 'Peccavi' I have sinned'.

Sindh was duly annexed by the British amid considerable controversy. Napier was appointed governor of Sindh, and knighted. He repulsed warring tribes on the northern Sindh border. He made Karachi the provincial capital and had great visions for it as a major city and port in the subcontinent; the town as we know it today, began during his tenure. He developed the cantonment town, the roads and the harbour.[2] He built the vital Napier Mole, connecting the island of Keamari to the mainland.[3] He set up the canal department to improve the irrigation in Sindh, and was keen to encourage trade and commerce. He adopted a policy of subduing the Baloch sirdars. Unfortunately, as an administrator, he was too quixotic an individual to implement his projects.[4] His one undoubted success was the efficient police force he created for Karachi. This was later replicated as a model throughout British India. Napier sailed from Karachi in October 1847. Two years later he was recalled to India as Commander-in-Chief, during the Second Sikh War, to replace Sir Hugh Gough who had suffered some reverses; but the war ended, with a final victory for Gough before Napier arrived. As Commander-in-Chief. Napier's plans for the army did not meet with the approbation of Lord Dalhousie, the Governor-General; the two men quarrelled and Napier resigned in 1851, having lost the support of his patron, the Duke of Wellington too. He died in 1853. A statue of him now stands in Trafalgar Square while there are many landmarks in Karachi which continue to bear his name.

HORMUSJEE JAMSETJEE RUSTOMJEE (1846-99)*

From the Sindh Gazette of 10 November 1891, over 105 years ago

The honour done to Mr Hormusjee Jamsetjee Rustomjee as one of the leading merchants of Karachi by His Excellency the Governor of Bombay is highly appreciated by the mercantile community of Karachi.

Mr Rustomjee's kindly feeling and liberality have made him as much liked as his shrewdness, ability and capacity for business have made him respected. He has identified his interests with those of the town, and the scale on which he carries out his operations and the superb pile in which they are conducted, stand as a record and an indication of mercantile property of the town. He has always evinced the keenest interest in all matters affecting the prosperity of the port and has been for years an untiring advocate of railway extensions of province...

Mr Rustomjee has taken the utmost pains to set off his huge building to the greatest advantage...the building itself is certainly one of the handsomest and imposing structures of its kind, not in Karachi or in the province only, but in India. The architecture is purely Italian and the facade closely resembles that of the New Dresden Bank at Berlin...The site is admirable, occupying a large space of over 8,000 square yards near the point where the two principal streets of the town, the Bunder and the McLeod roads converge, being thus in the very heart of the business parts of the city. Mr H.J. Rustomjee's mansion has a frontage of 100 feet and is constructed wholly of stone, having three stories, the total height being over 60 feet.

A handsome staircase leads from the basement to the roof, from which a superb view of the harbour, the sea, the fortifications of Manora, and the town of Karachi is obtained, with the hills of Balochistan which define the British boundary being plainly visible....

Attached to the office building are three huge warehouses from 300 to 350 feet in length by 50 feet wide...a 2-feet gauge tramway has been constructed to every part of the warehouses. Some eighty trucks for the storing and moving of goods are in constant readiness. Tramlines are also laid in the compound or yard....

The 'honour' done to H.J. Rustomjee by the Governor, Lord Harris, was to spend the afternoon of 4 November

H.J. Rustomjee:
who gave back far
more than he took.

that year inaugurating H.J's new office premises, the 'palatial building in which our enterprising townsman conducts his colossal mercantile business.'

H.J. was born in Bombay on 11 February 1846. Orphaned at an early age, he was brought up by an uncle, a watchmaker. They were amongst the first influx of Parsis, together with Cowasjee Rustomjee Variawa, to sail into Karachi in the wake of the British forces, following the annexation of Sindh in 1943. H.J. was married before he was twenty and at once began doing business on his own account. Whenever a ship came into port he walked to Keamari from Sadder where he lived, waited patiently till the vessel unloaded, bought cases or bottles of brandy, whisky and wine at a low price, and with a coolie to carry them he trudged back to town to sell his wares at a very substantial profit. His success came swiftly from this and from his wholesale dealings in other goods. His agents were spread all over Sindh, the Punjab, Quetta and the United

Provinces up to Cawnpore. According to contemporary accounts he was 'a strict disciplinatian, a man of enlightened views and extensive charity. He lived in comfort but there was no display of wealth.'

In 1897, two years before his death, he was described as one of the 'most interesting personalities amongst the merchant princes of India, the biggest businessman in Sindh, able to compete with any man in the land'.

Many of the flourishing Parsi families of today owe their prosperity to the initial aid given by H.J. which helped put their forefathers on their feet. Unhappily, after H.J. died at the early age of fifty-three from a heart ailment, at Karachi on 13 February 1899, none of the three of his six sons who worked in his business with him were able to carry on from where he had left off. In ten years time his firm went into liquidation.

H.J. and his contemporaries, one being Jehangir Kothari, all gave far more than they took. They gave liberally, both of their time and of their money, for the development and betterment of the port town of Karachi. In turn, they were given the trust, respect and affection of the citizens. H.J.'s and Kothari's names are engraved on the roll of honour of Trustees at the Karachi Port Trust.

COWASJEE RUSTOMJEE VARIAWA*

Cowasjee Rustomjee Variawa, came to Karachi about the same time as H.J. From the start, he ran a business in the harbour as a *Dubash*, supplying stores to vessels, first in partnership with Dubash Brothers and then with his own firm of Cowasjee & Sons.

With the advent of steam, the firm imported coal from south Africa and Wales and became coal bunkerers. Later on, his firm developed a stevedoring business and was involved in dredging work. Cowasjee Variawa had much to do with the development of the port at Karachi.

During the Afghan War of 1878-9 he and other Parsi commissariat contractors followed Lord Roberts and his army to Kabul, where many of them were captured and imprisoned by the Afghans. The British and the Indian prisoners were kept separately, so were the Parsis. The Afghans could not quite place them as they seemed paler than the Indians and not quite as white as the British.

The Afghan set about annoying the Indians. They horrified the Hindus by feeding them beef, they insulted the Muslims by feeding them pork, but were not quite sure what to feed the Parsis. One quick thinking Parsi told the Afghans: 'You may do whatever you like with us, feed us starve us, but please do not make us eat chicken.' Thus were they fed a chicken a day.

Early this century, when Cowasjee & Sons was handed over to be run by his two sons, Fakirjee and Minocher, Cowasjee Variawa retired to England, bought two houses in Torquay, one named 'Keamari' and the other 'Minora'. He lived through World War I in England and died there in 1919. He is buried at Brookwood.

A generous and philanthropic man, he put much of his money in trusts for charity with a concentration on education and health.

C.R. Variawa: names his two houses in Torquay 'Keamari' and 'Minora'.

---

* *These two pieces have been contributed by Ardeshir Cowasji.*

*Hotchand:
'the definitive
traitor in
folk history'.*

SETH NAOMUL HOTCHAND
1804-1878

Chiefly remembered today for his invaluable autobiography
The Memoirs of Seth Naomul Hotchand he provided a rare,
fascinating eye witness account of Sindh before and after
the British conquest, leading up to the First Afghan War.
The book is 'probably the only extant account of a British
"spy" and agent in India in the nineteenth century.'[5]
   There is considerable historical evidence to, however,
dispute some imperial myths fostered by Seth Naomul's
memoirs, including tales of Talpur bigotry and Seth
Naomul's claim that Karachi was a small fishing village in
the pre-British era, which was first fortified by his great-
great grandfather. In fact Karachi was already a small,
prosperous town before the Talpur rulers wrested it from
the Khan of Kalat in 1795 and built their fort at Manora.
Seth Naomul Hotchand was the second son of Seth
Hotchand, an eminent Karachi merchant. He joined the
family business when he was eleven and had a long, fruitful

association with the British, culminating with a grand durbar in his honour at Karachi's Frere Hall. There, Sir Bartle Frere, the governor, presented Naomul Hotchand with the Insignia and Grant of the Dignity of Companion of the Most Exalted Order of the Star of India with the words: 'You had great influence amongst your countrymen: you possessed information drawn from every part of northern and Eastern India: and you placed all unreservedly at the disposal of the Government. When many of your countrymen were appalled by the greatness of the danger, and believed that some catastrophe threatened the existence of the British Empire in India, you never faltered in your sagacious trust in the power of the British Government'.[6] Long before, in 1837, Captain Carless of the Indian navy had explored the potential of a harbour at Karachi, to facilitate the movement of British troops to counter Russian activity in Central Asia and Afghanistan. Seth Naomul provided Carless with vital supplies and information.

This marked the beginning of his work for the British. He then used his influence to obtain the necessary 1,000 camels for Colonel James Outram to transport the British army, through Sindh and the Bolan Pass into Afghanistan. He supplied boats and provisions to Reserve Brigadier Valiant, who captured the Talpur Fort at Manora, landed his troops in Karachi and planted the Union Jack within the city walls. Seth Naomul also reported the activities of the Talpur rulers of Sindh, to whom his family had access. He played a particularly important role in The First Afghan War. The Talpurs were well aware of his activities, but were too afraid of British ire to protest. He was probably regarded as no more than an opportunist by his contemporaries, although today he is remembered as 'the definitive traitor in folk history'.[7] He was greatly valued by Bartle Frere who became chief commissioner of Sindh in 1850. When Frere established the Karachi Municipal Corporation (KMC), Seth Naomul was the liaison between the commissioner and the townspeople; he was also on the first managing committee of the KMC together with Captain Preedy, the revenue collector and John McLeod, the collector of customs. As a reward for his services, Seth Naomul was sanctioned a pension of one hundred rupees per month, for three generations by the Government of India. He was also given a *jagir* in perpetuity, as well as other honours.

SIR HENRY BARTLE EDWARD FRERE
1815-84

Educated at Haileybury, the traditional public school for colonial administrators, Bartle Frere joined the Indian Civil Service in 1834 and was chief commissioner of Sindh between 1850-9. The post carried enormous powers, because Sindh had been merged with the Bombay Presidency after Napier, but was too distant to be administered from there; the commissioner was therefore given virtual gubernatorial control. In Sindh, the dynamic and imaginative Frere initiated 'one of the most remarkable pioneering periods of administration seen anywhere in the world'.[8]

Although he was greatly handicapped by financial constraints, Frere was able to translate Napier's dreams into reality. He laid down the framework for modern Sindh and the administrative infrastructure for the city of Karachi. To create an economic base in the province he constructed railways, canals, and metalled roads. He established the Karachi Municipal Corporation, made considerable improvements to Karachi harbour and introduced the first postal system in India, the Horse Dak. He paid considerable

Sir Bartle Frere

attention to education. He set up a network of vernacular schools, English schools and some engineering schools; he also pioneered the grants-in-aid system for schools, which was later adopted throughout India. He amended some of Napier's policies governing the jagirdars and zemindars, rooting out of injustice and ensuring the loyalty of important chieftains to the British crown to ensure peace.

As a result of his policies Sindh remained quiet during the Mutiny. In fact Frere's land settlement in Sindh 'may be said to have preceded and anticipated the post-Mutiny policies of Canning towards the taluqdars of Oudh'.[9]

To further protect the province and guard the Bolan Pass he garrisoned Quetta, long before it was established as an important military outpost in 1877. Frere's nine years in Sindh earned him a knighthood. Many Karachi landmarks continue to bear his name. He went on to have a very distinguished career in India. He joined the Viceroy's Council in Calcutta from 1859-62, was Governor of Bombay for five years and in 1867 returned to England as a member of The India Council. For the next ten years, he concerned himself with the development of Indian agriculture and communications. In 1876, he was made a baronet and in 1877, appointed high commissioner and governor of Cape Colony, to carry out the planned confederation of British South Africa and the Boer Republic. He did not understand South Africa as he had India. He regarded the Zulus as a menace and provoked a war. This led to the disastrous British defeat at Isandhlwane in 1878. Frere was officially censured and recalled to Britain in 1880.

THE HON. KHAN BAHADUR HASSANALLY BEY EFFENDI
1830-95

The founder of the Sindh Madrassah-Tul-Islam, the Hon. Khan Bahadur Hassanally Effendi, played a pivotal role in improving Muslim education in Sindh. He had to struggle very hard to educate himself as there were neither English schools nor law schools in Sindh, when he was young and education among Muslims was abysmal. The son of a religious and spiritual guide, he was born in Hyderabad, Sindh, orphaned young and educated in Persian at a local seminary. He learnt English and Sindhi while holding a humble post in the service of the British Government at Naushahro. In 1860, he was promoted to *serishtedar* of the district court in Karachi and learnt law. He so distinguished himself that he was

Effendi: a linguist who spread English education

appointed pleader, and later public prosecutor, a post enjoyed by few Indians. He was soon involved in public affairs and was appointed a member of the Karachi Municipal Corporation. He also became vice-president of the newly created political association, the Sindh Sabha, but resigned to start the Sindh Mohammedan Association of which he became the president, and which acted as a vocal and effective lobby for the Muslims of Sindh. Hassanally Effendi spoke English, Persian, Turkish, French and Sindhi and is particularly remembered for his pioneering work in spreading English education among the Muslims of Sindh. In 1885, he set up the Sindh Madrassah Board and worked tirelessly to set up a modern school, the Sindh Madrassah-Tul-Islam. He toured the province to collect funds; the KMC provided the land for the building which still stands today. The school originally took one bright boy from each of the fifty two talukas of Sindh, but soon broadened its base and became a centre of excellence, which provided many of Sindh's most eminent public and political figures.

EDULJEE DINSHAW C.I.E.

Eduljee Dinshaw was an exceptional, clever and successful businessman, who amassed a great fortune and made an enormous contribution to charities, public service and the betterment of Karachi. He was born in Poona into the Parsi community, grew up in Karachi and was educated at the Narain Jaganath High School. At twenty-one or twenty-two, he became an army contractor. He did extremely well, particularly during the Second Afghan War (1880-1), where he showed great courage and daring in supplying food, using the camel as means of transport. This earned him a fortune and the trust and respect of the British Government. His

Dinshaw: exceptional entrepreneur and philanthropist.

influential army friends advised him to buy land and invest in Karachi, which had a promising future. He used most of his profits buying up warehouses, shops and other buildings on land due for development. He even acquired 'swamps and tide-swept sands that nobody in those days imagined would be of any great value' around areas such as Victoria Road, City Station and Bath Island.[10] Eduljee Dinshaw always worked alone, never had any partners and would often supervise the construction of his buildings himself and make the payment due to the masons. But being a man of amazing commercial enterprise, he turned his attention to many other ventures. He became the largest coal importer in Karachi, and set up cotton ginning factories, wool and cotton hydraulic presses among others; he traded in Burma teak and other goods and exported Sindhi camels to Australia for transport between Fremantle and the gold mines at Coolgarlie. He owned property in Sydenham, Kent, and in Karachi was also involved with The Karachi Landing and Shipping Company, the *Sindh Gazette*, the Sindh Light Railways and numerous other concerns.

Eduljee Dinshaw erected a statue and fountain (now extinct) in Frere Gardens. He was a great philanthropist and did a great deal of public and charitable work. He was a delegate to the Parsi matrimonial court and served in the Karachi Municipal Corporation and the Karachi Port Trust. In 1903, he became the only Indian to be appointed honorary member of the Sindh Volunteer Corps. He founded and contributed to the maintenance of the Lady Dufferin Hospital in Karachi; he also set up well-known dispensaries for the poor in Saddar and Keamari and was also involved in other large scale charities in Karachi, Quetta, Poona and Bombay. In his will he left seven and a half lakh rupees to the University of Bombay for providing technical education for Parsi students.

RAJ RISHI DEWAN DAYARAM GIDUMAL SHAHANI
1857-1927

Born in Hyderabad, Sindh, Dayaram Gidumal, was among Sindh's first graduates. He did his B.A. and his law degree at Bombay University and in 1877 joined government service. He rose to the position of judicial commissioner of

*Diyaram Gidumal: set up educational,
political and literary institutions.*

Sindh, but refused the offer to become a
high court judge and retired in 1911. During
his years of service, he initiated many social
reforms and set up educational, political and
literary institutions. According to
Nagendranath Gupta[11]

> Whatever little public activity existed is Sindh at
> that time was due to the initiative of Dayaram.
> His was the brain that planned, his was the hand
> that worked. He had all the gifts of leadership,
> the power of organization, the great capacity of
> bringing men of different ways of thinking to-
> gether and making them work for a common
> purpose.

In those days political activity was comparatively mild and offered no conflict of interest for Government servants. Dayaram
Gidumal founded a political association, the Sindh Sabha,
which voiced the opinion of all communities in Sindh. He
helped establish its newspaper *The Sindh Times* and wrote its
leading articles, although as an official he could not hold any
other office. He set up the Seva Saran (Women's Home of
Service in Bombay) and the N.H. Academy in Hyderabad. Most
important of all, he initiated the idea for Sindh's first college
to make higher education more accessible to students in Sindh,
who hitherto had to travel to Bombay for a university education, as he had done himself, and which entailed finding guard-
ians in Bombay and other difficulties.

In 1885, he wrote a paper pointing out the benefits of a
college education and pointed out that Sindh had barely ten
graduates, while in the remainder of the Bombay presidency
there were very many and were represented in the judiciary,
army, commerce and other walks of life. He not only lobbied
with the Government for the Sindh Arts College and gave much
thought to its curriculum, but travelled throughout the province to raise funds: he collected Rs 80,000 which was then
matched by the Government. The college became the
D.J. College and still stands today. It was named after a public

figure Dayaram Jethmal, at the insistence of his family, who gave a large sum to the college, after his death.[12]

Meanwhile Dayaram Gidumal Shahani's contribution to the institution was largely forgotten. He moved to Bombay, spent his last years in spiritual and literary pursuits and was long remembered as one of the most generous, self effacing and remarkable men of his generation. Dayaram Gidumal was also a linguist and scholar. He did much to promote Sindhi literature and his translations and commentaries on religious books such as *Essence of the Bhagavad Gita* (1893) are said to be classics of Sindhi prose; he was well versed in Sufism too and wrote about Sufi saints, including Shah Abdul Latif in a book *Something about Sindh* (1882). He was one of the first writers of free verse in Sindhi which was published in the book *Mana-Ja Chahbook*.

CINCINNATUS F. D'ABREO
1865-1929

Cincinnatus F. D'Abreo was a very imposing, dignified man,[13] who was born in Karachi in 1865, educated at St. Patrick's High School and joined government service in 1888. He went on to became assistant collector and was the honorary treasurer of the Lady Dufferin Hospital and Louise Lawrence Institute, the D.J. Sind College and the Sindh Madrassah. After his retirement in 1920, he was associated

with a number of commercial enterprises, including the India Flour Mills and the Indian Assurance Company, of which he was the head. He was the leading figure in the Goan community to which he belonged and founded the Goa Portuguese Association. He also served for six years in the Karachi Municipal Corporation and was vice-president at one point. Cincinnatus d'Abreo was elected by popular ballot instituted by the *Daily Gazette* as one of the 'Twelve Leaders of Sindh' and lobbied for the government sanctioning and

D'Abreo: voted one of the 'Twelve Leaders of Sindh'.

construction of the Lloyd Barrage and Canals at Sukkur. These plans to irrigate Sindh had been drawn up in 1912 but had not been implemented due to the indifference of the Bombay Government. The scheme was finally pushed through, due to vocal Sindhi demands and completed in 1935: it transformed the entire agriculture, trade and economy of Sindh. Cincinnatus D'Abreo did a great deal of public work, served on many committees such as the Sindh Flood Relief Committee, the Sindh League of Progress and was known as a philanthropist too. Cincinnatus Town, where he lived and which was then a new suburb of Karachi by the Lyari river, is named after him.

SAHIBSING CHANDASING SHAHANI
1869-1931

Sahibsing Chandasing Shahani was born in Hyderabad, into an old Amil family of Sikhs.[14] He was the first Sindhi to do his M.A. from Bombay University and he took Persian and English as optional subjects. He was subsequently appointed Professor of Persian at Wilson College but returned to Karachi in 1896 as Professor of English at D.J. College, where he had studied earlier. Later he became the principal from 1917-27. As a teacher he made a profound impact on an entire younger generation of Sindhis. He did much to develop the D.J. College and encouraged a large number of girls to join, including his daughters, one of whom became the first Sindhi lady to be called to the Sindh Bar. It was also due to his efforts that a law college was set up in Karachi and he played an important role in establishing the Nadirshaw Edulji Dinshaw College for Engineering. S.C. Shahani, who owned lands near Jamesabad, was a keen agriculturalist too. He was among the first to grow Egyptian and American cotton, which the government was keen to introduce in Sindh. He made a substantial contribution to the Chatfield Committee in connection

Shahani: among the first Sindhis to grow Egyptian and American cotton.

with land settlement in Sindh and presided over the 1916 Social Conference in Larkana. In 1921 and 1931, he was elected to the Legislative Assembly from the Sindh Zamindars' constituency and took a keen interest in its legislation. He was also on the board of the viva voce examiners of ICS candidates in India and later, became its chairman.

SIR MONTAGU DE POMEROY WEBB C.I.E., C.B.E
1869-1919

A towering figure in the Karachi Chamber of Commerce and Industry of which he was elected chairman seventeen times, between 1901-22, Sir Montagu de Pomeroy Webb was the editor and owner of *The Daily Gazette* and general manager of Forbes, Forbes and Campbell. He was born at Clifton, Bristol in 1869 and arrived at Karachi in 1890. By this time, the Karachi Port Trust had been formed and Karachi's exports and imports equalled that of Bombay and Calcutta; it was also the largest exporter of wheat in the east, but movement of goods to and from the hinterland were hampered by Karachi's poor railway links. The Karachi Chamber fought a hard battle with the indifferent Bombay authorities over this. In 1907 Montagu de P. Webb informed the Indian Railways Committee that railway links in Sindh must be improved and the railway budget separated from the national budget.[15]

He was extremely vocal over the Indian Government's financial policies. He considered it utterly indefensible that the bulk of India's new Gold Standard Reserve was kept in London which 'provided the London bankers with valuable and utilizable resources while merchants in India, whether British or Indian, were coming to recognize the risk that was thereby created for them.'

He considered this as nothing short of misappropriation of India's cash and in 1910, with remarkable foresight said

> Were England unfortunately involved in a great European war, our artificial rupee, under present management would probably drop to 8d or 9d before the war was finished. That such a war is outside the realms of the possible, nobody who studies European armaments, for a moment imagines.

Webb: a towering figure in Karachi who was elected chairman of KCC seventeen times.

He built up a sufficient lobby in India and the British press for the matter to be brought up before a Royal Commission, headed by Austen Chamberlain which led to recommendations supporting the steps urged by Montagu de P. Webb and the Karachi Chamber. Later Montagu de P. Webb addressed inflation caused by World War I. He attended the All-India War Conference of 1918 and, during the aftermath of war, some of the recommendations made by the Chamber, pre-empted policies that were later adopted by the Commonwealth.

In fact Montagu de P. Webb played a very significant role in British India's monetary matters and built up the Karachi Chamber as one of the premier financial institutions in British India. He represented the Karachi Chamber at conferences in Calcutta, Montreal, London, and Sydney. He was a member of the Legislative Assembly in Delhi and Simla and of the Indian Fiscal Commission, 1921-2. He wrote extensively on economic matters and his books include *India and the Empire, Britain's Dilemma, The World Crisis and the Only Way Out.* During his tenure, the Karachi Chamber addressed many other issues pivotal to the development of Sindh, including education and the need to improve Sindh's irrigation. In 1912, the Chamber forwarded the Sukkur Barrage scheme to the secretary of state for sanction. This was part of a triple project which included barrages at Mithankot and Kotri, though the work on Sukkur Barrage did not begin until 1931, and the other two were only built after Partition. The many projects that Montagu de P. Webb helped to establish or initiate include the Sindh Light Railways, the Larkana Jacobabad Railway, Jacobabad-Kashmore Feeder Railways, the Karachi Electric Corporation, the Karachi Building and Development Company, the Saving and Helping Bank. He also took a keen interest in political affairs. In 1915 he attended the session of the Indian National Congress, not as a representative of the Karachi Chamber, but as a Sindh delegate. Among his many other activities he founded the Air League of India in 1922, which subsequently became the Karachi Aero Club.

HAJI SIR ABDOOLA HAROON
1872-1942

One of the most important political figures in Sindh, and a businessman of extraordinary prescience and acumen, Haji Sir Abdoola Haroon was born in Karachi *circa* 1872.[17] He was orphaned very young and brought up in straitened circumstances by his widowed mother. As a child, he worked as a hawker to augment the family income and although he had little interest in school, he learnt to read and write Gujerati. During his early teens he was employed as an apprentice by relatives, who were prosperous merchants, but encouraged by his mother he branched out on his own, selling bags of sugar. From a small shop in Jodia Bazaar, his business developed into a huge empire with dealings in the United States, Britain, Java, and South Africa and which earned him the title of The Sugar King. He was a delegate to the Imperial Economic Conference in Ottawa in 1932, was often consulted by the Government of India on commercial and financial matters, including the economic viability of separating Sindh as a province from Bombay.[18] He was among the foremost Sindhi leaders who strongly advocated provincial autonomy. He was knighted in 1937. He was later a director of a shipping company, Mughal Lines and the Indian Transcontinental Airways.

Long before that he was already involved in municipal affairs. He was elected to the Municipal Committee of Karachi from 1913-17 and 1921-34, during which he took a particular interest in health and education schemes for the urban poor, particularly in the Lyari quarter. He pioneered the education of Sindhi Muslim women and set up the Hajiani Hanifabai Girls School in 1926. He also took the unusual step of sending his own daughters to English medium schools and encouraged one of them to pursue medicine as a career. His enlightened outlook was shared by his dynamic wife, Nusrat Haroon, who became an eminent social worker in her own right. The many

Haroon: played a pivotal role in the political awakening of Muslim Sindh.

educational institutions that he established include the Jamia Islamia Yatim Khana to help poor students acquire a good education as well as a professional training.

Haji Abdoola Haroon played a pivotal role in the political awakening of Muslim Sindh and in crystallizing Muslim opinion. In 1920 he set up a newspaper *Alwahid,* but soon after the Masjid Manzilgah incident and the 1940 communal riots in Sukkur when 'the Hindu press adopted a truculent attitude towards the Mussulmans'[19] he turned *Alwahid* into a limited company and the first community daily paper for the Muslims of Sindh, to safeguard their interests. His political career began with the Indian National Congress and its ally, the nationalist, anti-British pan Islamic Khilafat Movement which he joined in 1917 and 1918, respectively. He became president of the Sindh Provincial Khilafat Committee, took part in the non-cooperation movement called by Gandhi in 1920, helped finance the Khilafat Movement and worked very closely with its founder, Maulana Mohammed Ali, who was subsequently jailed in Karachi. Haji Abdoola Haroon and his family also took to wearing home-spun cotton (*khaddar*). He turned his home into a centre of Khilafat activities and in 1927, he was appointed President of the Khilafat Committee although the movement had started to dissipate by then. Meanwhile in 1923, he was elected a member of the Bombay Legislative Council and gave voice to Sindhi issues; in 1926, he was elected a member of the Central Legislative Assembly, where he continued to be re-elected until his death.

He constantly criticized the autocratic powers vested in the Commissioner-in-Sindh and lobbied for provincial autonomy. This was originally demanded by the Hindus of Sindh who were more politically aware than the Muslims and wanted to end the domination of Bombay Hindus. The issue was later taken up by the Muslims and supported by the Muslim League. This was virulently opposed by the Hindu Mahasahba which projected fearful images of a 'Muslim Raj', because Sindh had a Muslim majority. Sindh was finally granted provincial autonomy by the Government of India Act, 1935. Haji Abdoola Haroon was on several committees to work out the details. By then, he was among the foremost political figures in the province who had fought hard for due Muslim representation at an all-India level, was general secretary of the 1930 All India Muslim Conference and attended The Round Table Conference in London to discuss constitutional issues. The politics of Sindh took many complex twists and turns over the next few years, during which Haji Sir Abdoola Haroon founded the Sindh United Party with Sir Shahnawaz Bhutto, but lost the election for the provincial assembly.

He was among the leaders who invited the Quaid-i-Azam to come to Sindh. In 1938 he arranged the historic Muslim League Conference in Sindh, presided by the Quaid-i-Azam. During this session, the subversion of Muslim culture by a Hindu dominated majority and the polarization between the two nations, Hindu and Muslim, were highlighted in a resolution which demanded that India should be divided on religious lines.[20] This proved to be a precursor of the 1940 Lahore Resolution. Haji Abdoola Haroon was the President of the Sindh Provincial Muslim League and also became Chairman of the All India Muslim League's Foreign Sub-Committee. He organized Muslim League branches in the province at different levels; in 1941 he was appointed Member of the Muslim League's Working Committee. During his travels he presented the Muslim League's point of view in foreign countries and through newspapers in India and abroad. He also addressed a wide range of problems pertaining to both Sindh and the Muslims of

India. He died shortly after presiding over the 1942 All India Seerat Conference in Allahabad.

THE QUAID-I-AZAM, MOHAMMAD ALI JINNAH
1876-1948

The Founder of Pakistan and its first Governor-General, Quaid-i-Azam Mohammad Ali Jinnah, fought for the political rights of India's Muslims against stupendous odds, made Karachi the capital of the new country, was born there *circa* 1876 and died there. The son of Jinnahbhai Poonja, a prosperous merchant, he was educated at the Sindh Madrassah-Tul-Islam, joined The Lincoln's Inn, London, and was called to the bar in 1896. He was clever, incisive, upright and hardworking and soon made his mark as a rising young lawyer in Bombay. He joined the Indian National Congress (established 1885) because he wanted to present 'a common nationalist front against the British.'[21] In 1910, he was elected to the Central Executive Council and in 1913, he joined the Muslim League (established 1906). He was the architect of the 1916 Lucknow Pact in which the Muslim League and the Congress agreed to work for a common goal: self-government. He was hailed as 'The Ambassador of Hindu-Muslim Unity'. In 1919, he spoke forcefully against the notorious Rowlatt Acts curtailing fundamental rights and was bitter at the Jallianwalla Bagh massacre, but believed that the battle for Indian independence should be fought from within the legislature, not outside it.[22] He criticized Gandhi for mixing religion with politics by using Hindu symbolism to gather mass support for his *satyagraha* (non-cooperation)

Jinnah: a colossus among men

campaign and for creating a wedge among Muslims by wooing the pan-Islamic Khilafat ulema.

In 1920 the Quaid-i-Azam resigned from the Congress. For the next decade, he was virtually eclipsed politically, but came to be known as one of the finest lawyers in undivided India. He also remained active in Muslim League politics, trying at every opportunity to safeguard the interest of India's Muslims. The Hindu revivalist movements of the nineteenth century had already given rise to Muslim fears of Hindu domination. In 1909, the Morley Minto reforms had conceded in principle to the Muslim demand for separate electorates. According to Dr Ayesha Jalal,[23] the Quaid-i-Azam never showed much enthusiasm for this: he believed that the real security for India's Muslims was to share power at the centre once the British left. The British, determined to hold on to power at the centre and diffuse nationalist sentiment at an all-India level, provincialized Indian politics, creating many conflicts and contradictions. The Quaid-i-Azam had to make many compromises to win over provincial leaders. He participated in the Round Table Conferences in London to discuss intricate constitutional issues. He became so disillusioned that in 1931, he abandoned politics and became a lawyer in Britain. Meanwhile, Congress policies and British tactics, increased insecurities and fears among many Muslims.

In 1934, the Quaid-i-Azam emerged from his London exile. He revitalized the Muslim League, broadened its base and participated in the 1937 elections to the provincial assemblies as laid down by the 1935 India Act. Since the country consisted of Hindu-majority and Muslim-majority provinces, he hoped the Congress and Muslim League would develop a *modus vivendi* to protect the minorities in each, and also come to a power-sharing formula at the central government. The Congress swept the polls and, heady with victory, chose to side-step the Muslim League. This increased Muslim apprehensions, made provincial Muslim leaders conscious of the importance of due Muslim representation at the centre; and led to more difficulties and a loss of faith. The Quaid-i-Azam described Muslims and Hindus as two distinct nations with a different culture and history. This was expressed in the momentous 1940 Lahore Resolution demanding the recognition of a distinct Muslim nationhood and which came to be known as The

Pakistan Resolution. According to Dr Ayesha Jalal,[24] the Quaid-i-Azam perceived the two nation theory as the means by which India's Muslims who were outnumbered by the Hindus by one to four could overcome the problem of numbers: it was only as a separate nation that they were entitled to equal bargaining power at an all-India level. She also draws a distinction between the assertion of Muslim nationhood which was 'non-negotiable' and the attainment of Pakistan as a sovereign state which remained open to negotiation until 1946.[25] There is a growing number of scholars who share her views, but many do not. The traditional, more well-known view is that the Lahore Resolution, was a clear and definite demand for Pakistan, as an independent state. This is borne out by his biographer, Stanley Wolpert.[26] At all events, the Quaid-i-Azam was a great constitutionalist, a very cerebral politician, who manoeuvred his way through many minefields, often using silence and ambiguity as a shield to unite and tread carefully between the disparate views of the minority and majority provinces, which had very different dynamics. He mobilized Muslim opinion; the 1945-6 election revealed considerable gains. The Muslim League and Congress vote was clearly divided between the Muslim and Hindu dominated electorates respectively.

He wanted much more for Pakistan than he was forced to settle for, as negotiation after negotiation collapsed. He twice rejected the 'moth eaten' and 'truncated' sovereign state that he was compelled to agree to in 1947. A year earlier, the Cabinet Mission plan *had* offered a three tiered federal power sharing constitutional structure, with distinct groupings of Hindu and Muslim majority states (virtually Hindustan and Pakistan) within a united India. The Quaid-i-Azam accepted this, but Congress rejected it: the subsequent amendments were not acceptable to the Muslim League. The British, having impeded Indian independence for decades, had voted in a new government after the World War II and were in a sudden hurry to leave. The Quaid-i-Azam was given the choice of accepting a much depleted and divided, sovereign Pakistan, or nothing. He presided over Pakistan's first Constituent Assembly at its new capital, Karachi, on 11 August 1947. One of his first speeches, upon assuming power as Pakistan's first Governor-General, was to urge communal harmony. As violence and carnage swept across India and Pakistan, he was only too conscious of how fragile Pakistan's newly won freedom and independence was and he tackled enormous economic, political, and other difficulties with great will, determination and courage. He died on 11 September 1948 and remains a colossus among the great men of that era.

JAMSHED NUSSERWANJI MEHTA
1886-1952

Jamshed Nusserwanji is often called the maker of modern Karachi. He was born into an eminent Parsi family. Though he joined the family firm, Nusserwanji and Company he was a man of austere and simple habits, greatly drawn to religious philosophies from an early age. He become a theosophist, influenced by Annie Besant, and took part in the Home Rule League. In the 1920s he encouraged the co-operative movement in Karachi. He set up co-operative housing societies to help the middle and lower middle class and established co-operative banks to finance them, although initially this meant going into debt[27] and met with much opposition. The scheme was so successful however that the municipality named an area, Jamshed Quarter, after him. In 1924, Jamshed Nusserwanji joined the Buyers and Shippers Chamber, became its chairman and turned it into a platform to focus on broader public issues, ranging from the need to improve the railways, to 'Indianization of the higher services' the stabilization of the rupee and taxation. He espoused the cause of the haris of Sindh and discovered that the plans for Sukkur Barrage and Canals 'were lying pigeon holed in some department of the Secretariat of Bombay'[28]. He brought this to the governor's notice and pressed for the implementation of the scheme. This took eight years, but transformed Sindh's agriculture, trade and economy. He also had many plans for rural reconstruction, through co-operatives, credit schemes, education and, ultimately, by abolishing the feudal *zamindari* system. An exceptionally able administrator, Jamshed Nusserwanji remained alienated from mainstream populist politics and is chiefly remembered for his work with the Karachi Municipal Corporation. He joined in 1918, became its president and was later Karachi's first mayor. He retired

Nusserwanji: one of Karachi's most remarkable citizens.

from the KMC in 1934 by which time he had transformed the city. He was responsible for restoring the large tract of land, the Artillery Maidan in central Karachi which was under the army's control, back to the city after travelling to Bombay to persuade the governor. He developed Karachi's underground drainage system, increased the city's existing fourteen miles of roads to seventy-two and asphalted them all. He constantly urged an improvement in arid Karachi's water supply, although it was only after his tenure that the government built the new Haleji Water Works. In fact, without the infrastructure that Jamshed Nusserwanji laid down, Karachi would have faced insuperable problems when it was made the federal capital of Pakistan in 1947. Jamshed Nusserwanji also built parks, encouraged the beautification and remodelling of the city and raised funds to erect a new KMC building, which still stands today. He opened Urdu primary schools throughout Karachi, and made primary education compulsory in the exceedingly poor, predominantly Muslim Lyari Quarter. He cleansed and broadened the Old Town Quarter and eradicated plague from it.

Nusserwanji was associated with countless charities, including the Hiranand Leper Hospital. He set up the Sobraj Maternity Home and the Gulbai Maternity Home. He spearheaded the relief work during the influenza epidemic of 1919, the floods of 1927 and 1929 and the Quetta earthquake of 1935. He streamlined administrative and bureaucratic procedures, and was elected into the Sindh Assembly from Dadu. Hatim A. Alavi, who worked with him in the KMC says, 'His intangible and unrecorded work was greater by far than his tangible and recorded activities.'[29] He realized that a highly developed civic consciousness was essential for any meaningful development and progress. He proceeded to educate citizens of Karachi, young and old, in their civic rights and responsibilities, through lectures and tours, aided by a group of young men and women, many of whom later became municipal councillors themselves. He continues to be remembered as one of Karachi's most respected and remarkable citizens.

HATIM A. ALAVI
1898-1976

Hatim Alavi was born in Karachi, into a prominent business family and was a partner in Yusafali Alibhoy Karimji & Co. He was also a well-known philanthropist and played an active political role in Karachi. He represented Sindh at the Indian National Congress's 1920 Nagpur Session when Gandhi called for a non-violent, non-cooperation movement to establish *Swaraj* or Self Rule for India. Hatim Alavi played an active part in this, as well as the pan-Islamic Khilafat Movement, which was then allied to the Congress. In 1921, he was appointed the secretary of the Swaraj Sabha, the new name for the All-India Home Rule League, founded by B.G. Tilak and Annie Besant. Hatim Alavi held office in various local Congress and Khilafat committees, helped to organize a public meeting for Gandhi in Karachi, and also the 1921 Khilafat Conference in Karachi, presided by Maulana Mohammed Ali. He stayed with Gandhi at the Satyagraha Ashram, and with Tagore at Shantiniketan and later, came to know the Quaid-i-Azam personally too[30]. He left the Congress Party in 1928 because of its increasing anti-Muslim communalism. By this time, the call for the separation of Sindh from the Bombay Presidency had become a burning issue.

Hatim Alavi joined prominent Sindhi leaders in their campaign for provincial autonomy which was finally granted in 1935. Shortly before this, Hatim Alavi had inaugurated the Sindh Muslim League, held municipal elections under its banner and joined the Karachi Municipality. In 1936, he was among those selected on the Muslim League's Sindh section parliamentary boards and joined the Council of the All India Muslim League. At this time, the Muslims of Sindh were riven by factions and the League's representation there was nebulous, particularly after the 1936 provincial elections. Throughout, Hatim Alavi's support for the Muslim League never wavered. He corresponded with the Quaid-i-Azam keeping him abreast of developments in Sindh. By 1938, the situation had changed radically in the Muslim League's favour. Hatim Alavi was elected the mayor of Karachi that same year, helped organize the 1938 Sindh Provincial Muslim League Conference in Karachi presided by the Quaid-i-Azam and organized a large meeting for him at the Karachi Municipal office. Hatim Alavi continued to work for the Muslim League, which formed a government in Sindh in 1942. When the Sindh Assembly voted in favour of the Pakistan Resolution in 1943, Hatim Alavi was appointed to the planning committee established to chalk out a social and economic programme for Pakistan. After Partition, he became chairman of the Pakistan Finance Corporation and made a significant contribution towards the inception and working of the State Bank of Pakistan. He remained on its board of directors till the end of his days and was a trustee of the Karachi Port Trust for twenty years.

He led Pakistan's trade delegations to many countries, was a member of the Sterling Balances Delegation to Britain and the United Nations and was appointed by the World Bank on the International Panel 'for the conciliation of commercial and industrial disputes between States and peoples'[31]. He was also vocal about corruption and the mismanagement of public funds. He had no hesitation in bringing to public notice some irregularities in the Karachi Electric Supply Corporation, although he was one of its directors. He was frequently critical of the Government of Pakistan's various trade and business policies and the slow rate of development due to political instability. He believed in Pakistani nationhood always, joined the Pakistan Democratic Party in 1972, as its chief

*Hatim Alavi:
an outstanding
citizen of Karachi.*

organizer and opposed the separatist movements in Sindh, after the creation of Bangladesh. He is particularly remembered for his welfare work. As president of the Karachi Medical Relief Society, he ran dispensaries in the remotest refugee settlements, after the carnage at Partition. He later set up a Red Cross dispensary in Lalukhet in 1953; he not only provided medicines but food and building materials to help refugees. He had a long and meaningful association with the Ida Rieu Centre for the Blind; he was on many other committees too, including the Sindh University Commission and the Karachi University Syndicate.

MOHAMMED AYUB KHUHRO
1901-80

The first Premier of Sindh after independence, the man who played a pivotal role in the separation of Sindh from the Bombay presidency and in bringing it into Pakistan, Mohammed Ayub Khuhro was born on 14 August 1901 in his ancestral village of Aqil in Larkana District in Upper Sindh. He was the eldest son of Shah Mohammed Khuhro, a leading *zamindar* of Larkana district. The Khuhros were an old *zamindar* family who had suffered reverses after the British conquest of Sindh, but were slowly recovering. Mohammed Ayub Khuhro was educated at the Larkana Madressah, and then at Karachi at the Sind Madressah and D.J. Sind College. He had to abandon his education early as his father died in 1920 and he had to return home to look after the *zamindari*.

Soon after his return to Larkana, Khuhro started taking part in politics and became a member of the district local board at the age of twenty one. Under the Montagu-Chelmsford Reforms of 1919, India had been given partial self government and the provinces had their own legislatures as a preliminary to eventual attainment of full autonomy. Sindh at this time was part of the huge Bombay Presidency, and the elections for the Bombay Legislative Council were due in 1923. Khuhro was elected to the Council and went to attend his first session in the spring of 1924.

From the very first Khuhro had set himself an agenda as legislator and representative of Sindh. He had identified the issues which needed to be addressed for the welfare of the Sindhi people. These issues were first and foremost the need for the Sindhi cultivators to be relieved of the debt burden by the passing of the Land Alienation and Debt Reconciliation Bill. They also needed some relief from the heavy tax burden which had been imposed on them by the colonial government. The ratio of Sindhi Muslims in services was quite inadequate and needed to be improved. Urgent measures needed to be taken to provide opportunities for the education and employment of Sindhi youth. Khuhro set about to work on all these issues and did make headway on all the fronts, particularly on the problem of getting representation of Sindhis in government services. He made it possible for a sizeable number of Muslim engineers, mukhtiarkars, magistrates, down to clerks and other lower staff to be employed by the government, and lobbied hard to get schools approved for areas where lower income Muslim areas could take advantage of education.

Realizing that the problems of Sindh were not getting adequate attention, Khuhro put his weight behind the demand for a separate and autonomous Sindh province to be separated from the giant Bombay Presidency. This demand was turned down by the Simon Commission which visited India in 1929 to assess the need for further constitutional reform. Khuhro realized that the most important factor in the consideration of the government was the financial viability of the proposed Sindh province, and set out to master the financial details of the province. He succeeded in convincing the expert committees, which worked on the subject, that Sindh was in a position to support itself and even pay back the Indian government for the huge Sukkur Barrage scheme. Khuhro went to London to give evidence before the third Round Table Conference for Indian Reforms. Largely as a result of

M.A. Khuhro: 'The iron man of Sindh'.

his efforts and persistence, Sindh was given autonomy in the Government of India Act of 1935. Karachi became the capital of Sindh, now for the second time since the departure of Sir Charles Napier in 1847.

Khuhro was one of the few Sindh leaders who invited M.A. Jinnah to preside over the Sindh Muslim League session in 1938 which established the Muslim League as the leading Muslim party in the province. Khuhro was also responsible for the public meeting which Jinnah held in the historic Tajar Bagh in Larkana.

Khuhro was also responsible, along with Abdoola Haroon and G.M. Syed, for the organization of the Muslim League in Sindh for the next ten years. Haroon died in 1942 and G.M.Syed left the Muslim League in 1946, thus leaving Khuhro as the most consistent and effective leader of the organization. It was Khuhro under whose leadership the two elections of 1946 were fought by the Muslim League. The second house elected in December 1946 brought in a majority of the Muslim League which voted for Pakistan.

After independence in August 1947, Khuhro became the first premier of the province of Sindh. When the Quaid-i-Azam decided that Karachi was to be the capital of the new country of Pakistan, it was Khuhro as the Minister of Post War Development and Public Works who prepared the city to receive the Government of Pakistan, to provide office and residential space for the thousands of incoming officers and staff and to improve the infrastructure to meet the heavy demands to be made on it. He did this most effectively by building barracks in the open spaces across the Sindh Secretariat for offices and housing officers in the houses, whether whole or in part requisitioned from the civilians of Karachi; as well as using the housing which had been used by army personnel during World War II.

At this critical time in the history of the subcontinent when the whole of the Punjab and the northern plains as far as Bengal and Bihar were enveloped in bloodshed, Khuhro kept Sindh peaceful except for some incidents which were quickly brought under control. Riots broke out in Karachi in January 1948 which quickly spread through the city, overcrowded with refugees and facing huge logistical problems. Khuhro took personal charge of the city in the crisis and called in the army when the police proved inadequate. He was able to control the city within two days, thus earning encomiums from the Quaid-i-Azam, who had been very anxious that the riots would mar the reputation of Pakistan's capital and also frighten the Hindus away. After the restoration of peace, Khuhro took the Quaid-i-Azam on a tour of Karachi to see for himself that the situation had been restored to normal.

During the early months of 1948 the central government decided that they were not satisfied with the arrangement that the Government of Sindh should continue to administer Karachi, which was the permanent capital of the province of Sindh. The central government wanted that Karachi be cut off from Sindh administratively and be taken over as a centrally administered area. There was a very negative reaction to this move in Sindh and it was regarded as an encroachment on the rights and territory of the province, as well as an unworthy return for the hospitality and self sacrifice of the Sindhi people. The Sindh Legislative Assembly passed a resolution that the Government of Sindh resist this move, and this was echoed by the Sindh Provincial Muslim League. Khuhro followed the decision of the Sindh legislature and refused to allow Karachi to be taken over. The end result of this resistance was that he was removed from the premiership of the province in April 1948.

In spite of being removed from office Khuhro continued to enjoy the support of the people of the province and became chief minister of Sindh three times altogether. He joined the Government of Pakistan as defence minister in 1958 but was removed and thrown into jail by the succeeding Martial Law government of General Ayub Khan.

The imposition of Martial Law in 1958 saw the end of the democratic dispensation in Pakistan for a long time and, although Khuhro remained active in politics and public affairs till the end of his life, the ground rules had changed. From now on there was no real role for the politicians trained in the old school of democracy. Khuhro died at the age of seventy-nine on 20 October 1980 and was buried in his ancestral village of Aqil.

G.M. Syed: 'The stormy petrel of Sindh's politics.'
GHULAM MURTAZA SYED
1904-96

'The stormy petrel of Sindh's politics', Ghulam Murtaza Syed was a unique phenomenon in the political life of Sindh'[32]. He was born into a family of religious leaders in the ancestral village of Sann near Dadu (in those days a part of Karachi district). Orphaned at sixteen months, he was brought up by an aunt and educated at the village school, but he had the instincts of a scholar. He read extensively, particularly religious and sufi texts, and went on to become the author of several books. He was also idealistic and possessed by a reformer's zeal. In 1919, he began to set up organizations to address and rectify a host of issues, ranging from oppressive social traditions among the Syed, and women's rights, to education and promoting Sindhi literature and poetry. He entered politics very young and soon made a name for himself in Karachi's political, intellectual and social circles, where he had many friends of all creeds. He also became very interested in theosophy. In his early twenties, Syed was elected to the Karachi District Local Board, having already participated in the Khilafat Movement. His main political thrust was towards self government and constitutional reform in India, but he also concerned himself with the Communist movement and the Hari Party in the 1930s. Prior to that, he joined Sindhi leaders in pressing for provincial autonomy for Sindh, which finally came about in 1935. For the next few years, several factions sprang up in Sindh, while politicians tried to resolve how the province should be divided politically. There was constant wrangling for power in the provincial assembly.

In 1938 G.M. Syed, exasperated by the constant Congress manipulation of Sindhi Muslim leaders, joined the group which invited the Quaid-i-Azam to come to Sindh. He helped organize the historic Muslim League session of 1938 in Karachi. He was present at Lahore, when the momentous 1940 Lahore Resolution was passed demanding a separate Muslim nation, Pakistan. That same year, he led the Muslim League's non-violent *satyagraha* protest over the Manzil Manzilgah, a mosque and historic buildings, which Muslims wanted to be restored to them and which the Hindus opposed. The vacillating government and administration lost control. There were riots. The Sindh Muslim League leaders, Abdoola Haroon and Ayub Khuhro, had already been ordered out of Sukkur and placed under house arrest; G.M. Syed was jailed. In 1943, he proposed the Pakistan Resolution in the Sindh Assembly and had it passed: this was the first time that such a demand had been approved by an elected, parliamentary body and was to have far-reaching consequences. Shortly afterwards he was elected president of the Sindh Muslim League. Throughout these years, he threw himself into working for the Muslim League, but 'idealistic and impatient he expected miracles from the governments which he supported'.[33] He developed differences with the Muslim League government which was in power at the time. This led to much unpleasantness, particularly over the nomination of candidates for the 1945 elections. The Muslim League's central parliamentary body censured Syed. He resigned, and with Congress support, became a bitter critic of the Muslim League. After Partition he was marginalized from politics for many years and devoted himself to literary pursuits, writing, giving lectures and attending conferences on philosophy, Sindhi literature and poetry, particularly on Shah Abdul Latif. He also wrote two volumes of life sketches of his contemporaries. During this period he remained very active politically, though he spent much of his time in jail due to his anti-establishment stand. During the 1970s, in the post-Bangladesh era, he became the rallying point for Sindhi nationalists and formed the Sindh National Alliance.

BEGUM RA'ANA LIAQUAT ALI KHAN
1905-90

The first Muslim woman ambassador and doyen of the diplomatic corps, the first Muslim woman governor and chancellor of a university, Begum Ra'ana Liaquat Ali Khan

Begum Liaquat: an untiring crusader in the fight for womens' rights.

was also the first Muslim woman to receive the Jane Adams Medal, the Woman of Achievement Medal and the UN Human Rights Award. In her citation for the medal by the 1978 UN General Assembly, she was described as 'the leading Pakistan women's rights activist, economist, educationist and diplomat, known not only to her countrymen but throughout the world for her outstanding contribution in the field of human rights...' She was born in Almora in 1905, educated at Wellesley Girls High School, and the Isabella Thoburn College, and was the only girl in her M.A. economics and sociology class at Lucknow University. She did her thesis on 'Women Labour Force in Agriculture in the United Provinces', made a study of the co-operative movement among the farmers of Bengal and became a professor of economics. In 1932, she married Nawabzada Liaquat Ali Khan. Soon afterwards, she accompanied him to England and the couple persuaded a disillusioned Mr Jinnah that the Muslims needed him, and he should return to India. She played a very supportive role while Nawabzada Liaquat Ali Khan, the general secretary of the All India Muslim League, worked tirelessly for the Muslim cause. At the behest of the Quaid-i-Azam, when fears of Japanese invasion were rife during World War I, she formed a small volunteer corps for nursing and first aid in Delhi. This was her first experience of organizing Muslim women.

In 1947, she was in Lahore, when refugees poured across the border and saw pitiable sights and untold suffering. In those days, it was rare for Muslim women to emerge from their homes to work, but Begum Liaquat Ali Khan mobilized them to defy the orthodox and help in the refugee camps, collect and distribute funds, clothes, food and medicines, drive trucks, train as nurses and para-military staff. In Karachi, the then capital of Pakistan, she formed the

Women's National Guard in which she held the rank of brigadier. With the help of her lifelong friend, the educationist Kay Miles, she established a home for abducted women, an employment bureau, a lost and found bureau, widow's home and other volunteer services. 'I was not a prime minister's wife,' she always maintained. 'I was really a social worker'.[34] She opened a cottage industries shop to encourage women and migrant craftsmen generate an income, and to provide support to existing indigenous crafts in Pakistan. The craftsmen colony she established in Karachi, now has a hospital, day care centre, schools and workshops. She also set up the flourishing Gul-e-Ra'ana Nusrat Industrial Home for women. Meanwhile from emergency relief, she extended her activities to every aspect of social welfare, particularly the uplift and empowerment of women. The key to her success was that she was an economist and a teacher by training, and an excellent administrator. She established the All Pakistan Women's Association (APWA) with centres and multifaceted projects throughout Pakistan; she also affiliated APWA with the UN and other international agencies to give it a higher profile.

To encourage female literacy and inculcate awareness among a largely indifferent population, she popularized the phrase 'You educate a woman, you educate a family.' She set up schools, dispensaries, maternity homes, family planning clinics in urban and rural areas. Her basic creed was 'health, education and training'. She encouraged her workers to acquire new, professional skills and to participate in official decision making bodies, such as the planning commissions where APWA's message could be heard. In fact, she firmly believed in integrated development and urged agro-technical training in rural areas. The many institutions that she set up in Karachi, include the Home Economics College for girls and the Professional and Business Women's Club and hostel. In the 1960s she defied the orthodox once more and persuaded President Ayub Khan to pass the Family Laws to protect women. In the 1980s she supported the Women's Action Forum and other women rights activists by speaking out vehemently against martial law ordinances discriminating against women. To support her family, after the assassination of Prime Minister Liaquat Ali Khan in 1951, in 1954 she accepted a diplomatic assignment in Holland and later, Italy, but she kept in close touch with APWA throughout. She spoke on many international forums, highlighted the social and economic needs of Pakistan, and spoke constantly of breaking down barriers and prejudices. She was showered with honours, including the Nishan-e-Imtiaz. She was appointed Governor of Sindh in the 1970s.

DR AKHTAR HAMEED KHAN

At eighty-three, Dr Akhtar Hameed Khan still has the fiery spirit of a rebel, a creative inquiring mind and the will to continue transforming society in a meaningful way. The basic concept behind his success is the principle of research and extension, learning then teaching. He has a methodical, scientific approach, is an inborn teacher and an excellent administrator. His pioneering work in Orangi, Karachi's largest *katchi abadi* (slum) with a population of one million is being replicated in Pakistan and has been recognized by UNESCO and other international agencies as a role model for Third World countries. He was born in 1914 in Agra, into a family strongly influenced by the reformist ideas of Sir Syed Ahmed Khan. His father was an upright police inspector who 'combined Muslim puritanism with the Victorian gentleman's strict self-discipline',[35] but it was from his mother that he learnt to love books. He did his masters from Agra University, joined the Indian Civil service and went to Cambridge. Over the years, he evolved from an admirer of Neitzsche's ideal 'superman', Iqbal's *Shaheen* and Allama Mashriqi's belief in 'the survival of the fittest' to find 'personal salvation' in the more reflective, caring philosophy of the sufis. As a civil servant, he came to dislike the role of master/superman, the entire system which divided the rulers from the ruled and led to arbitrary policies causing untold misery to millions, particularly during the Bengal famine. After nine years, he left the civil service and worked as a labourer and locksmith, before he joined the Jamia Millia in Delhi, as a teacher. In 1950, he became the principal of Victoria College in Comilla, East Pakistan and in 1958, was appointed Director for the Pakistan Academy for Rural Development there. He acted as peacemaker when ethnic strife broke out and encouraged Orangi's many communities to resolve their differences.

Dr Akhtar Hameed Khan: father of the Orangi project, who raised the concept of self help to new heights.

Furthermore, when the Baloch in Orangi were attacked and fled to their farming kinsmen on Karachi's outskirts, the OPP not only helped them to return to Orangi and rebuild their houses, but started a programme to help those arid Baloch villages or goths by building wells, windmills and introducing drip irrigation. The importance of Dr Akhtar Hameed Khan's work in Orangi cannot be overemphasized. He has provided an original, alternative and viable solution to the mismanagement and disorder that is generally considered synonymous with the proliferating megapolises of the third world. In less than two decades, Orangi has developed into a dynamic, thriving community with a literacy rate of seventy per cent, inclusive of both men and women. Orangi now has 15,000 business units, many run by women, and backed up by an easy system of loans and credit made available by OPP's Orangi Charitable Trust. The OPP has trained other organizations to replicate its work and disseminate that knowledge to countries with similar problems. The younger generation guided and inspired by Dr Akhtar Hameed Khan includes architect Arif Hassan and civil servant, Tasneem Siddiqui, who have received the International Year of the Shelterless Award and the Aga Khan Award respectively for their pioneering work in development.

MAULANA ABDUS SATTAR EDHI

One of Karachi's most respected and dedicated living social workers, Maulana Abdus Sattar Edhi has provided the nearest that Pakistan has to an alternative and comprehensive social welfare system. He has cut down paperwork and office procedures to the minimum, never accepted official funds and has demonstrated how much one organization can achieve. Abdus Sattar Edhi was born into a family of Memon traders and grew up in Bantva, a village near Junagadh. From childhood his thrifty mother taught him to give half of his daily pocket money to someone poor. Soon he developed a habit of seeking out people in genuine need.[37] In 1947, he migrated to Pakistan with his parents. The family settled in Karachi's Jodia Bazaar. By then, he had left school at thirteen, having no interest in academics. His father, a commission agent in a cloth shop, encouraged him to be independent and manage money by working as a street vendor, or running small businesses on his own. Abdus Sattar Edhi started to work for a charitable organization in 1948, run by the Memon community to which he belonged. He soon challenged its unrealistic, traditional concepts of hand-outs and patronage to people of the same community. He wanted to solve the real problems of people he encountered daily, regardless of community, caste or creed. His outspoken views offended his elders and he was ostracized, but he was determined to prove his worth. In 1951, he bought a small shop in Mithadar, put a tin collection box outside for charity and started a dispensary which never shut and where at night, he slept on the bench outside. He bought medicines at market rates and sold them to the poor for much less; he paid a regular wage to a physician, so that patients need not pay high fees; to save money he himself worked at the doctor's clinic in the mornings and trained in pharmacy and accountancy. He set up a maternity home and later trained midwives. To raise money, he sold animal hides that he bought wholesale from meat sellers or collected as donations over Eid. As word spread, he began to regain the goodwill of his community and of Karachi's inhabitants at large. During the 1957 flu epidemic he borrowed heavily to set up free camps stocked with medicines and injections throughout the city.

He made his 'first financial breakthrough'[38] when an impressed Memon businessman gave the organization Rs 20,000. He used some of this to buy a second hand vehicle that he named 'The Poor Man's Van'. He could then travel to other cities and also convey the ailing and sick to hospitals and clinics. This marked the beginning of Karachi's first, much-needed ambulance service which made him a household word by the 1980s, and which is now available in Pakistan's major cities. He also developed and trained a loyal band of volunteers that he called *razakars*. Whether

*Maulana Edhi: an angel
of mercy and friend of
the poor and destitute.*

there were floods, earthquakes, epidemics, wars, ethnic riots
in Karachi, or other parts of Pakistan, Edhi and his team
were always there, regardless of personal danger. He also
provided shelter for the destitute, orphaned, needy,
disabled, and dying. He helped rehabilitate drug addicts,
visited hospitals and met the wedding expenses of needy
girls. He was so enraged at public apathy and squalor
towards certain menial tasks which were regarded as
degrading, that he defied taboos and worked hours clearing
and unblocking drains himself, rescuing dead and
sometimes putrefying bodies from seas and rivers, bathing
them himself, and ensuring a proper funeral. His travels
abroad took him to Europe and also to war stricken
Lebanon and Somalia. He translated that newly acquired
knowledge and experience to his work in Pakistan.
Encouraged by Bilquis, his wife and colleague, he set up the
Edhi Foundation to continue the work he began in Karachi's
Mithadar. The foundation is the only charitable organization
of its kind and scale in Pakistan with centres throughout
the country. He was decorated with the Magasaysay Award
in the Philippines, and the Sitara-i-Imtiaz in 1989.

The KPT Building:
barometer of activity
at the port.

Chapter 6

AN ECONOMIC PERSPECTIVE

Shahida Wizarat

At the time of independence Pakistan was an agricultural country, exporting primary commodities, mainly raw jute and cotton and importing manufactured goods, mainly consumer goods. Karachi, which became the capital of the newborn state, was a small town with hardly any manufacturing capacity—the Dalmia Cement Factory and a few isolated manufacturing units being the exception. Areas that comprise Pakistan were by and large agricultural, growing raw material for industries located in areas that later became part of India. This colonial pattern of production and exchange between Pakistan and India continued even after Partition. However, as an aftermath of the Korean War all the major sterling area currencies were devalued, the Government of Pakistan decided not to follow suit as the country was experiencing a boom in demand for its raw cotton. The Indian Government refused to accept the new parity of the Pakistan rupee, as a result of which trade between the two countries came to a halt. This caused a major disequilibrium as Pakistan was left with a massive agricultural raw material surplus, a large market for industrial consumer goods, supplies to which had been disrupted. Lewis (1969) explained industrialization in Pakistan due to working off the disequilibrium created as a result of Partition, and the break up of the customs union between Pakistan and India, which made agricultural raw material available for domestic production on the one hand, while on the other, it made available a large domestic market for consumer goods.

Rapid industrialization has been pursued in Pakistan since its inception, and particularly after the disruption of trade with India. The reasons for promoting industrialization were three: first, in view of the surplus labour conditions prevailing in the country, it was argued that sustained growth of per capita income was possible only if there was a massive shift of labour from agriculture to industry and services. Second, on account of slow growth of demand for primary commodities in world markets, it was pointed out that a strategy based on export of primary commodities would result in slow growth of income and employment. And third, it was thought that long-term improvement in the balance of payments could be achieved through export of manufactured goods on a massive scale.

The forces of industrial agglomeration led to transforming Karachi, from its initial status of a small town to the metropolitan city and the centre of industry, finance and trade it is today. It has been observed that forces of industrial agglomeration are stronger in the developing countries than they are in the developed countries. The availability of social overhead capital and inter-industry linkages create 'growth poles'. The growth poles first attract the key industries, the key industries then attract other manufacturing and commercial activities through inter-industry linkages, leading to migration of labour from rural areas to the growth centres. As a result of brisk economic activity, financial institutions also get located in these areas. Studying the factors affecting industrial location in Pakistan, Papanek (1970) observed that immigration of Muslim traders from India after Partition in 1947 to Karachi was on account of linguistic affinity, proximity to the capital, and port facilities. This, along with public investment on infrastructure in these areas, resulted in very rapid growth of Karachi.

Rapid industrialization occurred in Karachi, or in the country for that matter, through the use of industrial policy. Import licences and quantitative restrictions were used to provide protection to domestic manufacturing. By giving unfavourable exchange rates to agricultural exports and curtailing import of manufactures, the domestic prices of manufactured goods were kept at a high level, while those of agricultural goods kept low. This increased the profitability of manufactured goods in the country, causing rapid increase in investment in the manufacturing sector. The import substitution encouraged by these policies was very rapid in consumer goods industries.

On account of high protection to manufacturing during the 1960s, most of the industries that came to be located in Karachi were consumer goods industries. Increased liberalization caused a slight increase in the share of intermediate goods industries. But it was not until the industrial policy laid out in the Sixth Five Year Plan i.e., 1983-8, that emphasis was laid on import substitution of capital goods and export oriented consumer goods industries. Among the capital goods, highest priority was to be given to the forward linkages of the steel industry, which include transport equipment, railway wagons, rails, electrical equipment, telecommunication, and industrial machinery.

The liberalization of the regulatory environment that was initiated in 1987 gained momentum from 1990. These include removal of the requirement for investment sanction, reduction in the list of specified industries that require government sanction to four, removal of non-tariff barriers and reduction of tariffs on raw material, intermediate and capital goods. Investors can now set up a project, irrespective of its cost, by applying directly to commercial banks and development finance institutions for finances. The procedure for obtaining a No Objection Certificate (NOC) from the provincial government has also been done away with. Most of the incentives to manufacturing being offered by the government are of an area specific nature with a view to dispersing industries away from developed cities like Karachi. However, the industry specific incentives apply to Karachi, as well as all other areas of the country. These are the key industries and include bio-technology, electronics, fertilizer, fiber optics, solar energy, engineering, cement, dairy and mining industries. Full benefits have yet to be realized from these liberalization measures, as the law and order situation and political instability have been the inhibiting factors.

As stated earlier, Karachi has been transformed from a small port city into a leading industrial, commercial and financial metropolis of the country. Agriculture, which still contributes the major proportion of the Gross Domestic Product (GDP) and employs a major proportion of the total labour force in Pakistan, is however, not a major contributor to Karachi's economy, as can be seen from Table I. Agricultural crops grown in Karachi include wheat, jowar, bajra, maize and sesame, although the proportion of these in total Sindh production is negligible. Among the fruits, dates, bananas, guavas and mangoes are grown in Karachi. Likewise, output from the livestock sector is also negligible due to scarcity of water and grazing land.

TABLE I
KARACHI'S SHARE IN MAJOR CROP PRODUCTION IN SINDH
1993-4

Major Crops	Sindh	Karachi	Karachi's Percentage Share in Sindh
	in m tons		
Rice	1,954,888	–	–
Wheat	2,120,750	179	0.01
Jowar	44,859	376	0.84
Bajra	7,708	24	0.31
Maize	5,555	113	2.03
Gram	65,969	–	–
Barley	10,808	–	–
Mustard	46,058	–	–
Sesame	623	25	4.02
Sugarcane	15,421,072	–	–
Cotton	1,517,903	–	–
Tobacco	398	–	–

Source: *Development Statistics Sindh 1994*
Sindh Bureau of Statistics, 1994

Moreover, fishing which happens to be a minor contributor to Pakistan's economy, is an important contributor to Karachi's economy. While the principal fish harbour is located at Karachi and contributed 60 per cent to the national value added in this sector in 1984-5, its share has declined from 76 per cent in 1972-3, due to the development of other fish harbours at Pasni and inland fishing in other parts of the country (Bengali, 1988). Table II shows total marine fish production in Karachi over the period 1984-93. We find that marine fish production has increased almost continuously during 1984 to 1992 when it stood at almost 294,000 m tons, after which there was a slight decline in 1993.

TABLE II
MARINE FISH PRODUCTION IN KARACHI

Year	Production (in 000 m. tons)
1984	221.5
1985	229.2
1986	240.4
1987	247.0
1988	247.3
1989	242.4
1990	260.2
1991	289.3
1992	293.8
1993	248.7

Source: *Development Statistics 1994*
Sindh Bureau of Statistics, 1994

Manufacturing happens to be a major economic activity in Karachi, with household, small-scale and large-scale manufacturing units contributing significantly. We find that of the total household units in Pakistan 11.4 per cent are located in Karachi. Their value of fixed assets are 5.5 per cent of the total, providing employment to 13.4 per cent of the total labour force employed by household units in the country, producing 4.2 per cent of the total output produced in the household sub-sector (Table III). The household units in Karachi are, however, 65.5 per cent of the household units in Sindh, with the percentage of fixed assets at 70.0 per cent of the total value of fixed assets, employing 67.5 per cent of the labour employed by household units in Sindh.

TABLE III
KARACHI'S SHARE IN HOUSEHOLD MANUFACTURING INDUSTRIES 1988

City/ Province/ Country	No. of Units	Value of Fixed Assets (000 Rs.)	No. of Employees	Employment Cost (000 Rs.)	Value of Output (000 Rs.)
Pakistan	27688	86000	59404	77710	569742
Sindh	4810	6800	11803	10529	69553
Karachi	3151	4763	7964	7059	24100
Percentage share of Karachi in Pakistan	11.38	5.54	13.41	9.08	4.23
Percentage share of Karachi in Sindh	65.51	70.04	67.47	67.04	34.65

Source: *Survey of Small-scale and Household Manufacturing Industries, 1988*

Household units have become a major contributor to Karachi's economy over the years. This has been possible due to the ingenuity of the people, one example of which is the Orangi Pilot Project (OPP) started in April 1980. Orangi is Karachi's biggest *katchi abadi* where settlement was started twenty-five years ago. The working family units in Orangi are completely integrated with the Karachi market. Many of the units operating in Orangi are supplying goods to well known firms that put their labels on the produce. OPP set up the Orangi Credit Trust (OCT) in 1987 for giving credit to family units, which borrowed credit from banks and lent it onwards to the family units. These loans were given without collateral and the rate of interest on these loans was not subsidized. Selection was on the basis of ability to pay back the loan with strict monitoring (Khan 1995).

Similarly, the Karachi Municipal Corporation decided to set up a Cottage Industrial Zone in Orangi and restore the Landhi Industrial Zone. These are estimated to benefit 20,000 families. The former is spread over an area of 300 acres with 4,000 cottage industrial plots of 200 square yards each. The scheme is provided with all types of civic amenities like water, power, Sui gas, large roads, sewerage, street lights, and green belts. Development of the Landhi Industrial Zone has been planned along similar lines. Loan facilities have been assured by the Small Business Finance Corporation.

Small-scale manufacturing units are also important contributors to Karachi's economy as revealed by Table IV. We find that of the total value of fixed assets of small-scale units in Sindh, 44.9 per cent is in Karachi, employing 45.8 per cent of the labour force in small-scale units in Sindh, and producing 38.9 per cent of the output. But it is the large-scale sector which is the major contributor to Karachi's output growth. We find that of the total number of large-scale units in Sindh, 72.7 per cent are located in Karachi with a value of fixed assets which is 71.4 per cent of the total, employing 71.6 per cent of the total employed labour force in the large-scale sector in Sindh. Value of output produced by these units is 74.8 per cent of the total large-scale output produced in Sindh (Table V).

TABLE IV
KARACHI'S SHARE IN SMALL-SCALE MANUFACTURING 1988

City/ Province/ Country	No. of Units	Value of Fixed Assets (000 Rs.)	No. of Employees	Employment Cost (000 Rs.)	Value of Output (000 Rs.)
Pakistan	184090	5410809	471094	1853925	12415321
Sindh	30416	982620	89045	461191	3123636
Karachi	1912	441093	40809	274312	1214070
Percentage share of Karachi in Pakistan	1.04	8.15	8.66	14.80	9.78
Percentage share of Karachi in Sindh	6.29	44.89	45.83	59.48	38.87

Source: Computed from the data contained in *Survey of Small-Scale and Household Manufacturing Industries, 1988*

TABLE V
KARACHI'S SHARE IN LARGE-SCALE MANUFACTURING 1990-1

City/ Province/ Country	No. of Units	Value of Fixed Assets (000 Rs.)	No. of Employees	Employment Cost (000 Rs.)	Value of Output (000 Rs.)
Sindh	1,751	57,863,527	254,647	13,797,957	181,493,076
Karachi	1,273	41,323,256	182,281	10,589,993	135,712,356
Percentage share of Karachi in Sindh	72.70	71.42	71.58	76.75	74.78

Source: *Development Statistics, 1994*, Sindh Bureau of Statistics.

Karachi's share in total manufacturing however, declined from 36.4 per cent to 32.3 per cent during the period 1972-3 to 1980-1, mainly due to government policy aimed at decentralizing industrial location.

Another major economic activity in Karachi is construction. This includes construction of housing, commercial buildings, public buildings, infrastructural projects etc. although Karachi's share in the national construction sector has declined from 36.1 per cent in 1972-3 to 25.8 per cent in 1984-5 (Bengali, 1988). The service sector has grown remarkably during the last few years as a result of the growth of services rendered by doctors, lawyers, chartered accountants, architects and consultants.

At the time of independence Pakistan did not have a capital market. The only source of long-term funds were a few insurance companies, while the banks financed commercial activities. In order to cater to the financial needs of industry, the capital market was developed. The capital market institutions in Karachi are commercial banks, specialized banks and financial institutions, insurance companies, non banking financial institutions, post office savings account, and the Karachi Stock Exchange. Government securities are mostly held by the State Bank of Pakistan, commercial banks, insurance companies, public corporations, local bodies and provident funds.

The head office of the State Bank of Pakistan is located at Karachi. All the major Pakistani banks like the Habib Bank, National Bank, United Bank, First Women Bank, Muslim Commercial Bank have head offices located at Karachi; Allied

Bank, being the only exception with its head office located at Lahore. Other important banks that have head offices located at Karachi include Faysal Bank Ltd., Habib Credit and Exchange Bank Ltd., Indus Bank Ltd., Metropolitan Bank Ltd., Schon Bank Ltd. and Prudential Commercial Bank. Of the total branches of Pakistani banks more than fourteen per cent are located at Karachi (Table VI).

TABLE VI
PAKISTANI BANKS

Bank	Total Number of Branches	Number of Branches in Karachi
HBL	1911	204
NBP	1517	136
UBL	1680	176
FWB	34	10
MCB	1315	125
ABL	900	121
ADBP	355	6
IDBP	20	3
Federal Bank for Cooperatives	1	–
Askari Commercial Bank Ltd.	19	2
Bank Al-Habib Ltd.	20	3
Bolan Bank Ltd.	31	6
Faysal Bank Ltd.	09	2
Habib Credit & Exchange Bank Ltd.	03	1
Indus Bank Ltd.	10	2
Metropolitan Bank Ltd.	10	1
Pakistan Commercial Bank	09	1
Prime Commercial Bank	15	1
Punjab Provincial Cooperative Bank Ltd.	160	–
Prudential Commercial Ltd.	10	1
Schon Bank Ltd.	10	1
Soneri Bank Ltd.	16	3
The Bank of Khyber	24	1
The Bank of Punjab	243	2
Union Bank Ltd.	25	3

Source: *Annual Report, 1995-6*, State Bank of Pakistan.

Banks were initially providing short-term funds to meet commercial needs, but later they got involved with term financing. Besides the commercial banks, there are development financial institutions that have offices in

Karachi, like the National Development Finance Corporation (NDFC), Bankers Equity Ltd. (BEL), Investment Corporation of Pakistan (ICP), Industrial Development Bank of Pakistan (IDBP), National Investment Trust (NIT), Pakistan Industrial Credit and Investment Corporation (PICIC), and House Building Finance Corporation (HBFC).

There are twenty-two foreign banks that have branches in Karachi, these include some of the well known ones like ABN-AMRO Bank, American Express Bank Ltd., ANZ-Grindlays Bank Ltd., Bank of America, Citibank, Deutsche Bank, Standard Chartered Bank, Bank of Tokyo, The Hong-Kong and Shanghai Banking Corporation Ltd. etc. (see Table VII). Of the total foreign bank branches a little over 52 per cent are based in Karachi.

TABLE VII
FOREIGN BANKS

Banks	Total Number of Branches	Number of Branches in Karachi
ABN-AMRO Bank	3	1
Al Braka Islamic Investment Bank	3	1
American Express Bank Ltd.	4	1
ANZ-Grindlays Bank Ltd.	14	7
Bank of America	4	1
Bank of Ceylon	1	1
Banque Indosuez	2	1
Citibank	5	2
Deutsche Bank	3	1
Doha Bank Ltd.	2	1
Emirates Bank International	9	1
Habib Bank A.G. Zurich	4	1
International Finance Investment Commercial Bank Limited	2	1
Mashreq Bank	3	1
Oman International Bank	1	1
Pan African Bank Ltd.	1	1
Rupali Bank Ltd.	1	1
Societe Generale	3	1
Standard Chartered Bank	4	1
The Bank of Tokyo - Mitsubishi Ltd.	1	1
The Hong Kong & Shanghai Banking Corporation Ltd.	3	1
Trust Bank Ltd.	2	2

Source: *Annual Report, 1995-6*, State Bank of Pakistan.

The Karachi Stock Exchange (KSE) was established in 1949 with ninety members and thirteen listed companies only. In the early years the stock market grew slowly, but with the passage of time, the growth rate accelerated, both in terms of listed companies and the paid up capital. The rate of growth increased substantially in the 1960s as a result of pro-industry policies of the government and the rapid industrialization that followed. There were two major setbacks. One, the dismemberment of the country in 1971. And second, the nationalization programme of the government during the early 1970s. But in 1977 these policies were reversed, and the decentralization and deregulatory policies of the government had a favourable impact on the market (Memon, 1995). As a result, the number of companies listed at the KSE increased from 438 in 1989 to 755 in October 1995 (Memon, 1995). The market capitalization of ordinary shares at the KSE increased from Rs 214.4 billion in January 1993 to Rs 368.2 billion in January 1996 (Table VIII). Total turnover increased from Rs 60.4 million in 1991-2 to Rs 436.0 million in 1995-6. The increase in the turnover between 1994-5 and 1995-6 is quite, spectacular (Table IX).

TABLE VIII
MARKET CAPITALIZATION OF ORDINARY SHARES AT THE K.S.E

Year	Month	Million Rs.
1993		
	January	214,428.7
	December	348,642.3
1994		
	January	404,578.3
	December	377,332.6
1995		
	January	293,326.8
	December	317,455.2
1996		
	January	368,213.8

Source: *Annual Report 1995-6,* State of Bank of Pakistan.

TABLE IX
TOTAL TURNOVER AT THE KARACHI STOCK EXCHANGE

Year	Million Nos.*
1991-2	60.41
1992-3	74.47
1993-4	152.58
1994-5	191.10
1995-6	436.04

* 12 Month average

Source: *Annual Report 1995-6,* State Bank of Pakistan.

The Karachi Stock Exchange is managed and governed by a fifteen member Board of Directors headed by a President. Two other directors are nominated by the ICP and the NIT. The KSE is regulated under the Securities and Exchange Ordinance 1969, while it is run by an administrative staff of 200, and is headed by a General Manager under the Companies Ordinance 1984. Corporate Law Authority (CLA) performs the function of a regulatory agency for the KSE.

Trading has always been an important contributor towards income generating activities in Karachi. This derives from the fact that more than 150 years ago, Karachi Port served the needs of a small fishing community. At the time of Partition in 1947 Muslim immigrant traders came to Pakistan and started trading and the profits earned in trade financed the industrialization of the country in the 1950s. At that time the total traffic handled at the Karachi Port was 2.5 million tons per annum. Since then the amount of traffic handled has increased manifold and the port has undergone modernization. Further modernization has been undertaken by the Karachi Port Trust (KPT), and in line with the Government of Pakistan's (GOP) privatization policy, private sector has been invited to participate in a number of port projects. Besides, Port Muhammad Bin Qasim situated fifty kilometres southeast of Karachi has been developed to handle conventional cargo, and provide port facilities to Pakistan Steel Mills and Bin Qasim Thermal Power Plant. The government has also allocated an area of 12,000 acres for developing a Free Trade and Industrial Zone. Moreover, a grain terminal to handle four million tons of grain annually, a fertilizer terminal to handle fertilizer in bulk, employing most modern methods, an oil terminal to handle nine million tons of oil annually, plus oil terminal number two have been planned.

TABLE X
CARGO HANDLED AT SEA PORTS

(Thousand Tonnes)

YEAR	IMPORTS			EXPORTS			TOTAL		
	Karachi Port	Port Qasim	Total	Karachi Port	Port Qasim	Total	Karachi Port	Port Qasim	Total
1984-5	12400	2150	14550	2497	862	3359	14897	3012	17909
1985-6	12509	2930	15439	3310	1504	4814	15819	4434	20253
1986-7	13180	2761	15941	3124	1126	4250	16304	3887	20191
1987-8	14332	2894	17226	3384	826	4210	17718	3720	21438
1988-9	14072	4599	18671	3792	556	4348	17864	5155	23019
1989-90	15023	4798	19821	4052	515	4567	19075	5313	24388
1990-1	14714	6503	21217	3996	1154	5150	18710	5657	24367
1991-2	15266	6352	21618	5187	808	5995	20453	7163	27616
1992-3	17257	7501	24758	4912	563	5475	22169	8064	30233
1993-4	17610	6766	24376	4960	676	5636	22570	7442	30012

Source: Karachi Port Trust and Port Qasim Authority.

While the bulk of the cargo is still handled at the Karachi Port, around one third of the total is handled at Port Qasim. Table X shows the growth of the Karachi Port and Port Qasim during the period 1984-5 to 1993-4. We find that the cargo handled at the Karachi Port and Port Qasim increased from 17.9 million tonnes to 30.0 million tonnes during the period under review. We also note that of the total imports of 14.6 million tonnes, only 2.2 million tonnes were imported through Port Qasim in 1984-5, which increased to 6.8 million tonnes of total imports of 24.4 million tonnes in 1993-4, while the proportion of merchandise exported through Port Qasim has declined, particularly after 1991-2. Table XI and XII show the number of vessels entered and cleared from the Karachi Port and Port Qasim respectively. We find that the number of vessels entered and cleared from both the ports has increased over the years.

TABLE XI
INTERNATIONAL SHIPPING-ENTERED AND CLEARED
AT KARACHI PORT

(Thousand Tonnes)

Year	Vessels Entered			Vessels Cleared		
	Net Registered Tonnage Number in Ballast/with Cargo			Net Registered Tonnage Number in Ballast/with Cargo		
1984-5	1649	685.2	11898.3	1614	6874.4	5345.1
1985-6	1828	828.1	12383.1	1787	6958.8	5937.1
1986-7	1922	674.0	12844.2	1885	7260.1	5975.2
1987-8	1901	705.6	13156.2	1888	7370.2	6427.9
1988-9	1873	780.7	12761.4	1869	7225.1	6333.1
1989-90	1940	833.9	13252.3	1940	7132.7	7000.2
1990-1	1805	920.9	13059.5	1787	7812.8	6096.0
1991-2	1968	1296.2	13280.0	1944	7351.3	7241.2
1992-3	2102	1020.3	14075.5	2077	8263.2	6904.0
1993-4	1930	921.8	13926.2	1901	8071.6	6675.0

Source: Karachi Port Trust

TABLE XII
INTERNATIONAL SHIPPING-ENTERED AND CLEARED
AT PORT QASIM

(Thousand Tonnes)

Year	Vessels Entered			Vessels Cleared		
	Net Registered Tonnage Number in Ballast/with Cargo			Net Registered Tonnage Number in Ballast/with Cargo		
1984-5	149	765	1393	143	1352	743
1985-6	239	1177	2109	243	2063	1218
1986-7	171	930	1892	171	1929	924
1987-8	152	664	2012	154	2019	713
1988-9	192	412	2429	191	2456	395
1989-90	176	284	2079	174	2092	265
1990-1	244	617	1997	243	1979	647
1991-2	274	440	3009	276	3011	451
1992-3	279	479	5325	283	5256	478
1993-4	293	603	4859	295	4943	609

Source: Port Qasim Authority

What lesson can the interior of Sindh learn from the development of Karachi and what can the government do to promote a mutually beneficial and reinforcing relationship between Karachi and its hinterland in the interior? These are important questions that need to be borne in mind by policy makers, when embarking on development and industrialization of the country, particularly the underdeveloped areas of the country. First, when formulating a development strategy for the interior of Sindh, the OPP model needs to be kept in perspective. It can be replicated in the interior with a view to developing the underdeveloped areas, and provide productive employment to the rural people where handicrafts, ethnic embroideries, fabrics, and other cottage industries can be developed. The decay afflicting most Pakistani institutions and the success of the OPP model reflects that in order for institutions to be successful they have to be built around personalities. Second, for industrial policy to be used successfully to promote regional industrialization, it is important to bear in mind that across the board incentives to industries have not been successful. These incentives were able to locate industries in the underdeveloped areas, but their withdrawal made the industries non-viable. A lot of the sick industries in the country have been the consequence of across the board incentives. The incentives offered to industries in interior Sindh should be industry-cum-area specific. They should be for specific industries that locate in the specified area; for example, only those industries should be eligible for these incentives that are based on the raw material produced locally and are located in the interior. This would ensure that the industries are viable even after the incentives have been withdrawn. By ensuring that these incentives are not available if these industries locate in the cities, the government can reduce the exodus towards larger cities. Replication of the OPP model in the interior, and the industry-cum-area specific incentives approach will mean that industries locating in the interior will mainly be cottage based household units, small-scale and medium scale industries, like textiles, mustard oil, cotton ginning, yarn and fabrics. These are generally labour-intensive in nature and will go a long way in increasing employment levels in the interior. Locating these outside Karachi will also mean a slower rate of urbanization, and thus less pressure on the already scarce civic amenities in Karachi.

Industries that are likely to get located in Karachi will be technology and capital intensive in nature, like engineering, electronics, petro chemicals, transport equipment, automobiles and railway wagons. Karachi's economy would thus become more oriented towards large-sized capital and technology-intensive industries. Moreover, services will acquire an even greater importance in the economy of Karachi. Liberalization and privatization policies, and the development of the capital market, will expand the demand for professional bankers, commercial consultants, cost and management accountants, doctors and lawyers. Not only will there be an expansion in demand for these services, these

Clifton Beach: cooling off after a hot day.

I.I. Chundrigar Road: Hub of industrial activity, where the head offices of many banks are located.

are expected to become more sophisticated as well. Further, accelerated development of the Karachi Port and Port Qasim, opening up of Central Asia and peace in Afghanistan, will mean that trading will contribute significantly to Karachi's income. The educational system in the city will have to be geared towards the needs of the economy that arise as a result of transformation and modernization of the city and its economy. This would entail improvement in the standard of education at the existing institutions, opening up of new institutions imparting quality education and a greater orientation towards vocational and skill-oriented education.

A street scene in a commercial district: traffic conditions become more chaotic by the hour.

Chapter 7

THE GROWTH OF A METROPOLIS

Arif Hasan

On the eve of independence, Karachi, the capital of Sindh, had a population of about 450,000. Slightly over fifty per cent of this population was Sindhi speaking. The other languages spoken by different communities living in the city were, in order of importance, Balochi, Urdu-Hindi, Punjabi, Gujrati, Kutchi, Brahui and Marathi. Fifty-one per cent of the population was Hindu, forty-two per cent Muslim, 3.5 per cent Christian and 1.1 per cent Parsi.

In physical terms, the city was clearly divided into two: the European city and the native city. The European city consisted of the Cantonment, Civil Lines and the Saddar Bazaar. It was inhabited by Europeans and Europeanized Indians and those who served them. Saddar Bazaar was the home of the Parsi and Goan communities and contained retail markets, shops and eating places very similar to those in European cities. It also contained social facilities, community centres, clubs and religious buildings belonging to the communities that lived here. Thus, it was dominated by churches, mission schools and Parsi institutions. Christmas and Nauroze were celebrated with fervour and May balls were held regularly. The city was well laid out with wide roads and open spaces.

The native city was close to the port and consisted of the old pre-British town and its suburbs. It was dominated by Hindu and Muslim merchants and the working classes. It contained most of the wholesale markets of the city (such as the *Dhan Mandi* and *Khajji* Market) and a large number of Hindu temples, *dharamshalas*, mosques, *imambaras* and shrines. Hindu and Muslim festivals, rather than Christmas

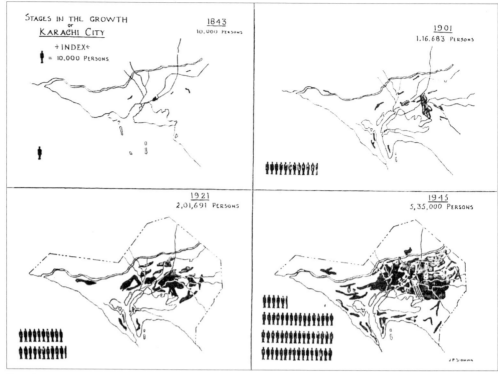

*Population growth
of Karachi:
1843–1945.*

and Nauroze, were celebrated here, and business and markets were very much in the Indian style. The streets were narrow and winding and within the old town there were almost no open spaces. The city proletariat lived to the west of the old town, in Lyari. In this settlement there were a number of tanneries and other manufacturing units.

The area between the two parts of the city consisted of the Bunder Road-McLeod Road-Kutchery Road triangle and extended south to the port. This area contained the Karachi Port Trust (KPT) warehouses and railway yard, port related business and commercial concerns, civic and municipal functions, and the major institutions of higher education such as the D. J. and S.M. colleges.

The three areas were linked by a diesel operated tramway system established in 1884, and at any point in Karachi one was never more than three kilometres away from the tramway. Karachi Port handled less than two million tons of cargo a year and all of it was handled by the railway and stored in the KPT yards.

To the west, the Lyari river was the frontier of the city, and on its western bank there were extensive orchards and fields. To the east was the suburb of Clifton. It was near the sea and was a place of recreation and holidaying. It was connected to the city by a narrow road which passed through mangrove marshes. To the north-east was the Malir oasis. Karachiites of all classes visited its gardens for picnics and recreation. It also supplied Karachi with much of its vegetables and fruits.

In addition to the city itself, the Karachi district also contained over 1,200 *goths* or villages. The coastal *goths* were inhabited by fishermen and the inland *goths* by agriculturalists and herders. The majority of these *goths* were Sindhi speaking and a sizeable number were of Balochi origin. Most of these *goths* have now been swallowed up by the city sprawl and in many cases their inhabitants have been forced to relocate elsewhere. The Karachiites were very proud of their city. It was supposed to be the cleanest

Population map of Karachi, circa 1947.

city in British India; its municipal committee established in 1853 was the oldest in the Empire; and the first aircraft that came to India landed first in Karachi in 1918.

Major changes took place in Karachi within a few months after independence. The most significant change was demographic. Within a few months after it became the capital of the country, Karachi received 600,000 refugees from India. In addition, it received a large number of government servants and support staff from other provinces of Pakistan. This huge influx was accompanied by an out-migration of the Hindu population from the city. By 1951 the population of the city had increased to over 1.137 million, and the number of migrants from India and other parts of Pakistan to 815,000. 170,000 Hindus had left the city. As a result, by 1951, over fifty per cent of the city spoke Urdu as its mother tongue and only 8.6 per cent was Sindhi speaking. The Muslim population constituted ninety-six per cent of the city and the Hindu population was reduced to less than two per cent.

This massive demographic change was also accompanied by physical and cultural changes. The Pakistan Secretariat was established in the Artillery Maidan next to Saddar Bazaar. Most countries established their embassies in the Civil Lines area. A university was established on what is now Baba-i-Urdu Road. All these functions were within walking distance from each other and from Saddar Bazaar, and the civic and educational institutions located on and around the Bunder Road-McLeod Road-Kutchery Road triangle.

The refugees squatted in most of the public and Hindu religious buildings in the native city, and occupied almost all the open spaces in the Cantonment area. These refugee colonies, especially in the Cantonment, were multi-class settlements. They contained government servants, poets, artists, journalists and intellectuals, as well as artisans and the proletariat. They were also within walking distance from Saddar Bazaar and cycling distance from the wholesale markets in the old city. Thus, Karachi became a high density multi-class compact city with no transportation problems.

The interaction between politicians, intellectuals, government servants, students, diplomats, businessmen, and the working classes, coupled with the sharing of a common urban space, enriched Karachi in cultural terms. Within a few years after independence, Saddar Bazaar emerged as the city's intellectual and entertainment centre. By the mid-sixties, it contained over twenty bookshops, sixteen cinemas, thirty-eight bars and billiard rooms, six libraries, and seven night clubs. In addition, seven of the most important schools of the city were located here and so were most of the public halls, auditoriums, and playgrounds.

Intellectual and political activity centred on coffee houses, eating places, and bookshops, of which the Indian Coffee House, Cafe Grand, Frederick's Cafeteria and Kitab Mahal (which claimed it had every Urdu publication ever printed in stock), were perhaps the best known. Political rallies and meetings were held at Jahangir Park, which was also in the heart of Saddar. Most student activities, such as variety programmes and debates, were held in the institutional buildings, such as Khaliqdina Hall or Sohrab Katrak Hall, in and around Saddar. The new eating places developed on the north Indian pattern, initially around Burns Road, where migrants from Delhi settled, and subsequently all over the city. *Nihari, paya* and *paan* became a part of Karachi culture.

The major problem that Karachi faced after the refugee influx was of housing the migrants, developing infrastructure for water and sewage, and creating space for the further development of the capital city. The new government very quickly took a number of steps to resolve this crisis. Housing was developed for government servants in and around the periphery of the city, and between 1949 and 1953 over 14,000 plots were developed by promoting cooperative housing societies. Most of this development catered to government servants, their relatives and to the more privileged or 'respected' of the refugee population. However, the vast majority of the poorer refugees and migrants from other provinces, continued to live in the squatter settlements within and around the city centre, and in public and religious buildings.

To tackle this issue, the state successfully removed the refugees from public-use buildings and settled them on land belonging to the Sindhi *goths* along the Lyari river. Displaced persons colonies were also developed on over 2,500 acres of land between 1950 and 1953. These colonies were at considerable distance from the city centre and transport, though inadequate, was developed to service them. These remarkable achievements were made possible by the establishment of the Karachi Improvement Trust in 1950. However, the solutions, especially for the poor, were on too

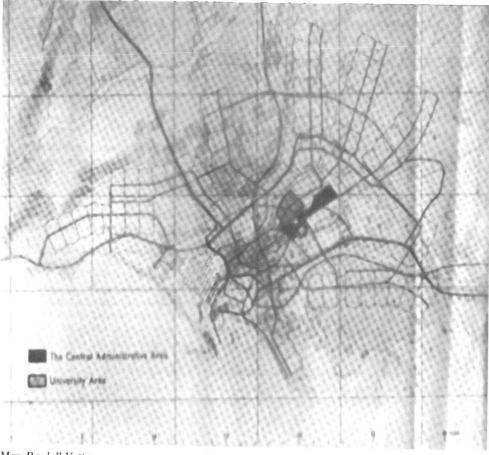

The Central Administrative Area

University Area

Merz Rendall Vatten
(MRV) Plan 1952.

small a scale and the problem of housing not only remained but intensified with further migration, natural growth and the passage of time.

The first attempt to tackle this issue comprehensively was undertaken in 1950, when the government of Pakistan hired the services of Merz Rendall Vatten (MRV), a Swedish firm of planners, to develop a 'Greater Karachi Plan'. This plan came to be known as the MRV Plan. It envisaged the upgrading of the existing civic centre around Bunder Road and its linking through Bunder Road with a new centre near where Sabzi Mandi is located today. The new centre was to contain the university city, and the federal secretariat and legislative buildings. The plan envisaged the resettling of refugees in ten storey apartment blocks within the city so that they would be near their places of work. In addition, the plan proposed guidelines, a road network, and a mass transit rail system for the future expansion of the city. It estimated that the city of Karachi would have a population of three million by the year 2000, a figure that was reached by the city in 1970!

The MRV plan was never implemented. Anti-government student movements rocked Karachi in the early fifties and were supported by the poorer sections of the refugee population. It is said that as a result, the government questioned the wisdom of having the university near the administrative and legislative centre, or having the poorer sections of society living within the city centre. Other plans were developed which proposed taking the administrative centre away from the city at Gadap, or on the New Karachi hills, and the university was relocated at its present site. However, apart from the university relocation, these plans were never finalized and a decision on whether the 'poor' or the administration would leave the city, was not taken till 1958. Meanwhile, the Karachi Improvement Trust was upgraded to become the Karachi Development Authority (KDA) in 1957, and it continued with the policy of developing housing schemes, mostly on the west bank of the Lyari river. In 1958, Ayub Khan established martial law in Pakistan. His government took a number of decisions that have had a major impact on the demography and development of Karachi since then. A number of external factors have also contributed to these changes.

The Ayub government decided to introduce green revolution technologies in the agricultural sector in Pakistan and also took aggressive steps to industrialize the country. This resulted in a mass exodus of peasants and small land owners, mostly from the Punjab, to the urban areas. Almost all of the industrialization took place in Karachi and hence people, displaced by the green revolution, migrated to the city in search of jobs. Thus, about fifty per cent of the city's growth during this period was due to migration. Also, in 1958 the Kotri Barrage on the lower Indus was commissioned. As a result, the Indus delta, deprived of water, shrunk from 3,500 square kilometres in area to 250 square kilometres. A large number of villages, mostly of fishermen, were left without drinking water. They migrated *en masse* to Karachi and catered to the newly developing fish industry. This development was the result of the

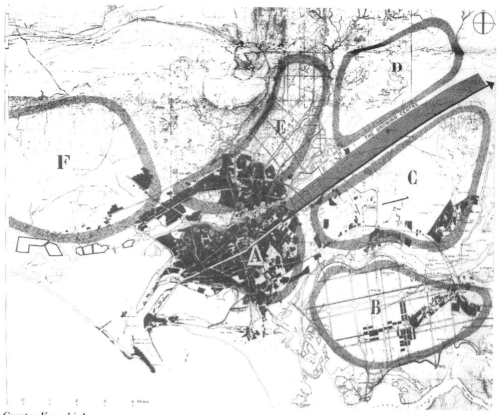

*Greater Karachi Area—
major community
grouping.*

establishment of the fisheries department, with the help of the FAO, which aggressively promoted mechanized fishing, nylon nets, and credit for fishing activity. As a result, fishermen from all over the riverine and coastal areas of Pakistan also migrated to Karachi. Due to this migration, fishing, which was previously entirely managed by the locals, came to be dominated by migrants from Mianwali. The sociology of the fishing *goths* in and around Karachi also underwent a change as an increasing number of self-employed fishermen started working for middlemen and contractors.

Two other decisions taken by the Ayub government were of great importance to Karachi. One, that the capital of Pakistan would be shifted from Karachi to Islamabad; and two, that the refugee colonies would be removed from the city. As a result of the first decision, diplomats and government servants had to leave Karachi. To facilitate the second decision, the government of Pakistan employed

*Greater Karachi
Preliminary Master
Plan—main road
system.*

Doxiades Associates, a well known Greek planning firm, to develop the Greater Karachi Resettlement Plan. The plan was to house 119,000 homeless families living in the city centre and to develop housing for 300,000 additional families in a fifteen to twenty year period.

As phase one of the plan, it was decided to create new townships fifteen to twenty miles to the east and west of Karachi in Korangi and New Karachi. In the vicinity of these townships, large industrial areas were also planned and incentives provided to the industrialists to develop these areas. Clearance of the inner city slums, and the shifting of the residents to the new sites was an integral part of the plan. It was felt that the residents of the new townships would be provided jobs in the proposed industrial estates and as a result, Korangi and New Karachi would become independent satellite towns. Initially, 45,000 one-room nuclear houses were planned for these two colonies,

179

complete with all urban services. However, only 10,000 units were built until 1964, after which the plan was shelved.

There were many reasons for shelving the plan. The main reason was that industrialization in the colonies did not take place and as such employment was not generated. As a result, many people came back to squat in the city centre. In addition, the state faced serious financial problems in providing housing as the expected repayment from the beneficiaries did not materialize.

The Greater Karachi Resettlement Plan also established the direction of growth for the city towards the north-east and developed a road network which has, to a large extent, determined the form the city has taken. It was also responsible for the development of the circular railway, which connects most of Karachi's work areas and links them to some of the working class residential areas.

The decisions of the Ayub government and the Doxiades Plan affected the city in many other ways as well, especially in the decade of the sixties. Since squatting in the city became difficult and housing was not available for the poor, squatter settlements developed along the roads linking the city to New Karachi and Korangi. Most of these settlements were developed by middlemen, and are located on or along natural drainage channels. This development was the beginning of large scale informal sector housing development in Karachi and the origin of the land 'mafia' which figures in most writing about Karachi today. In addition, the Doxiades Plan and the development of informal low income areas away from the city centre, laid the foundations for the physical division of the city into rich and poor areas.

Again, since jobs could not be generated in the New Karachi and Korangi townships, people had to travel from these settlements to the city, port area, and to the Sindh Industrial Trading Estate (SITE) on the city fringe. This was the beginning of the transport problems that have plagued the city ever since. In addition, since a rational road network had not been developed, most of this transport passed through Saddar turning the city's cultural centre into a transit area. With this development, and the evolution of a services sector to transport in Saddar, the city centre became increasingly degraded in environmental terms. The elite and the middle classes, unwilling to live in

Buses creating bottlenecks: a portent of the future.

environmentally degraded conditions, also moved out from Saddar to the new cooperative societies, and with them much of the retailing and community activities also moved out and were relocated in their new settlements. Civic and social functions could no longer be held in the degraded city centre, and they shifted to the newly developed four and five star hotel, or complexes. This further promoted the physical division of the city into rich and poor areas.

As a result of industrialization and surpluses produced by the green revolution, port activities expanded manifold. However, warehousing and the rail system, did not expand in the same proportion and, increasingly, road transport began to cater to cargo movement. This transfer from rail to road was facilitated by the support the oil and automobile lobby received from the state, at the expense of the rail road. As a result of these developments, Karachi's old city which is near the port, started to get converted into warehousing, and the city's roads started to get congested with heavy cargo carrying vehicles. In addition, the wholesale markets in the city which were made to cater to a population of under one million, expanded to cater to a much larger population. This expansion, coupled with the development of a supporting transport and services sector, started to further congest and degrade the old city. As a result, the more affluent residents also started to move out from the old city into the newly developed suburbs.

In demographic terms, the population of Karachi between 1951 and 1961 increased from 1.137 million to 2.044 million. Again, between 1961 and 1971, the population increased from 2.044 million to 3.606 million. Most of the increase between 1961 and 1971 was the result of migration from other parts of Pakistan. This migration introduced new communities in the city. The most important of these communities came from the NWFP. They were Pakhtoons or Hazarawals. Their migration was supported by the political patronage that was offered to them by the military rulers, whose leaders also belonged to the NWFP. These migrants, through their hard work and contacts, came to dominate transport, and building construction activities thus replacing the local population. They also acquired an important position in the police force in Karachi and were increasingly recruited as port and industrial labour. Meanwhile, in the absence of any major government programme for housing low income communities, squatter settlements continued to grow in the sixties and by 1971 it was estimated that there were over 1.3 million people living in them. It was against this background of transport problems, increasing inner city congestion and degradation, development of unserviced *katchi abadis*, and related infrastructure inadequacies, that the government of Pakistan in 1967 asked the United Nations for assistance in tackling Karachi's many problems. In 1968, the UNDP agreed to assist the government of Pakistan and, as a result, a semi-autonomous organization known as the Karachi Master Plan Department was established in the KDA to prepare the Karachi Master Plan (KMP) 1974-85.

The most ambitious programme proposed and implemented by the KMP was related to low income housing. The plan estimated that there were more than 1.5 million low income people living for the most part in squatter settlements. It further estimated that by 1985 there would be an additional 590,000 new households in Karachi,

*Life in a katchi abadi:
even the sunlight is
rationed.*

out of which 250,000 would be from the lower income groups. To provide for them, the housing programme undertook the development of 40,000 plots a year, complete with services, during the plan period. This was in addition to over 100,000 plots that were developed, or were being developed, for various income groups in Karachi through various KDA schemes. An important feature of this development were the 'metrovilles'. These metrovilles were to provide not only land and infrastructure but also technical advice, credit, and materials for construction. Social sector facilities were an essential part of the metroville progragrmme.

The housing programme managed to develop the plots and the required infrastructure. However, credit, technical advice, and other social sector facilities did not materialize. In addition, the cost of development was unaffordable to lower income groups, inspite of large subsidies. As a result, the schemes remained empty for years on end and much of them were subsequently purchased by speculators, or the middle classes. By the late seventies, the programme was all but abandoned.

The KMP also accurately identified Karachi's transport needs and stressed the development of an appropriate bus system, since the vast majority of Karachiites would always have to depend on road transport. It also identified the needs of the services sector to transport, and identified locations for bus terminals, depots and workshops. The plan also proposed the upgrading of the circular railway as a mode of mass transit. Studies were undertaken and proposals developed to expand the rail system into the suburbs and develop a rail corridor through the city, so as to serve Saddar and various locations in the business district.

A road network along with a number of bridges on the Lyari river was proposed. This proposal aimed at linking up various areas of Karachi to each other, so as to reduce distances and prevent unnecessary movement through Saddar and the inner city. In addition, a southern bypass was planned which would make it possible for all port traffic to bypass the city. A northern bypass was also envisaged and it was foreseen that much of the port and inland trade related activities would move from the inner city to these bypasses. This would reduce traffic, decongest the inner city, and make its rehabilitation possible.

The KMP also developed land use plans identifying areas for institutional development, recreation, environmental enhancement, and industrial growth. Locations for metropolitan and sub-metropolitan centres were identified in the suburbs of the city and the concept of cohesive and sustainable communities was developed for these areas. Some of these areas are Liaquatabad, NIPA Chowrangi, North Karachi, and Baldia.

Except for the development of the road network, building of bridges on the Lyari, and the part development of the southern bypass, none of the above proposals of the master plan ever materialized. The development of the road network, however, opened up new areas for development and shortened distances.

Other changes in the decade of the seventies also had a major impact on Karachi's development and planning. During this period, the state encouraged the construction of medium-rise and high-rise apartment buildings. Land at subsidized prices was allotted to developers, and credit from state institutions was made available for the construction of these housing complexes. As a result, Karachi's skyline started to change and a 'flat-culture', which has now become an integral part of Karachi's sociology, began to develop. It was also the beginning of the development of a strong developer's lobby which over the years was to increasingly determine state policy related to housing and land in the city in particular, and in Pakistan in general.

The building boom, described above, was facilitated by investments from Pakistani workers in the Middle East. It is estimated that almost fifty per cent of Middle East remittances from 1.25 million emigrant workers, said to average Rs. 30,000 per worker per year, were invested in Karachi in small businesses and real estate. This availability of finance has largely been responsible for the real estate speculation which has made formal sector land and housing unaffordable to the vast majority of the city residents.

The Dubai connection also generated a consumer culture and wholesale markets for electronic goods, motorbikes, and household appliances started to develop in Saddar and in the inner city. This development congested the inner city further and started to change the character of Saddar.

Saddar, in the seventies, underwent other changes as well. New building bye-laws were introduced, permitting the development of high and medium-rise buildings. This, and the related developments described above, led to the demolition of a large number of old buildings and the construction of new medium-rise structures. The inner city's architectural character and scale began to change. With the shifting of the university, the intervention of commercial interests, supported by new bye-laws, the availability of funds for construction, and the 'Dubai syndrome', Saddar's intellectual and cultural life declined.

However, connections with the Middle East and the availability of money brought about other changes in the city. Saddar's night life expanded and new cabarets, some featuring international groups, and discotheques surfaced. A casino was constructed in Clifton but was never commissioned. The Karachi Race Course acquired a reputation that was well known beyond the frontier of Pakistan, and people from the Middle East and the rest of the country came especially over the weekends to participate in its activities. Meanwhile, international film festivals continued to be held regularly in the Saddar cinemas.

It was in the seventies that the development of the Boat Basin and Kehkeshan was undertaken, and large areas of land along Clifton Beach and in the eastern parts of the city were reclaimed for high income residential and commercial complexes. At the same time, large scale development was undertaken towards the west of the city for housing low income and lower middle income groups. In this manner, the division of the city between rich and poor was further enhanced.

Most of the master plan recommendations were to be implemented in the late seventies and early eighties. Due to their non-implementation, the decade of the eighties created immense problems for the city. These problems continue to multiply.

The most serious problem has been the absence of planned infrastructure for the *katchi abadi*s that have grown as a result of the failure of formal sector housing delivery systems. The physical integration of these settlements into the larger Karachi framework has also posed problems of both a physical and sociological nature. The population of *katchi abadi*s increased from two million in 1978 to 3.4 million in 1988.

An aerial view of a megacity: a nightmare for town planners.

The failure to implement the transport related proposals of the master plan and the bypasses, has also resulted in a large number of problems for the city. Instead of proper buses or a rail system, the lower and lower middle income groups in the city rely for the most part on 13,000 uncomfortable mini-buses for commuting. These buses are individually owned. The owners purchase these buses by funds acquired from money-lenders at enormous rates of interest. The constant threat of having the bus taken away due to a default in payments, makes the bus owners (who are also the drivers and conductors) work overtime and violate traffic rules and regulations. In addition, the bus terminals, depots and workshops, were never built. They were encroached upon or were given away through a process of political patronage. Thus, the roads of the city have been turned into depots, workshops and terminals, and a services sector for transport has developed around them. In the absence of the bypasses, the inner city continued to develop as warehousing and storage for port related and inland trade. As its degradation increased, manufacturing, sweat-shops and the recycling industry started to locate itself here further adding to the degradation. Much of Karachi's traffic problems, environmental degradation, and congestion is the result of the issues discussed above.

In 1976, the Islamization process also brought about major changes in the culture of the city. Bars, billiard rooms, discotheques and cabarets disappeared and the race course was closed down. This development completely changed the nature of Saddar and parts of the inner city. Areas that remained open all night now closed down soon after sunset and, as a result, landuse changes were initiated which led eventually to a large number of cinemas, bookshops, and institutional buildings being replaced by markets and shops.

The seventies also saw the development of the Steel Mills complex, the Export Promotion Zone and Port Qasim. These developments took place towards the east of Karachi and created what is known as the eastern corridor. In the eighties it became the fastest growing corridor of the city. This development to the extreme east added to Karachi's already serious transport problems. Unfortunately, the existing rail link between the city and Pipri (where the Steel Mills and Port Qasim are located) has not yet been developed for commuter purposes.

The Afghan war and the Iranian revolution also had a major impact on the social, physical and political conditions in the city. About 200,000 refugees were added to the city's population, in addition to the 350,000 that had come from Bangladesh between 1972 and 1978. Karachi became the centre of the drug trade that financed the Afghan war and, as it always happens, this trade was accompanied by a trade in guns and the subservience of important state institutions to the mafia. This was also the period of dictatorship in Pakistan. The absence of space for a political consensus, combined with the development of the drug and arms mafia, increased alienation among certain sections of the population of Karachi, leading to ethnic politics, violence, and large scale administrative apathy and corruption. Armed gangs emerged to control various areas of the city, and kidnappings for ransom, and other crimes, became widespread.

This situation resulted in the ghettoization of the rich. Increasingly, they started to live surrounded by armed guards and security systems. They developed recreational, cultural, and educational facilities in their own settlements. Their relationship with the rest of the city ceased to exist, except for work purposes. This led to further degradation of Saddar and the inner city, and the development of new retail outlets and eating places in the affluent areas. Many of these retail outlets and eating places were old Karachi business houses that have relocated from the inner city to the richer areas.

However, in spite of these developments, Karachi continued to receive migrants, not only from the rest of Pakistan but from other countries as well. Bangladeshis and Burmese migrants replaced the locals in the fishing industry in the 1990s and a large number of Sri Lankans and a few Filipinos have become domestic servants to the richer Karachiites. It was during this period that Afghani food became popular in Karachi and is now available in all areas of the city.

In the late eighties, the government of Pakistan with UNDP assistance initiated another city planning exercise. As a result, the Karachi Development Plan (KDP) 2000 was prepared. Unfortunately, the plan did not take into consideration the informal development lobbies that had become important providers of services in Karachi during the eighties. These lobbies, which had by then become important interest groups were neither consulted, nor did they participate in the plan formulation. Furthermore, it assumed that the state planning and development institutions had the necessary organizational culture and skills to implement the KDP 2000. In addition, the steering committee of the plan, of which the chairman was the chief minister of Sindh, was unable to ever convene to approve the plan. As such, the plan has no legal standing and many of its recommendations are being violated. The non-approval of the plan and the non-convening of the steering committee, simply indicates that Karachi's planning has not been a priority with the four governments that have been in power since the plan document was completed in 1990.

Today, the population of Karachi is estimated at anywhere between ten and twelve million. Although it is said to be declining in percentage terms, it is rapidly increasing in statistical terms. The population growth is estimated at 4.8 per cent per year for the city as a whole. The *katchi abadis*, on the other hand, are supposed to grow at the rate of nine per cent per year. At this rate it is estimated that seven million people will be living in *katchi abadi*s by 2001. What the above statistics mean is simply that about 500,000 people (the population of Sukkur today) are added to Karachi's population every year.

According to the 1981 census, 54.3 per cent households in Karachi are Urdu speaking and 13.6 per cent Punjabi speaking. Pushto, Sindhi, Balochi, and Hindko were spoken by 8.7, 6.3, 4.4 and one per cent of households respectively. Surveys seem to suggest that in the eighties and nineties, migration from Sindh and the Sarai areas has increased considerably. Also, since there has been no major immigration of Urdu speakers, their number in percentage terms must have declined.

Surveys made for the Karachi Development Master Plan (KDP) 2000, established that an increasing number of Karachiites are living far away from the city centre. Projections of these surveys seem to suggest that by the year 2001, the vast majority of Karachiites will be living beyond fifteen kilometres from the central business district. These figures point to the necessity of developing a suburban rail system for the city.

The urbanized area of Karachi division has also expanded enormously. In 1971, it was 289 square kilometres, in 1974, 349 and in 1988, 3,520 square kilometres. The area of Karachi division is 3,527 square kilometres, and by the year 2001 the city will have expanded well beyond the frontiers of the division.

Housing and infrastructure remain Karachi's most pressing need. The city requires about 96,000 housing units per year over the next decade to meet the demand of housing backlog, population growth and replacement. However, the formal sector has produced no more than an average of 26,000 housing units per year over the last five years. The resulting demand-supply-gap is taken care of by the development of *katchi abadi*s, densification and postponement, or replacement or construction.

In terms of infrastructure there is also a serious gap between supply and need. According to the KDP 2000, sixty-seven per cent of Karachi houses have water connections, fifty-six per cent flush latrines, eighty-five per cent electric connections and fifty-five per cent gas connections. The major problem is of trunk sewers and treatment plants. The former are few and badly maintained, whereas the latter are almost non-existent. As a result, neighbourhoods and cooperative societies which develop their own sewage systems have no disposal points and over 400 million gallons of sewage goes into the sea untreated, causing large-scale marine pollution and threat of diseases. The sewage also contains industrial effluents. Tests on fish life indicate toxic pollution. Poultry and eggs are also contaminated since most Karachi poultry farms use fish feed. However, environmentalists agree that this situation is not yet serious.

Karachi's inner city and main corridors also contain some of the highest levels of urban air and noise pollution in the world. Studies have shown that this pollution is now adversely affecting the health of the residents of these areas, as well as of school children and policemen who manage traffic. As a result, inner city residents, mostly from low income areas, continue to move to the peri-urban *katchi abadi*s, where environmental conditions are comparatively better. They prefer to spend additionally on transport rather than live in the environmentally degraded inner city.

The natural drains that carried the rain water to the sea have also been encroached upon, or have been allotted to political beneficiaries who have built commercial and residential complexes on them. As such, the city gets flooded whenever it rains and alternatives for drainage have yet to be developed.

The infrastructure figures, however, are deceptive. There are major differences in the service levels between the planned areas of the city where the elite and middle classes live and the *katchi abadi*s. For example, eighty-four per cent of households in the planned areas have piped water, as opposed to forty-eight per cent in *katchi abadi*s. Similarly, eighty-five per cent of households in the planned areas are linked to a sewage system as opposed to twelve per cent in the low income areas. In social indicators there are similar differences. For example, there is over eighty per cent literacy in the planned areas as opposed to forty-eight per cent in the *katchi abadi*s. Infant mortality, gender distribution, crude birth rate, and education levels show an even greater disparity.

Solid waste management is another major problem that the city has so far failed to resolve. Only thirty per cent of the city's solid waste is taken care of by the KMC. Here again, there is a disparity between the planned and unplanned areas. sixty per cent of the solid waste of the planned areas as opposed to ten per cent solid waste of unplanned areas is lifted by the local councils. What saves Karachi from being swallowed by its solid waste, is the fact that all inorganic waste is collected by contractors and middlemen, appointed scavengers, and sold to the informal recycling industry. Thus, all waste paper is turned into cardboard, rags into fluff for upholstery, waste plastic into utensils and toys, while bones are ground and mixed with feed for poultry. This recycling industry has expanded to such an extent that it imports various types of inorganic waste from the Gulf and Saudi Arabia for recycling purposes. However, plastic bags are not recycled and they have become a major source of pollution for parks and beaches, and are responsible to a large extent for the blockages in the city's sewage and drainage systems.

Another serious problem that the city faces is environmental degradation, leading to the destruction of its architectural and historic heritage. As discussed earlier, this is due to the continued development of *ad hoc* cargo and bus terminals, and port-related activities, within the inner city. At the city level major planning interventions (such as the building of bypasses and development of areas for storage and warehousing) are required so as to create the necessary conditions for the development and implementation of a comprehensive conservation strategy for Saddar and the inner city. Here, it must be said, that Karachi has the finest and most extensive nineteenth and early twentieth century colonial architecture in Pakistan. In the periphery of the old town, almost all of this architecture has been replaced by ugly medium-rise buildings which have storage spaces on the ground floor and rooms for day wage labour on the floors above. Apart from the physical degradation, these areas have become male only areas and a culture of gambling, prostitution, and drugs has developed around them.

Another factor that is important in the case of Karachi is that about seventy-five per cent of its population works in the informal sector, in small businesses, workshops, manufacturing units, and in transport related activities. KDP 2000 surveys suggest that over thirty-five per cent of this population either works at home, or in its neighbourhood. Surveys indicate that formal sector jobs are not increasing in percentage terms and that for the near future this informal sector is the only employment generation activity in the city. However, this informal sector desperately needs credit and technical assistance for the improvement of its products, and expansion of its production. The only source of credit that is accessible to it is also from the informal sector at ten to twelve per cent rates of interest per month. This is in, most cases, beyond its affordability limits. Technical assistance, on the other hand, is not available at all. In spite of these constraints, the sector continues to expand and the lower middle income population of Karachi, mainly due to this sector's activity, increased from fourteen per cent of the total population in 1973 to thirty-one per cent in 1989. In actual figures this increase was from 70,000 households to 500,000 households.

The description of Karachi given above is, to say the least, dismal. However, the nature of its growth and its sociological conditions are no different from those of other Third World megacities. But it must be said that over the past decade and a half, the performance of its development and civic agencies, and its formal economy have declined considerably, whereas in most other Asian megacities there have been substantial improvements. Again, the increasing disparity between the rich and the poor, and the closing of a shared common physical and cultural space between them, are having serious political repercussions which are likely to become even more serious over time. This division between rich and poor is further complicated by a growing alienation of the city from the rest of the province. Urban planners, both in physical and socio-economic terms, will have to give priority to these two issues in the planning process for any future development.

It is true that the state has played a negligible role in Karachi's recent development, and much of the city's problems are related to the absence of this role. However, in sharp contrast to the state's indifference, the people of Karachi, who have migrated here from all over Pakistan and India, have managed to take care of themselves to a great extent. An informal sector provides employment, housing, education, health, and transport facilities. Households in low and lower middle income neighbourhoods join together to finance and build their local level infrastructure and lobby with the state for the services that they cannot develop themselves. Their efforts are supported by informal sector entrepreneurs and contractors. It is because of these activities that the housing stock in Karachi has improved considerably over time. In 1969, out of a total of 490,000 housing units 223,888 were permanent, 179,730 were semi-permanent and 86,382 were non-permanent. In 1986, out of 1,078,000 housing units, 452,760 were permanent, 534,688 were semi-permanent and only 90,552 were non-permanent. This is a remarkable achievement of the people of Karachi and of the recent migrants.

In addition, sports clubs, lending libraries, video halls, and thousands of social welfare and cultural organizations provide intellectual stimulation, recreation and entertainment, albeit of a substandard nature. On holidays the beaches and the badly maintained parks of the city are full of families and young people, both men and women. People play cards and carrom in whatever open spaces are available, families picnic wherever possible and children play cricket and football on holidays, or whenever there is a strike, in the empty streets and squares. In addition, in recent years, neighbourhood organizations are increasingly fighting off land speculators, who are often supported by politicians or bureaucrats, or both, from occupying the open spaces within their neighbourhoods. A struggle for protecting amenity plots from misuse is also underway. This struggle and other similar initiatives are bound to succeed and to create new institutional arrangements for governance of the city. They are bound to succeed because the majority of Karachi's population now consists of second generation Karachiites who have come of age. They are of various ethnic origins and unlike their parents and grandparents, they are not pioneers, but citizens who belong to the city and have claims on it. But these claims will only be accompanied by a sense of pride if these new citizens of Karachi know the history of the city and the forces that have created and sustained it. The city needs memorials to its heroes, such as the leaders of the guerrilla warfare against the British immediately after their conquest of the city; or the leaders of the rebellion against the British in 1857 who were blown up from the mouths of cannon in Artillery Maidan. They need to know about Mai Kolachi and about Moro, the hero of Shah Abdul Latif's *Sur Ghatto*, who lies buried off Manghopir Road and whose descendants now live in Rehri Goth. They need to know how Karachi has influenced the development of political ideas in Pakistan, contributed to the evolution of the student and labour movements, and laid the foundations of both leftist and rightist thinking in the country. To understand Karachi's history and its contributions to the political and cultural aspects of Pakistan, it is necessary that the city should have a metropolitan museum, and a museum of modern art.

In addition to neighbourhood groups and the informal sector, there are a large number of NGOs and citizen's groups who are involved in research and advocacy regarding Karachi's economic, social, and physical problems. These groups have only just started to have an impact on planning and governance issues in the city. Increasingly, their links with the informal sector, on the one hand, and with state agencies on the other, are being developed. These NGOs and groups cut across all ethnic boundaries and, as their work expands, class divisions are also becoming irrelevant. It can be safely said that some of the development and advocacy work done by Karachi's organizations is unique in the Third World urban context.

As Pakistan's population increases and capitalist farming consolidates itself in the rural areas, Karachi's population will continue to grow. It is estimated that it will be nineteen million by 2011, beyond which urbanization through migration is unlikely to take place in Pakistan. The present day and future politicians, and planners of Karachi will have to remember that, unlike the past, they will now be dealing with Karachiites, and not with migrants searching for a better future. In addition, instead of asking communities to 'participate' in their programmes as is common today, they will have to accept, facilitate and build on the work that the Karachiites, in the absence of government initiatives, have undertaken.

*The Habib Bank
Plaza: In the sixties
office complexes came
to symbolize the status
of the organizations
behind these.*

Chapter 8

HALF A CENTURY OF TRENDS

Noman Ahmed

Architecture is a dynamic subject. It changes its course with the passage of time and in the process evolves systems of built environment that mature with time. Each such system obtains its nourishment from the pre-existing and prevailing socio-economic, cultural, political and physical conditions. As this cyclic journey continues, its periodic change-overs furnish new dimensions to the process creating trends. These trends provide a comprehensive account of the architectural 'journey' and the in-built labyrinths of associated fields. It links time with space and presents a clear scenario of its origins, transformations, and the search for excellence.

Karachi has gone through numerous and distinctive phases in its brief history. The initial development of the city was influenced by a strong regional character which did not have time to mature because of the changes in the socio-cultural habitat. This is the main reason that buildings reminiscent of that era hardly exist, and those that do are not in a proper state. With the exception of a few Lohana residences and shrines that still remain in the Old Town, the urban fabric is devoid of building examples of the pre-colonial era. The British colonial period revealed its strength effectively in shaping Karachi according to its own standards. The variance in its built forms was subject to the scientific and technical excellence that the west was able to master during this period. Although the vernacular trend was able to survive till today, its apparent fabric absorbed a strong shade of the colonial impression. In fact, the hundred years of colonial rule produced a cultural dualism in which the

An early twentieth century house at Purani Numaish.

Civic Centre on University Road houses Development Authority offices.

A bank head office in the setting of Karachi's financial district.

PSO Building, Clifton, a modern structure of glass and steel.

cultural values of the British held sway over the private lives of people who were trying to sustain continuity of their regional relevance. Western values prevailed on the conduct of public affairs of the state, the government, in general, and urbanized elite, in particular.

With the Partition of the subcontinent and independence in 1947, Pakistan inherited a state structure set up by the British, together with a western concept of architecture that acknowledged westward-looking professionals only. This attitude is still with us. Today after the passage of half a century the country, in general, and the city, in particular, has not been able to release itself from western concepts and still follows them in every walk of life.

At the time of independence, Pakistan had few urban centres—Karachi being the most promising among them. The architectural forms that formulated the urban fabric of the city followed the pre-existing set of principles of early / mixed colonial styles. This is evident in the National Bank of India Building (State Bank of Pakistan Library), among the first eminent public buildings of the city in a typical simplified colonial style. As far as administrative buildings are concerned, the city inherited key edifices from the British regime that continue to serve till now.

During this period, public architecture attained premier importance, as Karachi was the state capital with all the state administration and activities that varied from trade to commerce. It was also a busy industrial production centre. These forces collectively intensified the construction activity in the city. The private sector also contributed, and office buildings, such as Qamar House and Mohammadi House, came up. Their architectural input was of a comparatively liberal and modern nature. At a later stage, Dawood Centre, near PIDC House, displayed the same modern outlook. The high grade of mannerism that is practised in these buildings was of tremendous importance, since it showed a turning point in the built forms, both in functional typology as well as aesthetic character. Cinemas and theatres started coming up early on, though their extrovert vocabulary was feeble and did not leave a lasting impression. Recreational and hotel architecture slowly emerged.

The Beach Luxury Hotel is another example of this mannered trend, as was domestic architecture in its very initial stages. The pattern of Bombay—styled facades became

*The Commercial
Union Building, a
forceful depiction of
modern construction
techniques.*

*An office building in
fair face finishes.*

common. Some vivid examples are still extant in Shikarpur
Colony and Muslimabad. This trend started to change when
houses inspired by the works of Frank Lloyd Wright and
Paul Rudolph began to be built. Houses showing Wright's
innovation appeared in the new housing localities of the
elite, e.g., PECHS, KDA Scheme No.1 and Muhammad Ali
Society. It should be noted that the rest of the city remained
at a mediocre level of development, without the appropriate
professional input.

The decade of the sixties produced some articulate
changes. Philosophies nurtured in the west made a forceful
entry in the local context. The building of the Karachi Arts
Council can be cited as among the first examples of a
Corbusian style. The amazing simplicity of the complex had
not been seen before; the contextual relevance of its built
forms reinforced the character of its facades as well as
interiors. Thus, such buildings were able to perform much
broader functions. An office complex was not simply a
building but symbolized the status of the organization
behind it. Such examples also served as a landmark in the
surrounding urban scape. Habib Bank Plaza is an admirable
example of this genre, other prominent buildings followed

Hotel Marriot on Abdullah Haroon Road.

the trend. Boldness of facade within a supportive scale frame that enabled it to show its depth of character continued to be built. Houses and house forms also under went change. Increasing land values and growing market pressures produced a direct impact on plot sizes. Plot dimensions decreased considerably; however, the owner's demands for added facilities increased. Designs in straight lines bearing plain facades were an outcome of this decade. The best evidence can be witnessed in the early developed sectors of Federal 'B' Area, that is Blocks 5, 6, 7 and 8, North Nazimabad Blocks A, B, C, D, F and H. The acquisition of durable goods, such as televisions, motor cars and other appliances created a need for their own proper spaces; TV lounges and car porches became household terms.

Monumental architecture, pertinent to its true definition, sprang up on the city scape. The Quaid's Mausoleum was built justifying its placement in the city layout with axial linkage and scale/height considerations. Despite controversies over the design competition that eclipsed the final choice, the Mausoleum is undoubtedly one of the strongest urban landmarks erected in the metropolis. Bye-laws and construction guidelines were prepared with respect to the

Hotel Avari Towers.

sanctity of this important edifice. During this phase, the first well-defined belt of industrial buildings began to appear on the urban landscape. Industrial buildings were, and are still, mostly built in an *ad hoc* fashion without considerations of functionality and aesthetics. The industrial zones of Landhi-Korangi, Sindh Industrial Trading Estate, West Wharf and the Industrial Zone in Federal 'B' Area are mediocre shack-like structures. As the population of Karachi continued to grow, additions to the commercial, recreational and administrative fabric also proceeded, giving a diversified outlook to the city.

A turning point in the architectural trend, initiated during the early seventies was the incorporation of multi-storey apartments, as an alternative to houses. Although this system was first introduced in the 1960s in Government Employees Housing at Federal Capital Area flats and Martin Quarters, they were not able to attract the private sector till the next decade, when they took off as economically viable dwelling units. The concentration of apartment high-rises remained in Federal 'B' area, along the Super Highway and its neighborhoods. Al-Azam Square was among the first range of lower middle income apartments. This trend gained pace with time to accommodate the increasing populace and to provide opportunities for sound investments. The quality of the buildings continued to improve and the typology of decorative elements diversified, as did the ratio of the covered area. Another change was the introduction of multi-storeyed shopping plazas. Previously linear shopping was considered to be the norm, with shopping districts performing proportionally to the needs of the people. However, increasing urban intensity and dispersion of shopping/commercial functions to various outer business districts created the feasibility of 'walk-up' shopping within walking distance. Shopping complexes came up in Saddar; later they spread to sub-metropolitan areas of Tariq Road, Bahadurabad and North Nazimabad. The architectural function of these building types was altogether different from prevailing typologies—new treatments of facades with extravagant glass usage, and huge neon publicity signs, were devised. The interiors were changed; a central open space was created to congregate the shoppers and disperse them according to the diverse attractions of the shops. To facilitate movement, lifts and escalators became a common feature. However, individual shops preserved the traditional cubical form, wherever it was possible to do so.

Towards the latter part of the seventies and in the beginning of the eighties, new architectural trends appeared. Four star hotels furnished the city with a true cosmopolitan appearance and linked it to the international transit circuit. The southern cordon of the city provides the evidence of this relatively new-born trend; Holiday Inn Crowne Plaza (former Taj Mahal Hotel), Karachi Sheraton Hotel and Towers (built at the site of Palace Hotel), Avari

Holiday Inn Crowne Plaza, formerly the Taj Mahal Hotel.

*The Sheraton Hotel
and Towers built at
the site of the old
Palace Hotel.*

Towers, Mehran, Marriot and Plaza International to name a few specific examples.

Alongside refinements in architectural input, variant ideas based on foreign and local styles continued to influence the fabric of the city, and mould it in relation to contemporary aspirations. Prestigious buildings such as the Aga Khan Hospital, and Finance and Trade Centre came up. Consequent changes in space usage, due to the vacillations of the business and financial markets, also produced a direct impact on specific building types. Cinemas and theatres were pulled down and replaced by shopping arcades, marking the failure and assumed success of two different commercial activities. Residential single family dwellings gave way to high-rise multi-storeyed apartment blocks or commercial complexes. A notable phenomenon that took the city by storm was the conversion of residential row type front houses into marriage halls. This change spread to most parts of the city but the major concentration can be seen along Rashid Minhas Road, Super Highway, and North Nazimabad. Another peculiar trend is the utilization of commercial or residential plots for private medical centres. Such structures have a typical built form; the first level is used to receive

Hotel Mehran—A landmark edifice of the seventies.

Four-star hotels give the city a truly cosmopolitan appearance.

Duplexes are increasingly being used for commercial purposes.

patients and comprises specialized consultancy clinics, the upper storeys, sometimes as many as fourteen, are used for ancillary hospital functions. One can regard these trends as ultimate offshoots of the changing socio-economic emphasis that prevails in the city.

Before analysing the ebb and flow of different architectural trends, a primary axiom has to be established. The professional architectural input in proportion to the net magnitude of the built environment is less than one per cent even today. Therefore, the role of the architect in constructing the new city of Karachi has been minimal.

There are four distinct categories of architects that have played important roles in shaping the built up environment in their respective areas. The first category comprises the architects trained during the pre-independence period. Most of them belonged to the J.J. School of Art in Bombay, while several received further education abroad, usually in England. In the early 1950s this small group of qualified architects came together to work towards obtaining official recognition of their profession. It was important to keep the direction of architectural development within proper guidelines. In unfavourable circumstances, they were still able to produce examples of architecture that were worth emulating, distinguishing their output from the works of non-professionals. Prominent names of the first generation of architects include M.A. Ahed, Tajuddin Bhamani, Minoo Mistry, Pir Muhammad, R.S. Rustomjee, H.H. Khan, Mehdi Ali Mirza, Peter Powell, Abdul Hussain Thariani and Zahiruddin Khawaja, Zameer Mirza Rizki, M.A. Farooqui, Pirzada A.R. Siddiqui and Naqvi. Their contribution to the profession has been overwhelming.

The next generation comprised architects who had studied abroad, and had practical working experience with international architectural firms. They introduced new trends into the local frame of reference. Trends like the modern movement, functionalism and Corbusianism were infused for the first time into the country, especially in Karachi. Architects Yasmeen Lari, Habib Fida Ali, Navaid Husain, Hasanuddin Khan, Ejaz Ahmed and Arif Hasan are some of the renowned names of this generation. Building examples from their work are: Burmah Shell Head Office by Habib Fida Ali, PIA Squash Complex by Unit 4 (Navaid

Houses in the posh Defence Housing Authority.

Houses built in the past decade are an interesting mix of the extravagant and the neo-classic.

Husain and Hasanuddin Khan), early residences by Yasmeen Lari, and Hasan Square by Arif Hasan, all demonstrating profoundly impressionistic shades of the styles they had absorbed during their experience abroad. One can consider that by virtue of these architects, Karachi was able to be linked to the international architectural network.

The proportion of trained professionals in the field of architecture was way below the required standards. To meet the urgent needs of Karachi there was no option but to rely heavily on the services of foreign architects, who were entrusted with some of the largest and most prestigious projects in the city and which, consequently, had considerable influence on its contemporary architecture. The work of these foreign architects had a mixed impact. Some of this architecture was not responsive to the local environment, and were imitations of academic conventions of the modern movement, such as the various complexes of Karachi University by the French architect, Echochard. In his campus buildings, louvres and perforated, fins are inserted to safeguard the interior space from the sun—kept as disciplinary elements of facades modified and incorporated to provide thermal comfort. Since no in-depth scientific calculations were involved, they became stylistic symbols rather than integrated functional and aesthetic design elements. On the other hand, a few architects, such as William Perry, produced buildings that rationally followed a well defined system. Dawood Centre depicts the efficacy of identical sun protection on each facade, and in a consistent manner. Similarly in the Institute of Business Administration, his detailing of beam and column joints seems almost symbolic of timber rather than of reinforced concrete, and presents an overall integrated design solution to a campus building complex. Another forceful architectural expression can be seen in the form of the Aga Khan Hospital designed by Payette Associates, in association with local consultants. The hospital leaves a strong impression on the contemporary architecture of Karachi. From subtle building details such as wind towers to the space utilization of the exteriors, the hospital complex has enveloped the indigenous spirit into the contemporary architectural form, with all the functional elements still intact.

At present, numerous private architectural concerns, partnerships and collaborations are working in this field.

Barren space adjacent to a well-developed residential area.

*The Finance and
Trade Centre.*

Most of these architects qualified abroad and tend to follow one or the other school of practice of western architecture. Amongst them foremost mention must be made of Arshad Shahid Abdulla. Predominantly followers of post-modern impressionism, their designed buildings depict serene facades, well-monitored finishes and a profound manipulation of internal spaces. PIC Towers by Ahed Associates have added yet another example, by treating the facades of a high rise with pure traditional elements from Sindh. Yasmeen Lari's Finance and Trade Centre has been at the centre of criticism by architectural critics for a long period. This building comprises multi-elemental implications derived from various styles, but the entity that out-rightly diminishes all other aspects of the building is its facade. Clad in gloss-vick imported granite, it displays the cosmetic look of a costly gem rather than that of a public-use building complex. Comparing it to the KDA Civic Centre designed by Rizki & Company, one can get a relative idea of the degree of practical significance that a design can impart to a building which an extravagant material cannot do. The distortion of plain-trix continuity of fabric along I.I.

Chundrigar Road by Habib Credit and Exchange Bank (former BCCI) Building (designed by architect Saleem Ahmed) is another example.

Alongside the established professional architects exists a second-rate group that is responsible for the majority of the built-up development in the city. Such practitioners are mere signatories for contractors/developers and are not qualified to take up large scale jobs. A large percentage of commercial fabric has been generated by these jerry-builders. Their products can be observed along Sharae Faisal, Tariq Road, University Road, partially I.I. Chundrigar Road and its by-streets. A majority of the city's public, office and commercial buildings are mediocre, copied from examples shown in international magazines and periodicals. The architecture of the city sub-centres is an example of this shortcoming. The office cum-commercial complexes built along North Nazimabad, Babar Market in Landhi and different phases of Defence Housing Authority are typical examples of this so-called 'architecture'.

The morphological impact of the squatter settlements which comprise forty per cent of the total housing stock in Karachi overshadows the entire urban landscape. This

Examples of taste and money in private housing.

Aga Khan Hospital Complex—a combination of well conceived aesthetics and functional requirements.

transient populist form of architecture is shaped by the people themselves and has its own aesthetic and construction logic. No less than half of the urban housing of the city is constructed in this manner.

Architects can be generally regarded as the main formulators of the architectural trends of a city. During the time of its emergence as a metropolis, Karachi was extremely short of architects and this gave rise to an era of extensive practice by the handful of architects then working in town. They can be regarded as the responsible creators of Karachi, turning imagination into concrete. Initial developments of Saddar, the central business district and linkages, prove this fact to a great extent. Parallel construction activity sponsored by the government, semi-government, and public agencies, outrightly refused the inclusion of private architects, engineers, and apprentices for their projects. True, Pakistan's Public Works Department had the pride of having Mehdi Ali Mirza and Zahiruddin Khawaja on its team but their involvement was not spread to all aspects of its work. Government buildings, in most cases, do not display or attain proper architectural performance standards.

Opinion holds that society is responsible for their cities because it inflicts its influence on its architects. According to this opinion, the architect produces what society demands—his/her power of influencing the clientele is very limited. Within these parameters, how successful has the

Post-modernism hits Karachi.

architect been in contributing qualitatively to the inputs of the clients, in particular, and generally to the metropolis? Unfortunately, in the majority of cases, the results have been disappointing. Architects cannot be relieved of their complicity, they are supposed to act as directional leaders for trends. This is not only valid for the 'architecture created by architects' but also for the imitators who follow. In the light of the words of Mehdi Ali Mirza, 'Just any thing written is not literature, anything built is not architecture'. Therefore, this 'architecture' becomes the responsibility of all architects who are equipped and trained to set the guidelines towards a proper course.

It has been forcefully stated that an architectural trend is 'elite-borne'. This statement bears considerable weight as far as domestic architecture is concerned. The client possesses every right to shape his abode according to his desires. However, in public architecture this may not be true. As can be observed in Karachi, the in-practice paradigms of a state directly interfere in the formulation of architectural trends. The seventies saw a liberal government and marvellous hotels, bustling restaurants, elite clubs, lavish night clubs, casinos, and pent-houses came up. This trend came to a sudden halt with the new government which had an entirely different outlook towards life for its subjects. Under its regime a wave of Islamization swept across the country. Numerous mosques were built on new and old sites, and public and commercial buildings began to show symbolic Islamic motifs. The subsequent regimes continued this confused policy.

It should be understood that architecture represents the actualities that a society possesses. The curves are clearly dependant on trends that take place in the cultural or socio-

Apartment blocks in Parsi Colony.

economic systems. However, when the population is divided into those that are aware/unaware, and literate/illiterate, the intensity of an architectural trend shrinks. As one descends from higher to lower degrees of awareness, the masses accept or are made to accept whatever is given by the trend-setters. This phenomenon spirals downwards in society with a gradual decrease in its vocabularic intensity. This can be observed with the help of examples—in an affluent locality the town house concept is angular facades, pitched roofs and Manglore tiles, the same trend is replicated in the mid-level localities on a smaller and more limited scale. This establishes an indirect relationship between architect and the non-paying client. Such replications are not restricted to house forms, they can be found in public and commercial buildings as well. The usage of mullioned exposed glass on outer facades was introduced by architects of the first grade, and on some of the best edifices. It has been copied in buildings in informal and lower income settlements without the formal input of the architect. Similarly, marriage halls, a recent addition to the surface fabric of streets, also present the same phenomenon. If one of them develops a hyper-expressive facade with lustrous treatment, the others produce its replicas within the fortnight. Car show-rooms along Khalid Bin Waleed Road (PECHS) and Sharae Faisal, with stretched glass facades are another recent fad. This process ultimately stabilizes whatever an architect creates, good or bad, relevant or irrelevant. It is accepted as a model, the fashion spreads and becomes a legitimate architectural approach.

To conclude this account of present day architectural trends in Karachi, it can be said that architectural progression appears to be in a more promising state, compared to the immediate era after independence. Whereas there exist various constraints that demand practical efforts from the professional architects and allied personnel, the primary recognition that the term 'Architecture' needed to firmly germinate itself has been attained. One key factor that can play a vital role in the acceleration of this process would be to increase the awareness of the masses. However, poor literary rates, current civic upheavals, and narrow-minded investment directives concerned with profit, make this an almost unattainable solution. On an optimistic note, one may concude that if architects and other related professionals will try to comprehend the broader socio-economic realities of the context they live and practice in, positive changes can occur. After all, it is always a small group of like-minded people that paves the way for the first step towards the betterment of society.

New apartment blocks, home to the majority of the city's middle and upper-middle income families.

A painting by Salim Mansuri depicting the crowded lanes of Karachi. The overhanging balconies of first floor dwellings and the canopy stretched across the lane cast dappled shadows on the street below.

Chapter 9

THE LITERARY SCENE—ENGLISH

Tariq Rahman

W hen Pakistan emerged on the map of the world, the areas comprising West Pakistan changed. But where this change was most manifest—almost like a magical transformation—was the city of Karachi. Let our first witness of change be the census reports of 1941 and 1951.

Whereas in 1941 Muslims were only forty-two per cent of the total population of the city; in 1951 they were ninety-six per cent.[1] So, Karachi became an almost wholly Muslim City. This brought about a complete change in the culture, the essential character of the city. For most the new Muslims who had come to Karachi were Urdu-speaking immigrants—called *Mohajirs*—from northern India. Indeed, about 57.55 per cent of the total population of Karachi—the majority was Urdu-speaking in 1951.[2]

These *Mohajirs* were different from the Sindhis, Balochis, Gujratis, Sikhs and Hindus who lived in Karachi before 1947. Their literacy rate was 23.4 per cent whereas it was only 13.2 per cent for Sindh as a whole;[3] they were more urbanized; they depended on employment for a living. In short, in Hamza Alavi's terms, they were predominatly a 'salariat',[4] though in time their less educated members also went into business. At that time however, the educated *Mohajirs* were generally either employed or, as was often the case, in search of employment.

The *Mohajirs* had reached Pakistan after the trauma of the Muslim, non-Muslim riots about which much literature has been produced. Most of it is, of course, in Urdu but some is in English too.[5]

However, in this article we shall ignore this vast literature in order to focus upon the experiences of the *Mohajirs* in Karachi.

Surprising, there is not much literature in English about this highly significant experience of the *Mohajirs* psyche. There is, however, a novel called *Refugee* (1974) by Linda and Khalid Shah.[6]

Khalid experienced the flight from India at the age of ten when, having run away from Aligarh, the family came to Bombay and sailed for Pakistan. Eventually 'by nightfall the ship had eased slowly into Karachi harbour'.[7] And now here they were in an alien city 'swollen to its very limits by the haunted faces of the homeless and destitute'.[8]

The rest of the novel captures the essence of life for the immigrants in those uncertain days of transition: the protagonist, Rehman, hunts desperately for a job and all he finds is manual labour. But in the quest for a new life a map of the city, the new city of refugees, emerges: *Phopi* Fatima's house on Martin Road; the officers of the bureaucracy; the crowded streets; an abundance of cheap labour—a condition of flux with human beings living through a quantum leap between an orderly agrarian existence to uncertain modernity. The rest of this novel is about the family's onward journey into the Punjab to work in salt mines. The essence, however, is the experience of migration and of this Karachi is the symbol.

This aspect of Karachi is also the theme of M.A. Seljouk's short story *The Bandit*. The narrator begins the story with the words

'I was living in the slums of Karachi then. The year was 1958... even the slums of Karachi looked like paradise to me. For here I was at least free.'[9]

The story then describes vividly the Karachi of 'tin shacks, tent-extensions, mudrooms...bursting with refugees looking for work'.[10]

In this Karachi of chaos and desperation a man takes to stealing and is killed by the servants of a rich man into whose house he breaks in. But this isolated incident does not make Karachi a city of violence. It is the city of desperation; of hectic activity; of the pursuit of money and respectability.

But there is another side to the city also—that of power, fabulous riches and corruption. There are two novels on these themes: Adam Zameenzad's *The 13th House* (1987) and Mirza Raquib Beg's *A Blossom in the Dust* (1992).[11]

Zameenzad, probably a *nom de plume* spent his childhood wandering along the eastern coast of Africa. He then went to live and work in Pakistan and now lives in England.[12]

His first novel is set in the lower middle class neighbourhoods of Karachi. The protagonist Zahid and his beautiful wife Jamila live in 'an ordinary house: the type that is always springing up somewhere in the numerous potpourious suburbs of Karachi since its continual expansion after the fateful birth of Pakistan.'[13]

The ordinariness is symbolically significant for it is the ordinary man who is cursed by all sorts of arbitrary forces in Pakistan. In this case the forces are medieval, symbolized by Shah Baba, a spiritual guide—as well as modern.

The latter are symbolized by the narrator, the I, who is from a rich family and whose friend Shamsie, a leftist, is killed in Zahid's house. In this clash of the medieval and the modern, Zahid, the ordinary man, suffers the most. His wife and daughter are abducted, for beauty is conquered by the powerful in a lawless land, and in the end he is left mutilated, violated and desecrated. The symbol which stands for the politics of the country is the skeleton of a boy in whose orifices insects go in and out freely. Zahid sees this[15] and becomes like this: 'the flies that kept moving in and out of Zahid's living holes seemed happy enough with him'.[16]

Such is the macabre message of the novel, but then the situation of the ordinary man was, and remains, desperate.

Mirza Raquib Beg's novel, too, is about the ordinary person. But his Jamshed Ali, alias Jimmy, is a beer-quaffing, English-using Anglicized naval officer. In his middle class Urdu-speaking home, an atmosphere of genteel poverty prevailed but the values were Indian Muslim (Mughal). In his social circle, on the other hand, the values were westernized—one said 'hello', drank, shook women's hands and talked of the 'figures' of girls. Caught among these two worlds—a condition common to many young people educated in English-medium schools or working in elitist institutions Jimmy tries to get married. But at this point let us stop and consider the other side of the coin—the life of people like Zameenzad's Zahid.

In this novel such a man is Anwar Khan, a servant in the house of Jimmy's European friends. His daughter Kulsoom, too, is supposed to get married. But while Jimmy is leaving the arrangements of his marriage to his mother, in Kulsoom's case it is her father who controls her destiny. While Jimmy dates the beautiful Anita, Kulsoom hardly leaves her home without a chaperone. While Jimmy's Karachi comprises posh hotels, beaches and beautiful drawing rooms, Kulsoom's is made of squalid little houses in narrow alleys. But the two worlds impinge upon one another. When Jimmy and Anita's relationship breaks up they come back from the beach and 'the stench and ugliness at the last turning of Mauripur road was appalling'[16]—the world of the ordinary citizen is appalling! And in this 'appalling' world Kusloom lives her insecure life. But when she enters the world of the rich—indeed she is forced into it after having been abducted, she comes to a world which looks impressively grand and beautiful but which is appalling in its cruelty and exploitativeness. She has been brought to the big house to be raped but she escapes. The escape, however, is *deus ex machina* and quite incredible. And after this the novel becomes melodramatic as Jimmy eventually marries Kulsoom and vows never to 'indulge in any sort of unlawful sex' or drink alcohol.[17]

But, however flawed the novel may be as a piece of art, it describes the city of Karachi in the fifties better than other works of fiction in English. Here, for instance, is a description of Nazimabad

> The streets of Nazimabad were full of people in their colourful clothes, with varying headgear, ranging from thin muslin caps shaped like slices of melon to those made of velvet and fur. Intestines of sacrificed animals were strewn all over. Beggars, who had said their prayers earlier than the others now came out in hordes, seeking alms.

The colourfulness of Karachi comes out in a number of prose writings too. Anwer Mooraj, for instance, has captured the spirit of the life of the city in a number of articles in *Sand, Cacti and People* (1960), *Wild Strawberries* (1992) and *Harbour Lights* (1992).[18]

Mooraj's first book, *Sand, Cacti and People,* comprising small prose pieces, is mostly about Karachi. They are enjoyable because of their wit and clarity. Here, for instance, is a note on 'the cup that cheers',

Tea is the most popular beverage in Karachi. Almost everybody drinks it. But unlike England where people work in between cups of tea, in Karachi the beverage is consumed before, during and after work.[20]

Whether it is speech-making, getting a haircut or commuting, chewing betel leaves (*pan*), or getting married, Mooraj has something delightfully witty to say about it. For instance in *Memories of Old Elphi* the city comes alive with its gramophone records, Greenwich Bookshop and the 'Manhattan soda fountain where boy met boy and sometimes girl'.[20]

In another article 'Amado Mio on Sundays' one learns of Bohri Bazar where someone sold sherbets and the author and his friends 'sampled every bottle of nectar that was arranged on the dusty shelves during the hot summer evenings'.[21]

Mooraj's command over English and his humour make his articles a treat. Laughter, after all, is always a part of life and so is the exuberance of youth. The Karachi of the fifties was, after all, not such a violent city as it is now and for the young—or at least those who were not completely destitute or ill it was a city of innocent fun, and a culture of diversity and tolerance.

In fact, one might say that Anwer Mooraj's humorous prose has succeeded in presenting us with, the social history of Karachi just as Khalid Hassan had done for Lahore in *Scorecard* (1989).[22]

Other humourists such as Omar Kureishi have also used wit, humour and irony in their descriptions of life in Karachi. For instance, here are a few lines from an article on the bad drainage system of Karachi

It is our conviction that it does not rain in Karachi. That it has never rained in Karachi. That it will never rain in Karachi. Everything in this city is anchored to this conviction.

But when it rains, it does not just rain, it pours. Then there is much activity described as follows:

The politicians emerge out of hibernation, charity workers start looking around for old blankets. Speeches are made, press statements are issued, civic leaders undertake tours of the city.[23]

This description has interesting parallels with Mooraj's description of a 'ten minute torrential downpour' in Karachi.[24]

Omar Kureishi's satire, in his own words, attempts 'to convey some of the frustration and some of the exasperation that is being felt by a lot of us'.[25]

To this frustration and its consequences we will come later. For the moment let us dwell a little more on the Karachi of the peaceful years.

In the fifties and sixties, Karachi was the centre of cultural activity in general. It was also the centre of poetry written in English. Ahmed Ali, who is famous for writing *Twilight in Delhi* (1943), a well-known novel about the downfall of the Muslim elite of Delhi, lived in that city.[26]

He was also a poet as were a number of other people. Most of these others were younger people linked with the Department of English at the University of Karachi. Syed Ali Ashraf edited *Venture* which gave the young poets a platform. The first anthology which was published was *First Voices* (1965) and this was followed by *The New Harmony* (1970); *Pieces of Eight* (1971) and *Wordfall* (1975).[27] The poets of Karachi were never in a numerical majority but Karachi itself was the centre of activities. However, Maki Kureishi, Ahmed Ali, Syed Ali Ashraf, and Masood Amjad Ali lived in Karachi. Later Kaleem Omar too settled down there. The point, however, is not the physical location of the poets, but the fact that most of these anthologies were published by the Oxford University Press, Karachi and it was that city which co-ordinated English-literary activities. The only rival to Karachi was Lahore, and later on what little was left of creative writing in English had no focal point not even in Islamabad where groups like the *Margalla Voices* held irregular poetry sessions.

This aspect of Karachi—the intellectual and cultural life—is mentioned in passing by many people notably, Anwer Mooraj. However, Nasir Ahmad Farooqi makes it a focal point in his novel *Faces of Love and Death* (1961), and it is mentioned (as a city in which one gets anything one desires) in *Snakes and Ladders* (1968). In both he describes the days of the early years of Pakistan when intellectual debates went on in the press and bureaucrat-intellectuals lorded it both in the drawing rooms and in the press. However, in the first novel, where Karachi gets wider coverage, the heroine, Annie (possibly Qurrat ul Ain of the *Aag ka Dariya* fame?) operates the equivalent of a sophisticated Parisian salon of the eighteenth century. The bureaucrats and intellectuals surrounding her write in the leading newspapers and one of her cousins, Dr Alam Ali 'had studied with Harold Laski at the London School of Economics' and 'remained at heart a Fabian socialist'.[28]

People discussed Islam, socialism, Islamic-socialism and other fads. Although the Pakistani intelligentsia did, and even now does, try to walk a tightrope between the west and the east; tradition and modernity, these serious concerns are trivialized in the drawing room world of Faruki's novels. Even politics, which could have been given serious treatment, only becomes a side reference one can use for dating the events. In Mehr Nigar Masroor's novel *Shadows of Time*, Mehr Nigar where it is central, Karachi gets only a passing reference though Lahore is given detailed treatment. But Faruki's snobbery—his reference to intellectuals and their ideas without the necessary distancing and irony which should have gone with it—mars his novels

The English Department at the Karachi University.

even though they do portray an essential aspect of life in Karachi upto the sixties.

Surprising, there is very little response in fiction to the changes which took place in Karachi in the nineteen eighties and nineties. Even the language riots of January 1971 and July 1972, which contributed towards creating the *Mohajir's* ethnic identity, have not been treated in fiction. Off and on a writer, like Kamal Jabbar, tells us that 'people in this city would use guns everyday'[30] but he does not use this fact to create a story. Unemployed young men are to be met with, to be sure, in Diana Storr's novels. In *Solar Dust* (1990), we are given a journalistic description of the city

'Karachi had become the scene of gang crimes, dacoity, daylight robberies and bank hold-ups had taken on an ominous regular colour. Valuables and human life were no longer safe. The ethnic battles had created pockets of opportunists.'[31]

But the description of a burglary and rape in a rich area of Karachi are merely sensational. Indeed, Diana Storr's novels use the formula of violence, action and sex to catch the readers' attention which may create readable popular fiction but not the qualities one looks for in a classic.

Aspects of life in the eighties in Karachi also come to us from unusual sources: a brief biographical essay by Hanif Kureishi—of the play *My Beautiful Laundrette* fame—and poems. Describing an upper-class party in Karachi, Kureishi tells us that he 'once walked into a host's bathroom to see the bath full of floating whisky bottles being soaked to remove the labels, a servant sitting on a stool serenely poking at them with a stick'.[32]

But, having made fun of the elite's hypocrisy, he says

> The family scrutiny and criticism was difficult to take, as was all the bitching and gossip. But there was warmth and continuity for a large number of people; there was security and much love. Also there was a sense of duty and community—of people's lives genuinely being lived together, whether they liked each other or not that you did not get in London.[33]

But this upper-class life was under attack. Unemployed youths made gangs to rob individuals and business; poets wrote about fabulous riches cheek by jowl with abject poverty; and people like Abdus Sattar Edhi and Akhtar

Hameed Khan tried to create a welfare state on their own. Being concerned with literature let us look at some of the poems of this period.

Let us first take the occasional poems by poets who generally write on other themes. In one such poem Ejaz Rahim says

Karachi, you have become a symbol
of all our wasted words
And still-born runes.[34]

In another poem, by Parveen Pasha, we have the following haunting words

In the vast prescient ebbing-light
in radiance of fading dust,
horizons ringed with sorrow,
an end—to end the endless
fear of morrows,
coppercalm gleam of the sea
a perverse hope for tranquillity;
where roads erase
where silence ends
the day *pounds:* fully armed
the lidless sun pours brilliance
on terraces of noon

Is this only dust, the taste of dust?

But in addition to such occasional poems, there is a collection of poems by Arif Viqar which is entitled *Karachi* (1983). In this it is not violence or ethnicity but class differences, or rather the injustice of the co-existence of great wealth with degrading poverty, which is the major theme. The Defence Housing Society is the symbol of fabulous riches while Lyari, Korangi and slums symbolize squalor. One representative poem is as follows

Why is it
That there is
So much water
In the sea
In front of Korangi
And no running
Cooking or drinking
Water in Korangi
Why is it
That there is
So much money, wealth
In Defence Housing Society
And so little money
In Korangi or Lyari
And why are
So many hands, eyes
Turned towards the heavens
When there is
So much sorrow, poverty
Down on this earth
In which we live
Our life[36]

A typical katchi abadi.

And here is Omar Tarin's comment

Urban warfare
Six more die
Karachi cries
Blown brains
And rapid fire rains
....
Some still say
We are *quite well*, thank you,
And going to be an
Asian Tiger,
A stuffed one
I'm sure....

Such comments, however trenchant, are not enough to create a body of literature. Indeed, although some of the novels mentioned earlier have been published only recently, there is no significant delineation of life in Karachi after the rise of ethnic violence in the eighties—at least in English.

I cannot think of an explanation for this. Those who claim that great literature is born out of human anguish seem to be wrong. Indeed, it would appear that if the savagery is excessive, literature too is killed. And even if it were not; even if a great epic is born out of all the torture, all the dehumanization which the people of Karachi have endured in the past fifteen years; would it compensate them? I think not! Indeed, when it comes to real life one wishes that all the suffering there is should only be in the world of fiction. That of course, is a dream, but dreams are the stuff of literature, not bullets!

Baba-e-Urdu
Maulvi Abdul Haq.

Chapter 10

THE LITERARY SCENE—URDU

Muhammad Ali Siddiqui

Karachi has been a literary centre of Sindhi literature ever since its elevation to the administrative seat of Sindh. But like every cosmopolitan city of the subcontinent, Karachi has always had a group of Urdu writers struggling to make their presence felt.

One need not go into the genesis of Urdu poetry in Sindh. A well-known scholar of Sindhi language and literature, Dr N.A. Baloch, has traced its origin to the time of Mughal Emperor Shah Jahan (1592-1666), and he has marshalled arguments and a 3000-year old *Kalam* of some poets to prove his point.

Some Sindhi poets like Sachal Sarmast (AD 1739-1829) and Mir Hasan Sanghi (AD 1851-1924), a Talpur prince who was kept in forced exile in Calcutta, have important collections of Urdu poetry to their credit. During the British period, many a Sindhi scholar enjoyed facility of expression in Urdu as well. They may not be called bilingual, but it is a fact that a branch of Anjuman Taraqqui-Urdu was opened in the twenties in Karachi and, under its auspices, Urdu *Mushairas* were held on a regular basis.

In an article published in *Quarterly Urdu*, Delhi, in its July 1937 issue, there appeared the names of some important Urdu poets of Sindh. They are Pir Baksh Asar, Sher Ali Khan Asad, Afzal Ghulam Hussain Asad, Makhdum Muhammad Moin, Bairagi Tasleem, Munshi Paras Ram Birbal Mushtari, Syed Fazail Ali Begaid, Dhanpat Rai Baikas, Jafar Ali Be Nawa, Muhammad Zaman Habib, Ghulam Mohammad Khan Khair, Makhdum Muhammad Ibrahim Khalil, Mian Muhammad Shakirani Zahid, Mir Mahmud

Rizvi Sabir, Muhammad Yusuf Khan Zaheer, Syed Ziauddin Zia, Qazi Abdul Qadir, Qazi Ghulam Ali Jafri, Mir Sher Ali Qaney, Makhdum Abdul Karim Karam, Syed Ghulam Muhammad Hashmi Gada, Mir Ghulam Mustafa Mehzoon, Mohsinuddin Shirazi, Seth Muhammad Ismail Maghmum, Munshi Muhammad Munir, Mir Subedar Khan, Mir Ebdul Mulk Ghaziuddin Khan, Nizam, Saadullah Ansari, Wali Muhammad Wali, and William Burwaite William.

Karachi was a city of some half a million people when Pakistan came into being. The Gujeratis and Rajistanis formed the second biggest chunk after the indigenous population. The Punjabis and Pathans also lived here, along with a small pocket of Urdu-speaking people. The Partition of the subcontinent brought a change in the demographic complexion of the city. The incoming refugees from India replaced the out-going Hindu population of Karachi. Of the city's 1951 population of one million, over 600,000 were refugees from India.[1] In fact, most of the towns of West Pakistan came to receive a substantial number of refugee populations[2] and the social fabric of Pakistani society acquired a new factor which could be termed 'the migrant factor.' In areas where this factor was insignificant, compared to the indigenous population, it became part of the local mosaic. However, in some areas like urban Sindh, it did not have to contend with the immediate need to assimilate with the indigenous population, because the migrants were numerically a bigger chunk of the population in areas where they settled.

The status of Urdu as the national language also fostered a feeling of self-sufficiency, and much of the present day ethnic character of the politics of urban Sindh, comprising Karachi, Hyderabad, and Mirpur Khas—owes its genesis to the fact that Karachi, being the capital of the newly born nation, became for obvious reasons the home of the government servants and their kith and kin who had opted for Pakistan. Urdu became the most widely spoken language of Karachi by 1951. And naturally, Karachi appeared on the scene as an important centre of Urdu language and literature.

The other category of migrants comprised those who were uprooted in the communal riots in India and they set their eyes on the 'promised national home'. The capital cities of Lahore and Karachi became their primary destinations, and hence the present-day demographic realities of the two cities. Both are cities of 'migrants'.

The preceding list includes Muslim, Hindu, and Christian poets and shows that the appeal of Urdu poetry transcended the religious divide. Some of the poets mentioned were accomplished figures.

It was but natural that many a poet and writer—some of them government servants—settled in Karachi, and we find a galaxy of intellectuals grappling with the problems which the *hijrat* (migration) posed. It is obvious that the bulk of the refugee population could not be settled in evacuee homes and lands. Some had to live the ghetto life, similar to the chaotic conditions existing in some of the *katchi abadis* of Karachi inhabited by mostly workers from the Punjab and NWFP.

The Urdu writers of Karachi did not belong to any single school of thought. They brought their own schools of thought with them. Most of them portrayed mixed feelings of rootlessness and disenchantment with the prevalent situation. Some could not come to terms with the sudden change that came into their life.

The literature of Partition denotes an unusual experience. For most it is more or less similar to the eighteenth century *Shehr Ashob*. The feelings of bitterness, pessimism and ennui became the warp and woof of some writers. Others burst into euphoric hysteria of sorts and they thought the birth of Pakistan had given them a Muslim homeland—a substitute for the lost glory of Muslim India. They could not adjust to the paternalistic and highhanded administration which was the characteristic of the British. Hence a clash of political cultures was inevitable.[3]

Three schools of literature made their presence felt among Urdu writers of Karachi in the late 1940s. The Progressive School, the Traditional School and the Modern School, and it is interesting to observe that the same stratification obtains even today.

Karachi has made a great contribution to Urdu literature in various genres. The city attracted writers of all persuasions in the late 1940s, and it is quite interesting to go through some of the names. They are Maulvi Abdul Haq, Qazi Muhammad Akhtar Junagadhi, Mirza Muhammad Saeed, Prof. Abdul Aziz Memon, Dr Ishtiaque Hussain Qureshi, Shahid Ahmed Dehalvi, Raziq-ul-Khairi, Sadiq-ul-Khairi, Rais

Amrohvi, Syed Muhammad Taqi, Nashoor Wahidi, Arsh
Taimuri, Tabish Dehalvi, Yousuf Bokhari, Fazal Haq
Quraishi, Jalil Kidwai, Mumtaz Hasan, Qurratul Ain Hyder,
M. Hadi Husain, Mumtaz Husain, Kh. Abdul Waheed, Nihal
Seoharvi, Adeeb Saharanpuri, Nazar Hyderabadi, Seemab
Akbarabadi, Arzoo Lucknavi, Behzad Lucknavi, Mahirul
Qadri, Hadi Machli Shehri, Raghib Moradabadi, Agha Abdul
Hameed, Abdul Khair Kashfi, Akhtar Ansari Akbarabadi,
Saleem Ahmed, Jamiluddin Aali, Altaf Gauhar, Iqbal
Safipuri, Mehshar Badayuni, Aijaz ul Haq Quddosi, Ibrahim
Jalees, Tehseen Sarwari, Abdul Raoof Urooj, Muslim Zaidi,
Zaheen Shah Taji, Z.A. Bukhari, Ikram Lucknavi, Khwaja
Moinuddin, Badshah Husain, Sehba Lucknavi, Aley Raza,
Aziz Hamid Madani, Ziaul Qadri, Mulla Wahidi, Mubarak
Husain Shamim, Akhtar Husain Raipuri, Syed Muhammad
Jafri, Zareef Jublepuri, Habibullah Khan Ghazanfar, Kh.
Aashkar Husain, S.A. Zeba, Saba Akbarabadi, Dr Ahsan
Faruqi, and Mujtaba Husain.

The preceding list comprises writers who were already
known as writers when they arrived in their adopted country.
A decade or so later, a new crop of Urdu writers appeared
on the scene and they also impressed lovers of literature
with their works.

They were Shamim Ahmed, Aslam Farrukhi, Abdul Khair
Kashfi, Jamil Jalibi, Habib Jalib, Athar Nafees, Asad
Muhammad Khan, Farid Jawaid, Nigar Sehbai, John Elia,
Obaidullah Aleem, Saqi Faruqi, Shahid Ishaqi, Hasan Abid,
Wahid Bashir and Qamar Sahiri.

In order to have a bird's eye view of the contribution
made by Urdu writers of Karachi let us begin with fiction.
Subsequently, we will take up poetry, criticism and humour.

FICTION

The only prominent writer who used to contribute to Urdu
literary journals from Karachi in pre-partition days was
Mahmuda Rizvia, whose daughter, Rasheeda Rizvia, later
wrote some beautiful short stories and novels. From amongst
those who migrated to Karachi, there were quite a few
important writers whose literary output was quite impressive.
Some of the fiction writers who helped Karachi become an
important literary centre in this field were Abdul Fazal
Siddiqui, Akhtar Husain Raipuri, Ghulam Abbas, Jalil

Kidwai, Zamiruddin Ahmed, Muhammad Ahsan Farooqui, Fazal Haq Quraishi, Aziz Ahmed, Mirza Haider Dehalvi, Ibnul Hasan, Ibne Saeed (M.H. Askari), and Nasir Shamsi.

Some of the above mentioned writers enjoyed also subcontinental fame. Shahid Ahmed Dehalvi editor of *Saqi*, Delhi, brought out his magazine from Karachi. Other important editors such as Raziq-ul-Khairi, whose monthly *Ismat* had played a very important role in awakening Muslim women of the subcontinent through fiction and educative reading material, also made Karachi his home followed by Sehba Lucknavi, who brought out the monthly *Afkar* from Karachi. *Afkar* is now a fifty-one year-old literary magazine and enjoys the reputation of being the vehicle of liberal and progressive literature. Mulla Wahidi also became a Karachiite. His inimitable prose was popular throughout the subcontinent. He wrote some memorable works in Karachi, namely *Mere Zamane Ki Delli* followed by Shah Ahmed Dehalvi's *Ujra Dayar*.

The uprooted writers of Delhi, the capital of Muslim and British India, generated so much nostalgia about the historic city that a great deal of it went on reverberating and still survives. Some writers continue to write about the 'good old days'. These works gave birth to reminiscing, and other writers meandered along familiar paths down their respective memory lanes. A lot of nostalgia similar to the one generated by the East European writers of the United States, such as Isaac Bashevis Singer, was produced.

Not before long a new generation of writers came along and Karachi became the focal point of their creative expression. Qurratul Ain Hyder had her beginnings as a writer in India, contributing to Shahid Ahmed Dehalvi's *Saqi* and other literary magazines, but her real career began in Karachi. She seems to have devoted her attention to the pangs of Partition. Her first novel *Mere Bhi Sanam Khane,* completed in Karachi, is the first ever 'modern' Urdu novel which made full use of the techniques of contemporary Western novelists. She used the techniques of creative monologue, association of ideas, montage and flash-back. This novel portrays the fast dwindling feudal class of Oudh. She writes about why the custodians of Oudh culture, migrated to distant lands of a different political culture to face untold humiliation. Another novel *Safina-e-Gham-i-Dil* was written in 1953. This novel could be termed an extension of the first novel. It is more or less a biographical work written on her famous father, Sajjad Hyder Yeldram; perhaps the first effort of its kind in Urdu.

Her novelette *Seeta Haran* is a sympathetic study of the great culture of Sindh. Her novelette *Housing Society* is a candid criticism of those Mohajir elements who were indulging in the loot of evacuee homes, and were busy constructing new homes in Karachi through unscrupulous gains. Perhaps this is the first candid work on the subject. Her novel *Aag Ka Darya*, written in 1959, is the most important work written in Urdu fiction so far. A novel which covers India's past and present—right from the Vedic period to the emergence of Pakistan. Qurratul Ain Hyder migrated to India after *Aag Ka Darya* and is busy creating monuments of Urdu fiction there. It could be easily said of her that she provided a turning point in Urdu fiction. Employing Virginia Woolf's technique of the stream of consciousness successfully employed in *Orlando,* she opened the floodgate of inspiration for young writers to imbibe the new stylistic and thematic currents from the New Writings group of England. She is truly a writer whose contribution to enrich the Urdu language will always be remembered with gratitude.

Another writer who enriched Urdu fiction is Aziz Ahmed. His novel *Aisi Bulandi Aisi Pasti,* is a full-length account of extreme decadence and depravity of the Hyderabad aristocracy.[4]

He studies the whole of society in the grip of the worst type of depravity. His novels *Aag* and *Gurez* are also important works. There are two collections of his short stories, *Raqs-e-Natamam* and *Bekar din Bekar Raten.* He migrated to Canada and wrote some good books on the Muslim community of the subcontinent from there.

The other important novelist from Karachi is Shaukat Siddiqui whose novel, *Khuda Ki Basti,* has for its theme the *katchi abadis* of Karachi. Dealing with the seamy side of the socially downtrodden who are consequentially crime-prone, this novel on Karachi could very well be representative of any urban centre bursting at the seams. This work shows how a city, left to its fate, comes to acquire an inhuman character. It contains, however, a ray of hope which is the organized effort to right the various wrongs being perpetrated by unscrupulous characters.

Other works which could be mentioned in this context are Razia Fasih Ahmed's *Aabla pa* and *Laho Laho Zanjir*, Syed Anwar's *Ek Aur Somnath*, Dr Ahsan Farooqui's *Sangam*, and Ikram Barelvi's *Lawa* and *Pule-e-Sarat*.

THE SHORT STORY

Karachi has also played a commendable role in the development of the Urdu short story. Some of the stories written after partition by Quratul Ain Haider, Zamiruddin Ahmed, Ibnul Hasan, and Ibne Saeed represented different approaches to the art of depicting life. These artists had heralded a new sensibility.

It could be said that the traditional style of story writing was on the wane and that western writers had come to acquire the distinct status of 'tutelage'. The English departments in Pakistani universities had became 'clearing houses' of western influences and the university professors, a good number of them having a natural tendency of no more sitting in judgement over the works of others, presented themselves as writers as well. There was in evidence a certain claim that only writers who had a command over English could write criticism and fiction. Poetry was not excluded from this dictum and we witnessed a time when writers, not having English literature as their background, were playing second fiddle to the English-background writers of Urdu.

Most of the novelists were basically short story writers. We see very few novels upto 1958 for the simple reason that a newly born country which was busy creating a state structure for itself—including a federal capital and a provincial capital at Dhaka—couldn't provide its writers, some of whom were serving the government in different capacities, enough time and patience to try out the form of the novel which needed a whole society to be successfully portrayed. The short story, on the other hand, could look at a slice of life and any aspect of a character or event. Even a monologue could provide a semblance of a short story to give the readers a feel of the kind of tension which the writer is busy negotiating for eventual release.

As regards the other short story writers of Karachi, the most important authors who immediately come to mind are Muhammad Hasan Askari, who came in the 1950s, and

Hajira Masroor, who came in the 1960s. All of them have contributed a great deal, and it is interesting to note that in the first two decades Karachi's short story writers have been in the forefront of the Urdu short story, even though some notable writers belonged to the north.

It is only after 1958 that we see a new crop of short story writers: Asad Muhammad Khan, Muhammad Umar Memon, Ghazi Salahuddin, Khalida Shafi, Rashida Rizvi, Umrao Tariq, Nazrul Hasan Siddiqui, Nasim Durrani, Firdous Hyder, Afsar Azar, Naim Aarvi, Mehmood Wajid Hashmi, and Sultan Jamil Nasim. The latest crop of short story writers comprises Ali Haider Malik, Zahida Hina, Asif Aslam Farrukhi, Nasir Baghdadi, Saeeda Gazdar, Shamshad Ahmed, and Saghir Malal.

Zahida Hina has quickly acquired a place for herself. Her first collection *Qaidi Sans Laita Hai* was a great success. She is heavily influenced by Qurratul Ain Haider and has the knack of mixing politics with literature so well that one element doesn't cancel out the other.

POETRY

Most of the writers who settled in Karachi, soon after partition were, of course, poets. Poetry has been the main vehicle of our literary tradition since the beginnings of our literature. The situation has somewhat changed, but even today the ratio of poets to prose-writers is heavily in favour of the former.

Karachi was fortunate in having celebrities such as Arzoo Lucknavi, Seemab Akbarabadi, Irum Lucknawi, Behzad Lucknavi, Hafeez Jullundhari, Saba Akbarabadi, Hafeez Hoshiarpuri, A.D. Azhar, M. Hadi Husain, Jalil Kidwai, Syed Aley Raza, Rais Amrohvi, Soz Shehjahanpuri, and Tabish Dehalvi as its post independence citizens.

The second line of poets comprised Mehshar Badayuni, Jamiluddin Aali, Salim Ahmed, Aziz Hamid Madani, and Akhtar Ansari Allahabadi. Not before long, in the late 1950s, there was a new line-up of poets such as Zia Jullundhari, Hameed Naseem, Abdul Raoof Urooj, Sehba Akhtar, Jalil Kidwai, Nazar Hyderabadi, Raghib Muradabad, Ibne Insha, Majeed Lahori, Zaheen Shah Taji, Bahar Koti, Z.A.Bokhari, Himayat Ali Shair, Sehba Lucknavi, Shabnam Roomani, Sarshar Siddiqui, Shahid Ishaqi, Qamar Hashmi, Syed

Muhammad Jafri, Habibullah Ghazanfar, Mustafa Zaidi, Khalid Alig, Rahman Kiani, Mahir-ul-Qadri, Nigar Sehbai, Shahid Naqvi, Habib Jalib, Anjum Azmi, Qamar Hashmi, Ahmed Hamdani, Wahid Bashir, Qamar Sahiri, and Karrar Noori.

There is another young group soon after which registered its presence on the landscape of Karachi's poetry. They are John Elia, Saqi Farooqui, Obaidullah Alim, Farid Jawed, Sahar Ansari, Naseer Turabi, Hasan Abidi, Sarwat Husain, Ather Siddiqui, S.M.Shaukat, Naqqash Kazmi, and others.

The poets enumerated in the preceding passage do not constitute a complete list. A conscious effort has, however, been made not to leave out important names in all the age-groups.

The Karachi poets, like other poets of the country, belonged to different schools of thought, such as the Progressive School, the Halqa or Modern School and the Traditional School, including the poets who subscribed to the Islamic ideology.

The birth of Pakistan had generated a kind of euphoria in the majority of poets. Some were carried away by the very emotion that the dream of Pakistan had, at long last, come true. Some thought that the politicians had created a mess and were insensitive to people's sufferings. Some poets went to the extent that they subscribed to the idea that Pakistan obtained freedom only in name. According to them, power had changed hands from the white sahibs to the brown sahibs. Generally, the progressive writers and poets had borne the brunt of the government's rough handling.

The early years of Pakistan saw curbs on the freedom of the press and the first two years witnessed the suppression of the press on a big scale.[5] It may be attributed to a lack of tolerance on the part of the dissenters. Perhaps it denoted the beginning of the manifestations that authoritarianism was on the way to becoming the characteristic outlook of the ruling elite, and a pliant bureaucracy agreed to work as its willing tool. The notion that the Islamic State of Pakistan was bedevilled by many internal and external threats led to erecting barriers to the functioning of the fourth estate. The liberals and progressives abounded in the fields of literature and journalism, and they became sitting ducks to the reactionary politicians, who wanted the implementation of Islam which the government professed to promote and implement.

The people of East Pakistan did not subscribe to the language policy of the Muslim League and they began to feel as if they were a colony of West Pakistan. And in West Pakistan, the elections in NWFP, the Punjab and Sindh alienated the intellectuals and dissenting politicians. The formation of One-Unit in 1955 created a great deal of dissatisfaction and mistrust in the smaller provinces. East Pakistan also took it as a ploy to deny them a majority in the Lower House.

The above scenario spurred the progressives to write protest poetry and anyone who has studied the Urdu poetry of the first decade of Pakistan will not fail to find a protest wave coursing through the works of the senior as well as junior progressives. They invited the ire of the government in 1954 when the Progressive Writers Association was declared a political organization, along with the Communist Party of Pakistan. The year 1954 saw Pakistan becoming an American satellite. The Dulles Doctrine was in the ascendant and the police, reared in colonial times, didn't require any adjustment in its role towards the progressives. Their integrity to the state was suspect. Progressivism being a forbidden fruit attracted all those who believed in the right of dissent.

The 1958 Martial Law was equally hostile to the progressives as to the militant Islamists such as the followers of the Jamat-i-Islami and Jamiat-e-Ulema-Islam. Both regarded Martial Law as a negation of Islam. Field Marshal Ayub Khan's hostile remarks against the syllabi of Deeni Madressahs (religious schools) invited their ire. Ayub Khan was a Kamalist whose friends even forget to call Pakistan an Islamic Republic in the draft of the 1962 Constitution. The word 'Islamic' was inserted on the pointation of a Jamat-i- Islami member of parliament. The majority of writers was opposed to Martial Law as a first response, except for a motley of writers such as Baba-i-Urdu, Qudratullah Shahab, Majeed Mufti, and Ibne Insha. Their statements were published in a government booklet entitled *Bunyadi Jamhuriatain*. The formation of the Pakistan Writers Guild enjoyed Field Marshal Ayub Khan's blessing, and not before long quite a few writers joined the Guild to escape possible victimization at the hands of the Martial Law government. Perhaps the government's tilt towards Communist China synchronized well with the esteem some top office bearers of the Guild felt for the rising Asian power.

Until 1961 Pakistan was not in sight of its second constitution. The Basic Democracies were conceived as a system to be worked under the thumb of the government. Quite a number of Pakistan poets in the post 1958 phase took to symbolism and other literary fads to escape the wrath of the government. Many writers were sent behind bars for their dissent. The progressive writers were the main sufferers while the modernist and traditional poets found ways and means to express their dissent more indirectly. Quite a number of collections appeared in Karachi in the Ayubian era. Aziz Hamid Madani's *Dasht-i-Imkaan,* Faiz's *Dast-i-Tah-i-Sang* were some of the important works of the 1958-69 era.

It was in the 1970s that we come across scores of poetry collections, regardless of the schools of thought. Karachi, compared to Lahore, has always leaned towards traditional and progressive poetry. Rais Amrohvi's collection of Ghazals *Alif,* and his four volume collection of *Qataat*—a socio-economic-political commentary on the affairs of the country, are the landmarks of the 1960s and 1970s. The other poets who came out with their important collections in the seventies, eighties and nineties are Ibne Insha, Salim Ahmed, Nigar Sehbai, Ather Nafees, Sehba Akhtar, Shabnam Roomani, Qamar Hashmi, Anjum Azmi, John Elia, Ahmed Hamdani, Sahar Ansari, Sarshar Siddiqui, Fahmida Riaz, Obaidullah Aleem, Mehboob-Khizan, Qamar Jameel, Mohib Arfi, Shor Alig, Mohsin Bhopali, Himayat Ali Shair, Sabir Zafar, Pervin Shakir, Salim Kausar, Nazar Hyderabadi, S. Aley Raza, Hadi Mohammad Shah, Saqi Farooqui, Tabish Dehalvi, Saba Akbarabadi, Hasan Abid, Anwar Shaoor, Pirzada Qasim, Irfana Aziz, Fatima Hasan, Shahida Hasan, Khwaja Razi Haider, Rais Faroogh, Saba Ikram, Absar Salim, Hasain Akhtar Kamal, Shaid Ishaqi, Naqqash Kazmi, Saeeda Safdar, Adeeb Sohail, Muhammad Afzal Syed, Raghib Mooradabadi, Rehman Kiyani, Rashid Turabi, Qamar Sahiri, Hasan Abid, Sara Shugufta, Rashid Mufti, Sarwat Hasan, Muslim Shamim, and Hameed Naseem.

CRITICISM

Among the critics who soon after Partition made Karachi their home, were Dr Akhtar Husain Raipuri, Aziz Ahmed, Ahmed Ali, Mumtaz Husain, Dr Ahsan Faruqi and Mumtaz Husain. Some other writers wrote critiques or appreciations but they did so by way of research articles. Maulvi Abdul Haq, crusading for Urdu's status for over thirty years in 1947, wrote scores of prefaces and introductory articles to Anjuman's publications. Yet he cannot be called a critic. So were Dr Shaukat Sabzwari, Shanul Haq Haqqi, Yusuf Bukhari, Qudrat Naqvi, Muslim Zia, Tehseen Sarwari, Dr Abdul Qayyum, Prof. Ghazanfar and Faiz Ahmed Faiz.

During 1947-57 not many works of criticism were produced. The Progressive Writers Association (PWA) was declared a cultural front of the Communist Party of Pakistan and banned in 1954. It is, however, needless to say that the majority of the Urdu writers in the 1950s had progressive leanings and they had, as their ideological adversaries, the exponents of Halqa-i-Arbab-i-Zauq.

The Halqa writers started their journey soon after the founding of the Anjuman Taraqqui Pasand Musanaffin in Lucknow in 1936, which had among its supporters such stalwarts as Munshi Prem Chand, Maulvi Abdul Haq, Jawaharlal Nehru, Allama Iqbal, Zaheer Kashmiri, M.D. Taseer, Sajjad Zaheer, Akhtar Husain Raipuri, Ahmed Ali, S.Sibte Hasan, Dr Abdul Aleem Nami, Ali Sardar Jafri, Majnoon Gorakhpuri, Faiz Ahmed Faiz, and many others. Miraji, who could be considered the leading light of the Halqa-i-Arbab-i-Zauq, was an active progressive writer upto 1943. But he found to his dismay that the progressive's primacy of content over form, and that too an abiding sympathy for the underdog, was a non-literary concern. He felt that it was not economics which was the key factor in reaching out to the true meaning of human life. Miraji thought, and so did the Halqa writers, that economics was not the only determinant. For him the sex motive also played a vital role. This was an obvious influence of Freud. The progressives took a U-turn against Freud and all those writings which titillated the senses.

Most of the progressive writers accepted the decision with a pinch of salt. They thought that it was not proper to follow a lead which came from elsewhere. Pluralism is the essence of democracy and the Writer's Association which claimed to be democratic should not have acted arbitrarily. Soon after Partition the decision to expel Askari, Mumtaz Shereen, Manto and Dr Taseer was taken during the Progressive Writer's meeting in 1949. This was a controversial decision and remains so even today.

Halqa writers were mostly government servants, and thought the Halqa's abhorrence of politics didn't make them suspect for the government of the day. The progressives were, in comparison, mostly free agents and therefore could go to the extremes. From amongst the senior critics, Dr Akhtar Husain Raipuri and Aziz Ahmed didn't offer much criticism after Partition. Mumtaz Husain was quite active and his book *Adab Aur Inquilab* proved a much applauded work of criticism. Mumtaz Husain provided the theoretical basis for progressive criticism. His work on Ghalib, Amir Khusro, and Hali towards the last twenty-five years of his life could be regarded as the milestone of his career. He was a critic who proved to be an astute researcher.

Muhammad Hasan Askari, and Mumtaz Shirin are other critics who have contributed a great deal to the criticism of fiction. Askari's *magnum opus* in this field remains *Insaan Aur Aadmi* between 1947 and 1958. This work proved to be something different. Muhammad Hasan Askari was also declared a renegade by the progressives, along with Manto and Mumtaz Shirin, for his disagreement with them on certain issues, such as Pakistani ideology, Kashmir and the progressive's subservience to the communist line emanating from Moscow. Deeply immersed in French literature, he was for the autonomy of art. He did not subscribe to the idea that literature ought to act as a second fiddle to politics.

Later on he underwent a sea change in the late 1960s and 1970s. He became an exponent of Rene Guenon's view and was influenced by Maulana Ashraf Ali Thanvi, a Deoband scholar and a mystic having a large following among those devotees who complemented the religious fiats with mystical leanings. The majority of Muslim mystics, under the influence of Wahdat-ul-Wujood, have stood for the primacy of *Tariqat* (the mystical perception of God). It is an interesting development that Muhammad Hasan Askari made a monumental leap into mysticism from his life-long predilection for the French symbolists. He wrote an important book *Waqt Ki Ragini*—a collection of critical writings in which he developed the theory that the societies which broke loose from their tradition ended up in chaos. He contended that Islam demanded of its followers to live a life wedded to tradition, and no deviation from it was desirable. His other book was *Jadidiat Ya Maghribi Gumrahion Ka Ek Khaka* (Modernity, or a conglomeration of Western waywardness).

Another important work was Muhammad Ali Siddiqui's *Tawazun,* adjudged the best work of criticism in 1976. The main burden of this book was a critique of Wittgenstein's logical construction which made a dent in Urdu criticism. Lahore's New School of Literature under the advocacy of Iftikhar Jalib and Anis Nagi came up with the idea that conventional language could not express a writer's thought, owing to the built-in linguistic inadequacies and, therefore, the need was for evolving a universal mathematically verifiable language. But they failed miserably to evolve one, and the whole effort fell flat. *Tawazun* played a key role in this school's retreat.

Abdul Khair Kashfi, Dr Farman Fatehpuri and Dr Aslam Farrukhi also contributed with their research and critical writing. There were scholars and university teachers. Salim Ahmed, Shamim Ahmed, Jamil Jalibi have also contributed in their specific fields with great gusto. Ahmed Hamdani and Atiq Ahmed also made their presence felt. Hamdani's book *Qissa Nai Shairi Ka,* and Atiq Ahmed's books *Istafada,* and *Sajjad Zaheer* also helped the progressive trends.

Majnoon Gorakhpuri, the doyen of progressive criticism, also made Karachi a place to be known for the fact that he came up with a work on Ghalib which is a remarkable addition to the corpus of Ghalibeana. But the surprise of the 1990s was Aziz Hamid Madani's *Jadeed Urdu Shaeri* which is a summing up of an eminent poet's criticism of his contemporaries—both senior and junior. This work could not be as candid as Madani was capable of making it.

Karachi's contribution, however, was not confined to fiction, poetry and criticism. In humour, Mushtaq Ahmed Yousufi is blazing a trail which is significantly important. At the time of Partition, Karachi had two humourists of note, Maulana Irshadul Haq Gangohi of the Church Missionary School and Majid Lahori. Soon after, Ibn-e-Insha, Ibrahim Jalees, and Tufail Ahmed Jamali appeared on the scene.

Rais Amrohi also tried his bit. However, Ibn-e-Insha succeeded in writing a variety of humour which was not tainted by satire or sarcasm. Ibrahim Jalees abounded in the last two fields and Tufail Ahmed Jamali combined in his writings humour and satire in good measure. Ibn-e-Insha, however, rose to the top and he achieved an eminence which is unrivalled.

It was only during the prime of Ibn-e-Insha that a new humourist appeared on the scene. He was Mushtaq Ahmed Yousufi, whose first book *Charag Tale* became a modern classic. Yousufi has rightly placed Karachi in the fore-front of Urdu humour. Karachi's contribution is an outstanding one also in autobiography, travelogue and Urdu journalism. Taking all these aspects together it is no wonder that the city of Karachi has achieved a wonderful position in Urdu literature which no other city could surpass.

Mirza Kalich Beg:
the Renaissance man
of the Sindhi
language.

Chapter 11

THE LITERARY SCENE—SINDHI

Hamida Khuhro

The earliest extant written work in Sindhi in its modern form is the poetry of Kazi Kadan who lived and wrote in mid sixteenth century. The eighteenth century saw a flowering of the poetic talent which reached its full bloom in the poetry of Shah Abdul Latif of Bhit. The *Risalo* of Shah expresses the full richness and versatility of the Sindhi language and established it as a literary language of the first rank. So far the writings in Sindhi had largely been of a religious nature, beginning with the Maktab teachers and the Ulema who produced a large number of readers and treatises for religious instruction in Sindhi verse early in the seventeenth century. Manuscripts of thirty-nine such treatises have been recently discovered deciphered and published by Dr N.A. Baloch under the title, *Sindhi boli jo agato muazum zakhiro* (The earliest versified record of the Sindhi language).[1] These early pioneers used the Arabic script unmodified by any dots or signs to specify the Sindhi sounds. The modifications were first made by Mian Abul Hasan of Thatta who composed the first work in Sindhi verse *Muqadimat i Salat* (*circa* AD 1700) in which he adapted the Arabic *Naskh* script to Sindhi phonetics by adding dots to represent a greater variety of sounds than were available in the Arabic script. 'Abul Hasan's Sindhi' became the standard for the Sindhi writing which was used for the next two hundred years. A large number of religious works were written in this period, particularly in Thatta, (just sixty miles or so from Karachi) which was the centre for learning. Makhdum Mohammed Hashim Thattavi, who flourished after Abul Hasan, was the most famous and prolific writer of the period on religious subjects and wrote in Sindhi (as well as in Arabic and Persian), which was essential in order to communicate with the people in their own language. While the official language continued to be Persian, the language of commerce was Sindhi, written in the local *Khudawadi* script. With the advent of the British in 1843, English became the official language, but the rulers needed to communicate with the people. This could only be done in the local language which was Sindhi. The Governor of Bombay minuted

> We should introduce the language of the country (namely, Sindhee) as the medium of official intercourse. I do not see in what way our Revenue and Judicial officers(however their offices and courts may be constituted) can work effectually through a foreign medium of communication, such as Persian or English.[2]

Thus by, 1851 Bombay Government Circular No. 1825 of 6 September 1851, Sindhi became the language of administration, of the courts, of police, and revenue administration, and above all, of education. So far although Sindhi had been written in the Arabic *Naskh* script as adapted by Abul Hasan, there was no longer any standard adaptation of the script which could be used for the purposes of a modern government, and a modern education. Adopting Sindhi as the official language required that the alphabet be standardized. The Government of Sindh asked its Sindhi language experts to give their opinion. Richard Burton, who was starting out on his career as an orientalist and linguist from Sindh, and had become a scholar of the Sindhi language, gave his opinion that it was 'copious, expressive and capable of high refinement' and George Stack, linguist and scholar wrote

> Far from being a mere patois, or Provincial dialect, it is an ancient and distinct tongue, differing from its neighbours in some very important points... it is exceedingly copious and exceedingly clear... The grammatical structure too is most exact and minute and in some points almost curious from its nicety. In short we will find in Sindhi, the most complete means of expressing every subject, except the arts and sciences as yet unknown to the people. Here we must borrow from more learned tongues, as has been needful in our own language.[3]

Although Stack advocated the adoption of the *Devanagiri* or *Khudawadi* (Sindhi *bania* script) as the official script for Sindhi, Richard Burton made out a powerful and eventually irresistible case for the adoption and adaptation of the Arabic *Naskh* script. He pointed out that all the existing literature in Sindhi was written in the Arabic script, and that the *Khudawadi* was not used as a language for literary or official work, but only for keeping *bania* accounts which were written in so abstruse a script that often the writer himself found it difficult to decipher. The adoption of the Arabic script was advocated not only by Burton, but also by Dr Ernest Trumpp, the German scholar who wrote a grammar of the Sindhi language (1872). Other nineteenth century grammars included one by Wathen, which was very poor in Trumpp's opinion, and one by George Stack, both earlier than the one by Trumpp who had (in 1866) published a collection of the poetry of Shah Abdul Latif. The Arabic script was also advocated by influential officials who had studied the language. Thus Arabic *Naskh* became the base of the standardized Sindhi script which was adapted with fifty-two alphabetical letters. The Court of Directors (East India Company) in their Despatch No.46 of 8 December 1852 decided 'in favour of the Arabic characters.'

With the standardized script in place, the government established secular Sindhi schools which in great measure replaced the old Madressah education in the province. The introduction of the new education gave rise to the need for Sindhi books on different subjects. Sindhi was also made compulsory for English officers serving in Sindh which meant that books of interest to a more mature readership were required. A large number of translations were made of English books on basic sciences, as well as other branches of learning. Translations were also made of books of English literature. Lamb's tales of Shakespeare, Aesop's stories, as well as other books for children, were translated and excellent books of primary education were written for Sindhi schools. Popular works of English fiction were also translated into Sindhi, including Tolstoy's shorter stories, as well as other books with philosophic and fatalistic themes which would find a ready response in a Sindhi, or indeed Indian, readership. Persian works such as Sa'adi's *Gulistan* and *Bostan* and Nizami's *Sikandernama* were taught in schools in Sindh, but were now translated. So were Arab classics, such as *Alif Laila* and religious books. Translations were also made from Urdu and Bengali. Thus in the 1850s, when the new school system was started, school text books for the use of classes from the primary to matric had been prepared. The best known among the scholars who prepared them were Nandiram Mirchandani, Udharam, Pribhdas, Akhund Abdul Rahim, and Qazi Ghulam Ali among others. Miran Mohammed Shah was among the earliest to translate a work of fiction (*Sudha toro and kuda toro*, 1855) into Sindhi from Hindi.

The father of modern Sindhi writing is undoubtedly Mirza Kalich Beg. Originally in government service in the newly organized colonial government, his duties included translation from and to Sindhi. He used his skills to translate works from English, Persian, Arabic, and Urdu into Sindhi, including the earliest work of history written in the subcontinent *Chachnama*, which he also translated into English. Kalich Beg not only translated numerous books into Sindhi but also authored many books on a variety of subjects. He wrote more than three hundred works. He also wrote a dictionary of old Sindhi, a history of Persian, and a book of Sindhi proverbs. The subjects he covered in his books included grammar, Sindhi vocabulary, logic, medicine, economics, philosophy, culture, religion, and gardening. He wrote the first Sindhi novel in which he dealt with the position of women (*Zeenat*). Mirza Kalich Beg was the Renaissance man par excellence of the Sindhi language, and played a very important part in expanding the horizons of the Sindhi language in terms of subject matter for writing and research.

An important contemporary of Mirza Kalich Beg, also based in Karachi and Hyderabad, was Dayaram Gidumal Shahani who played an important part in the writing and publishing of books in Sindhi. Although not anywhere as prolific as Kalich Beg, Gidumal wrote on a number of subjects in English and Sindhi. His object was the religious and moral revival of the people. He covered mainly religious and social subjects. His important works in Sindhi were the *Jap Sahib, Bhagwat Gita,* and *Yoga Darshan.* Another very important work on philosophy was *Mana ja chabuka* which was regarded by him as his spiritual diary. He depicted the social problems of women in *Mau ain dheeu* (mother and daughter). Dayaram Gidumal did a great deal for the spread of education. He wrote a memorandum to the Government of India stressing the need for establishments of higher education in Sindh and was the moving spirit behind the establishment of D.J. Sind Arts College. The intellectual tradition of the family was carried on by his son, Kewalram Shahani, who published journals and translations into Sindhi, and established libraries, and an art school in Karachi, which were housed in the elegant red sandstone Sarnagati building in the square near D.J. Sind College.

The establishment of Karachi as the capital of Sindh saw a flowering of cultural and literary activities in the city. These had an important focal point in the educational establishments of the city, such as D.J. Sind Arts College and Sindh Madressah, which included literary, poetic, and dramatic activities. The first four decades of the twentieth century saw the growth of the intellectual and literary life of Karachi which flourished around a number of personalities, which brought this new city into the mainstream of culture and intellectual pursuits of British India. This group consisted of scholarly personalities such as Rai Bahadur Seth Vishindas Nihalchand (d.1929), who moved from Manjhand to Karachi and who sponsored the translation of books on *tasawwuf* (sufiism) and Hindu religious teaching. He also published an anthology of poetry which included Persian, Urdu, Sindhi, and Seraiki poetry, and had translations of the Holy Quran published and distributed free of cost.

One of the most active literary figures of Karachi was Hakim Fateh Mohammed Sehwani who moved to Karachi *circa* 1910 from his ancestral town of Sehwan. Hakim Fateh Mohammed was an eminent Sindhi prose writer and a poet of Persian and Sindhi. He edited and published a weekly paper *Islah*. He wrote a series of Sindhi text books for different grades, based on Islamic values. He also wrote a number of literary and biographical books, notably *Abul Fazl* and *Faizi, Makhzan al Raz,* a biography of Qalandar Shahbaz, a book about the rule of the Talpurs, *Miran ji Sahibi,* and *Aftab i Adab,* a literary work. He also wrote a life of the Holy Prophet (PBUH), *Hayat al Nabi* and other religious books. Another notable literary personality of Karachi was Ghulam Ahmed Nizami (1895-1951), who was born in Karachi. He set up *Bazm i Adab* in Shikarpuri Mohalla in 1923, under the auspices of which literary meetings and *mushairas* were held. He played a leading part in calling literary conferences and eventually set up a poets organization known as *Jamait i Shuarai Sindh*. In 1929 Nizami started a monthly journal *Durra-i-Haidari*. His publications included two books of poems *Biyaz e Nizami* and *Riyaz e Nizami*. He also produced a versified Sindhi translation of *Mussadas e Hali*. Nizami also wrote two works of fiction *Hur e Damashq* and *Muhammad Namo*. A very elegant writer of Sindhi prose was Dr Gurbaxani who taught Persian at the D.J. Sind College. His *magnum opus* was the collection of Shah Abdul Latif's poetry *Shah jo Risalo*. He also wrote a number of Sindhi books, among them *Nurjehan*—a romance about the famous Empress of India.

Among the personalities who led the intellectual life of Karachi were Jamshed Nusserwanji, a notable theosophist and friend of Dr Annie Besant, Ghulam Ali Chagla, Khan Bahadur Wali, Mohammed Hassanally Effendi, Seth Tayyabali Alibhai, Hoshang Nadirshaw Edulji Dinshaw, Mohammed Hashim Gazdar, Khanbahadur Ardeshir Hormusji Mama, Khanbahadur Shahryar Dadabhai Contractor, Mir Ayub Khan Aliani, Mir Maqbool Khan Aliani, Barrister Abdur Rahman, Mrs Gul Minwalla, Mrs Dinshaw Pestonji D. Dastur, G.M. Syed, and Jethmal Parsram.

The earliest poetry society was founded by Allama I.I.Kazi in Khairpur in the twenties which had a great impact through its branches in other towns, such as Larkana and Karachi. Sindh Sudhar Society was set up by Hakim Fateh Mohammed and its first poetry session was held in D.J. Sind Arts College on 16 January 1932, under the chairmanship of Mir Ayub Khan of Lasbela, himself a poet and literary figure. Mir Ayub Khan and his brother, Mir Maqbool Khan, were poets and writers, and composed poetry in Sindhi, Persian and Urdu. Mir Ayub Khan's later poetry reflects nationalistic thinking, and at this stage he was associated with the Jamiat-i-Ulemai Sindh which had its headquarters in the famous Madressah at Khadda in Karachi.

On 19 December 1933, the second *Mushaira* was held under the chairmanship of Ghulam Ali Chagla, and the third on 2 March 1934 under the chairmanship of Dr Daudpota. In 1939 the *Mushaira* was held under the presidentship of Hakim Sehwani. Other literary organizations in the first half of the twentieth century were *Majlis Mushaira Naoabad* which was established by the poet,

Shaikh Abdullah 'Abd'; *Anjuman Taraqqi-a-Urdu,* which held Urdu and Sindhi *Mushairas* which were regularly attended by Sindhi as well as Urdu literati. *Mehfil e Ahbab* Karachi was set up by Ghulam Ahmed Nizami, Allah Baksh Uqaili and other eminent Sindhi poets in 1950, as was also *Bazm Nizami* by Nizami. In 1962 *Bazm Sarshar* Karachi was established by Allah Baksh Uqaili, and *Bazm Mushaira* D.J. Sind College which held regular *mushairas.* At the Adabi Conference in 1949, concern was expressed for the future of the Sindhi language and a leading *misra* was proposed on which all the poets were to compose poems on the theme of *Quam zindah thi rahe par je zaban zindah rahe* (the nation lives only if its language lives).

The fourth All Sindh Literary Conference was held in Karachi in 1941(*Kul Sindhi Adabi Conference*) under the auspices of *Sindhi Sahat Sabha.* In April 1954 the fourteenth All Sindh Adabi Conference was held under the auspices of *Bazme Nizami* and *Jamait Shuara Sindh* in the Sind Madressah.

The major themes of the literature in the twenties to the end of the forties were political. The militant nationalism of the early twentieth century, the appearance of Gandhi on the political scene, and the Non Co-operation and Khilafat movements had inspired writers, both Hindu and Muslim, to produce political and patriotic literature in which colonial oppression and the struggle for freedom were the subject of a large number of books. This period also saw the popularity of short stories which appeared in the numerous literary journals which flourished at this time. From the later twenties, however, the common themes shared by Hindu and Muslim writers ended in a bitter communal confrontation. The Hindu writers were accused of vilification of Muslim rulers and even of disrespectful references to the Holy Prophet(PBUH). Novels like *Rang Mahal* and *Sheesh Mahal* were scandal sheets of the Mughal and other Muslim rulers and *Satyarath Prakash,* which was virulently anti Muslim, was translated into Sindhi. Muslim writers retaliated in kind with books, extolling Muslim rulers and heroes and denigrating Hindus. The most famous and popular writer of books in this genre was Mohammed Usman Deeplai who wrote a vast number of books and developed a huge following among the young and old. Deeplai depicted the darkest corners of Indian religious practices, such as *suttee* and *devadasis* (*Somnath ji Sundri,*

Dahiri Rang Mahal etc.*)* and did not spare the obscurantist aspects of the religious practices of Muslims, such as excessive devotion to *pirs* (notably *Dada ji Sarangi*). Deeplai wrote many popular books extolling Muslim historic personalities, such as *Mustafa Kemal, Tipu, Fateh Spain, Shere Iran* etc. He played an important role in popularizing the idea of a separate Muslim state in the shape of Pakistan by explaining the idea through his widely read fiction, and thus made the task of the politicians much easier.

Most writers of the Sindhi language in the colonial period started their work in the columns of that new phenomenon on the political and literary scene—the journal and the newspaper. Most writers first came to the notice of the public through 'the press'. The earliest newspaper to be published in Karachi was *Fawaid al Akhbar* (15 May 1858), barely fifteen years after the conquest. This weekly newspaper was published in Sindhi, as well as Persian. In 1866 *Sindh Sudhar* was published by Narain Jagganath Varya on behalf of the educational department of the Sindh government. Narain Jagganath Varya was a Maharashtrian educationist who devoted his life to the spread of new education in Sindh. His services are commemorated by N.J.V. School in Karachi which is named after him. In 1870 Mirza Mohammed Sadiq published *Aqlil* in Persian, and in 1880 he published *Mueen al Islam* a wholly Sindhi newspaper. In 1884 Sadhu Hiranand published the twice weekly, *The Sindh Times*. The Government of Sindh published the Sindh Official Gazette in 1868 with a complete Sindhi translation. In 1889 a weekly Sindhi newspaper, *Muawin Majmua*, was started with the joint efforts of Hassanally Effendi and Syed Amir Ali. Associated with them in this effort were Maulvi Mohammed Usman Nauranzada, Allahbaksh Abojh, and Shamsuddin Bulbul. The latter two were to become well known names in Sindhi literature. The first Sindhi journal was *Sarsawati*, published by Sadhu Hiranand in 1890 and, in the same year, *Sarsawati Sahitia* was published by Mulchand Naromal, also from Karachi. In 1895 Seth Haji Ahmed Memon brought out *Aftab-e-Sindh*, with Shamsuddin Bulbul as editor. Also in the same year Diwan Tarachand Showkiram brought out *Patra.* The next year, the fortnightly *Jaut* was brought out by Parmanand Mewaram. In the next year, 1896, Rais Ghulam Mohammed Bhurgri started his newspaper *Al Amin* from Hyderabad, which became a very influential political newspaper throughout Sindh, highlighting the problems of the Muslims of Sindh, as well as other political issues. It was edited in the first instance by the newly converted Shaikh Abdul Majid. In the same way as *Al Amin*, although published in Hyderabad was important for the intellectual life of Karachi and other towns, *Sindh Zamindar* which was published by Mohammed Ayub Khuhro starting in the twenties and continuing for over three decades, was to play a very important role in championing the cause of Muslims and in raising awareness in the Muslim community well beyond Sukkur, in nothern Sindh, where it was published. Other journals and newspapers, *Desh Mata*, *Sindh Sevak*, *Sadai Sindh*, were also published in these years and, although there is some doubt, the probability is that they were published from Karachi. In 1916 the well known writer and intellectual brought out *Sindhri*, and in 1923 Deen Mohammed Wafai brought out the monthly journal *Tauheed*. In 1901 Satan Dharam Sabha brought out *Satan Dharam Parcharak Patar* as a monthly journal under the editorship of Maharaj Sobhraj Sharma. The following year, Maulvi Allahbaksh Abojh published *Risala Madressah*. In 1905 'Mukhlis' published *Tuhfatul Ahbab*. In 1909 Mohammed Ismail Sirhindi brought out a monthly journal, *Islah*. In 1916 *Sansar Chakar* was published by Maharaj Harumal Premchand which came out without fail on the fifteenth of each month. In 1919 *Sindh Samachar* was published by Pandit S.Totaram. In the community and welfare tradition of papers *Sikh Tract* was published in 1926 by K.R. Lalchand.

So far the newspapers and journals published in Karachi, and in Sindh in general, had been predominantly concerned with social and religious problems and politics were a side issue. But as constitutional reforms were brought, in and particularly after the Great War of 1914-18, politics became the primary concern of the newspapers. In 1920 the Sindhi leaders of the Khilafat movement decided that the movement needed a newspaper to propagate its point of view and started *Al Wahid*, which was to become the foremost champion of Muslim causes in Sindh. It was first started by Shaikh Abdul Aziz, an intellectual and pan Islamist who then made the *hijrat* from the *Darul Harb* of India to the *Darul Islam* of Afghanistan, in accordance with the programme of the Khilafatists. *Al Wahid* was then acquired by Seth Abdullah Haroon, Kazi Abdur Rahman, and others and started work initially under the editorship of Shaikh Abdul Majid, himself an important Khilafat leader. Deen Mohammed Wafai was also associated with the newspaper.

In the three decades till independence, the major concern of the newspapers continued to be politics and, on the whole, they were strongly partisan. Thus *Sansar Samachar*, perhaps the most popular Sindhi newspaper after *Al Wahid*, was unequivocally pro-Hindu as the latter was pro-Muslim. In 1924 Abdul Khaliq Morai brought out *Tarraqi*, and in 1925 Khemchand Advani published *Desh Mitr* in Sindhi and English. In the same year Hakim Fateh Mohammed Sehwani published *Al Jame*, and some years later in 1936 the weekly *Islah*. In 1925 also, *Hindi Hindu* was published by the Hindu Press. An illustrated educative magazine was brought out by Kazi Abdur Razzaque in 1927. Also largely educative and non political were two weeklies, *Chaudas* and *Paigham* published in 1929 by Assudomal. The latter weekly was in the form of a booklet and was written by Abdul Karim. In 1934 Pir Ali Mohammed Rashdi, who had started out on his journalistic and writing career as editor of Khuhro's *Sindh Zamindar*, published one of the many papers he would edit or publish. At this time it was *Subah Sindh*. In 1931 Virumal Begraj started his newspaper *Qurbani*, which was bought by G.M.Syed after Partition and would run for a few years afterwards.

In the immediate post independence era, Sindh lost many of its prominent writers and publishers who emigrated from Pakistan. With their departure Sindhi writing was in a state of stagnation for some time. The issues changed, and with the huge influx of the non-Sindhi speaking immigrants after 1947, the Sindhi reading public diminished considerably in Karachi. Only major Sindhi newspapers like *Al Wahid* could continue undiminished, as its readership was intact and its position as the major political mouthpiece of the Muslims of Sindh unchallenged. But soon other newspapers, such as Khuhro's *Nawai Sindh* emerged. Khuhro also owned and published *Sindh Observer*, one of the three major English newspapers of Karachi (the others were *The Daily Gazette*, and after 1947, *Dawn*). It became a victim of political vendetta however and was forced to close and go into liquidation. *Qurbani* was published by G.M. Syed and became the voice of Sindhi nationalism. Numerous journals and weeklies were started. Unfortunately, however, the major Sindhi newspapers became victims of the political infighting of the political forces in Pakistan. Each new government would ban the newspaper belonging to the outgoing political leaders, and the result was that most of the newspapers found themselves unable to keep going. Thus by the middle of the fifties, most of the major Sindhi newspapers in Karachi had disappeared. Although the Urdu press came in with full force and produced hugely circulated popular papers, the need for a Sindhi press continued to be felt. This need was eventually filled by the appearance of a number of newspapers, some of which survived and some did not. Hyderabad became the centre of Sindhi newspapers and of Sindhi intellectual life. But gradually as time went by, Sindhis living in Karachi gained enough confidence to be able to support newspapers from the city. The number of these gradually increased so that in the nineties more than half a dozen newspapers are being published from Karachi. Thus *Hilal-e-Pakistan*, owned by the government, nevertheless found a wide readership, and so did papers which were published in the eighties, a time of political revival. These included *Awami Awaz, Barsaat,* as well as others. The Sindhi newspapers published from Karachi were acknowledged as 'quality' newspapers with a high standard of reporting and writing.

The late fifties and sixties saw a great revival of writing in the Sindhi language after the difficulties of the years immediately after Partition. The impetus for the revival of writing came from the perceived anti Sindhi actions of the first Martial Law regime, downgrading the status of the language for education and for government purposes. Apart from public protest there was the outpouring of writing in journals and newspapers. Short stories and poetry became particularly the vehicles for the expression of protest and disillusion with the rulers. Journals proliferated, many of them published from Karachi, and gave opportunities to younger Sindhi writers and poets to hone their skills.

The post Martial Law decades were seen as inimical to Sindh and its interests, and this feeling of deprivation was reflected in the writing in this period. The renaissance of Sindhi writing in the sixties has been sustained by three generations of writers which has resulted in a vast growth in the Sindhi reading public and the publications of dozens of Sindhi newspapers, with about half a dozen being published in Karachi alone.

Mohammedali Building: tasteful embellishments and old world elegance.

Chapter 12

SADDAR—HEART OF THE CITY

Asif Noorani

Saddar, which has been a North Indian term for the cantonment area, was not a part of the old town. It was built by the British when they captured Karachi way back in 1839. And in the fifties, soon after Partition, when the immigrants from India and the work force from up north in Pakistan, came to what was then the capital of the country, found it to be the main shopping area of a city whose population was growing in geometrical progression.

When you spoke of Saddar you had certain boundaries in mind. Empress Market on one side and Masjid-i-Khizra on the other. The roundabout near what used to be the Rex cinema, where they once had a musical fountain was the boundary in the north, though some people thought Hotel Metropole was the outer limit. And on the southern side was the Bunder Road-Victoria Road (now M.A. Jinnah Road and Abdullah Haroon Road) junction.

For buses Saddar was an important junction. Only a few of them plying between the newly developed areas of Nazimabad, PIB Colony, and Liaquatabad plied directly through Bunder Road. Most of them were routed through Saddar.

And for the diesel-operated trams (all other tramway systems in the subcontinent were powered by electricity), run by Mohammad Ali Tramways, Saddar was an important hub. There were three routes that operated from Saddar, near Empress Market. One went to the Cantt. Railway Station, and two continued on the same line up to Bunder Road, later renamed M.A. Jinnah Road. The trams that turned right on reaching the rechristened road didn't have

St Patrick's Cathedral: reverential, austere, majestic, built when Napier was still governor of Sindh.

much distance to travel. They terminated at Soldier Bazaar, while those that turned left proceeded right up to Keamari, the harbour, except for a few that ended their journey at Merewether Tower. When Garden Road, an extension of Elphinstone Street (now Zebunnisa Street), was turned into a one-way street in 1954, the trams continued to enjoy a rare privilege, they could move both ways, but not without causing a few accidents. One of the persons to suffer was Zain Noorani, a veteran Muslim Leaguer. One fateful morning he was rudely reminded by a tram that rammed into his Chevrolet that the street cars, as the Americans call them, operated from both sides on Garden Road.

The trams were considered to be a traffic hazard since they stopped in the middle of the road. By the end of the sixties their routes had been curtailed, and they were sent packing in the early seventies, unlike their counterparts in Bombay. The last tram in what is now called Mumbai ended its journey a few years earlier at the stroke of midnight, with several celebrities, disembarking the double-storey electrically operated tramcar. They were highly nostalgic about trams and were wistful at the end of their sentimental association with the city's cheapest form of transportation. Currently, the only city in the subcontinent to have trams is Calcutta.

Horse-drawn tongas operated from the peripheries of Saddar near Empress Market and carried passengers to Abyssinia Lines, charging them on a seat-by-seat basis. They are rarely to be seen anywhere in Karachi. But the victorias are still there, except that they now cater to tourists only.

Cycle rickshaws, were forbidden to enter Victoria Road and Elphinstone Street, the two prestigious passages in Saddar. They were withdrawn from Karachi some time in the mid-sixties. They all moved to Bahawalpur, and the adjoining towns of Ahmedpur East and Lodhran.

Since shopping areas in the newly emerging suburbs, such as First Chowrangi Nazimabad and Tariq Road, did not emerge till the late fifties, Saddar remained the main place for shopping. For groceries, people came all the way to Empress Market. Though there were markets in the older sections of the town, Empress Market offered a much wider range of wares to the shoppers.

Built in 1884-9, it was designed by James Strachan of the Great Indian Peninsular and the Bombay and Baroda Railways, and remained one of his most celebrated buildings. It was named after Queen Victoria, the Empress of India.

One Mr Ruknuddin, who manages a grocery store at Empress Market, ruefully remembers the time when Empress Market had four small gardens, which were converted into shops after Partition by traders who came from across the newly created borders. One of the most memorable personalities of Empress Market in the fifties was a grand old man, Mr B.D. Sethna, who bought a shop from a Hindu migrating to India in 1947. In the mornings, my younger brother Asad, and I would see Mr Sethna engrossed in his copy of *Dawn*. It was customary for us to say 'Sahibji' (the Parsi style of greeting) to him, and in return hear him say 'God bless you'. During the cricket season we would ask for the latest score, because our copy of the morning paper was delivered at home well after we had left our Nazimabad house for our school in Saddar.

'Your favourite Fazal Mahmood took five wickets yesterday,' or 'Hanif has scored yet another century', the septuagenarian would say, sporting his endearing toothless smile. He is still remembered by the shopkeepers and some of the older shoppers at Empress Market with a tinge of nostalgia.

Until the seventies this grand edifice had not suffered at the hands of the encroachers and, though not as clean as it was before Partition, it still was much more presentable than it is today.

For buying consumer durables such as cloth and crockery, the market of choice remained Bohri Bazaar. Built before the country achieved independence, its narrow streets, meant only for the pedestrians, criss-crossed each other. Karachi was in a way an exception in the province, because all other towns in Sindh, and even in lower Punjab, had long Shahi Bazaars. Bohri Bazaar substituted for a Shahi Bazaar.

In a city where you see very few women on the streets, Bohri Bazaar always attracted more women shoppers than men. But, surprisingly enough, on 5 March 1958, when fire crackers in a shop caused a fire in the bazaar, more men were burnt to death and injured than women. As many as thirty-five people were burnt to death and many more were injured. At least ten people jumped to death out of panic when their buildings caught fire. The fire brigade vehicles, which were quick to come from their station, next to Empress Market, were handicapped by lack of water. A ban, now no more effective, was imposed on the sale of fire crackers.

Bohri Bazaar and some other parts of Saddar were destined to see a worse calamity when a number of bombs exploded in 1988, but that's another story.

Until the eighties, the fast food culture had not hit Karachi. Only Hanifia, a burger joint in New Town, with a branch at Nursery in PECHS, offered fast food.

More than any other place in the city, Saddar had some of the finest restaurants. The three Chinese restaurants which the early fifties saw were all in Saddar. South China Cafe, on Clarke Street (now Shahrae Iraq) near Masjid-e-Khizra, had a packed hall. The only one to survive is the ABC Restaurant, which was supposed to be popular with the GIs before Partition. Its decor remains much the same.

A more pricey Chinese eatery that emerged in the sixties on Victoria Road was Hong Kong Restaurant. It continues to attract Chinese food buffs even though many eateries have sprung up all over town.

A popular haunt for racing enthusiasts was Frederick's Cafeteria, which had a separate enclosure for families, and a small courtyard that opened only in the evenings. Cafeteria, as it was commonly called, was a rendezvous for punters, twice a week, after the races. Their review of the afternoon's proceedings didn't quite interest others who made it their meeting point on a daily basis, a large number of whom were those who assembled at other cafes in the afternoons, but preferred the cooler open air environs of the cafeteria.

Air-conditioning in restaurants was not in vogue. There were just two, one which sprang up later in the fifties was a part of Hotel Jabees, but the place was somewhat down market. On the other hand, the pricey Shezan on Victoria Road, served good food and tasty snacks. It was quite spacious and the hall inside, and the one on the first floor, were reserved for parties. Shezan opened its first branch in

An impressive Imperial-Vernacular building recreating the glory of the past.

the shopping area of the Service's Club, opposite Hotel Metropole, which was named Ampis. The restaurant is still there. But Shezan is not. It yielded place to an ugly building which houses small electronic goods stores. Shezan was not the place for students for it was one restaurant where you read the menu from right to left. Next door to Shezan was a sister company, Shahnawaz, which had a workshop and service station for Volkswagen cars and vans. The gate was locked sometime in the eighties and has remained so to this date.

The Indian Coffee Board, which ran a chain of India Coffee Houses in many principal cities of the subcontinent, sold its Karachi establishment on the corner of Victoria Road and Frere Road to Zelins, who had two more coffee houses—one at the Bunder Road-Victoria Road junction, and was aptly christened Zelins' Corner, and the other opposite ILACO House (now Siemen's House) on Victoria Road. But Zelins didn't continue with the Victoria Road-Frere Road junction branch for too long. They sold it to an Irani, who renamed it as Eastern Coffee House. It remained the haunt of writers, poets, student leaders, and small time politicians who sat there for hours. The owner wasn't making good money, but he continued to run the establishment until such time that he succumbed to a lucrative offer. When the Coffee House, as it was commonly called, closed down its clients were uprooted. A few of them moved to Jabees Restaurant for a short while, and some to a new small nondescript cafe next door, but a large majority were left in the lurch. They couldn't find any other rendezvous.

Incidentally, the Coffee House inspired writer Hameed Kashmiri to do a TV serial in the eighties. Its central character was, of course, the venue itself.

KWality had two restaurants, one diagonally opposite Regal cinema and the other opposite ILACO House. While it had an impressive menu of snacks and normal meals, the speciality of the two establishments was their ice-creams. The ones made of seasonal fruits were the best and the most popular among them was Peach Melba. In those days when tinned fruits were not so widely used, one had to wait for the peach season to enjoy the restaurants' speciality.

KWality was run by a man called G.M. Naz, who played the agony uncle in the columns of a popular woman's magazine. In the evenings, he ran a clinic. He was a psychiatrist, too. A middle-aged lady who happened to be my mother's close friend, once visited him with a problem. Her husband of ten years was planning to marry again—to a lady who was much younger than her. Naz's advice proved only fifty per cent fruitful. She could not make her husband give up his obsession, but she did learn to live with the idea of sharing him with another woman.

KWality was not the only place for Mughlai food. Cafe Firdous on the site of the present Mahboob Bakhsh Cloth Market, and Farooq Restaurant off Elphinstone Street served mouth-watering North Indian food. Farooq had the distinction of introducing chicken tikkas in Karachi. Cafe Firdous was the first restaurant of repute in Saddar to draw its shutters, but Farooq continues to exist in the same premises, probably because its restaurant is a part of its modest hotel. In 1963 when Captain Ihtesham, the producer of the East Pakistani hit film brought an entourage of East wing artistes (which included a bashful teenager by the name of Shabnam), they stayed at the economical Hotel Farooq. It offered a clean sparsely furnished room with an attached bathroom, and the single room's rent was a mere seven rupees.

For those who loved the Bombay style *khichra* or the Parsi-style *dhansak*, the ideal place for lunch and dinner was the Pioneer Coffee House which was set up by one Mr Merchant, who started his career as a coffee-taster with the India Coffee Board in the forties. During the Partition riots in Bombay, when no Hindu or Sikh was willing to work at the Mohammad Ali Road branch of India Coffee House, Merchant was sent by the management to manage the branch. Soon after Partition, he was transferred to Karachi, where he ran the branch until the Coffee Board sold the only branch in the city to Zelins. Merchant set up Pioneer Coffee House on Victoria Road and ran it with distinction. He introduced several dishes, and on meatless days the one speciality which attracted a lot of gourmets was the vegetarian *thali*. He tried to establish another branch on Allama Iqbal Road in PECHS, but had to give up soon, when his under-study and half-brother abruptly left him to start Alpha Coffee House on Inverarity Road, which offered more or less the same cuisine as Pioneer. But Alpha, though still there, was never anything more than a clone of Pioneer's.

· The senior Mr Merchant, who later on ran the canteen at the newly set up Aga Khan Hospital, and made an abortive attempt to start Pioneer Coffee House in a small premises close to the Liaquat National Library on Stadium Road, was an obliging person. He refused to charge anything from those who supported him in his earlier days, and when they insisted on paying he gave them a fat discount. Once I took a vegetarian friend of mine, Kishore Bhimani, the former sports editor of *The Statesman*, Calcutta to Pioneer on Victoria Road. It wasn't a meatless day so *thali* was not on the day's menu, but when I told Merchant about Bhimani's culinary limitations, he offered to make two *thalis* specially for us. All he asked for was a one hour notice period. Returning from the shopping spree we found hot vegetable delicacies and freshly fried puris waiting for us. The last that we heard about Merchant was that he had migrated to Canada, where his sons had settled.

A more economical restaurant, serving Bombay style food was Cafe Oxford. It was known for its tea, which was pre-mixed with milk and a rather generous quantity of sugar. Quite a few people thought that the management added something to it which made the tea quite addictive. But the food was also quite tasty. The Bombay-style *nan chanp*—a flat rounded bread served with delicious mince meat— attracted gourmets from far and wide. They felt that it was Karachi's answer to Bombay's Pydhonie *nan chanp*. On the two meatless days, Mondays and Tuesdays, one could find seats relatively easily both on the ground floor and the mezzanine floor, which was meant for families.

Cafe George, still remembered for its succulent mutton patties, and Cafe Parisian, whose bakery continues to exist, were the haunt of people who had quite a lot of time at their disposal. That was well before fast food, or as one cynic calls it fast fodder, became a fad in Karachi. The food at these Irani restaurants, as also in the more economical Boman Abadan Irani, was reasonably good. The advantage of going to Boman's eatery was that you could give your pair of shoes to one of the many Pathan shoeshine boys who sat in a row on the footpath, and borrow a chappal from him. By the time you were through with your cup of tea and his famous saltish puff biscuits, your pair of shoes were ready—shining like a piece of mirror, as each one of the shoeshine boys claimed.

*The Real Life Assurance
Company's Building:
turn-of-the-century charm.*

*Old Elphi: whose ebb
and flow is the very
pulse of Saddar.*

On the upper storey of the nearby Capitol cinema, was the Flamingo Restaurant where they served the best cold coffee in town. With the demolition of Capitol cinema, the restaurant also died. But the one to disappear much earlier, in fact, before the onset of the sixties was the chic Gaylords Restaurant.

The one place where you could get the best chicken patties in town was Pereira's Restaurant, which was housed in the same building as Pereira's Bakery. But the speciality of the restaurant was its Goan cuisine.

A stall in Bohri Bazaar served mouthwatering *chaat, dahi badey* and *choley*. It was a haunt of the ladies who went there to shop. Two places, one opposite the Parsi Fire Temple and the other on the opposite footpath, served Bombay style *bhelpuri*. They are both there even now but they cease to enjoy the kind of clientele they did until a couple of decades ago. Baloch Ice Cream in Bohri Bazaar, is one place, which has gone from strength to strength. Its *faluda* was as popular as Pioneer's, and in so far as ice creams were concerned, it was second only to KWality. However, for those who could afford to pay in double figures, there was nothing to beat Shezan Surprise, which was both filling and extremely delicious.

There was also Gulzar Restaurant, which was there from pre-Partition days. Years after Partition when the Indian singer C.H. Atma, visited his native town, he made it a point to go to Gulzar Restaurant for a cup of steaming *chai.*

Of the many restaurants in Saddar, hardly two or three remain. The rest have yielded place to shopping centres. Running restaurants and coffee houses became a non-lucrative business. The main reason behind their disappearance was that the price of real estate became too attractive to be resisted, which was why the owners disposed of their restaurants.

Until prohibition was introduced in the seventies bars were not too uncommon a sight in Karachi. The Palmgrove on Elphinstone Street-Inverarity Road junction had a large garden which came to life in the evenings. The poor people went to toddy shops, and the biggest one of them was opposite the Empress Market.

The navy marches past: Saddar wore a festive look on ceremonial occasions.

Floor shows and cabarets were a regular attraction in quite a few three-star and four-star hotels in Karachi. In Saddar the only place which offered this kind of fare was Hotel Excelsior, and the cover charges until the end of the sixties were to the tune of twenty five rupees per head, which was more than adequate to cover a sumptuous supper as well. The floor shows were banned in the seventies during the Martial Law regime of General Ziaul Haq.

The most popular form of entertainment during the fifties and sixties, going to the movies, used to be an outing for the family or for a group of friends which had to be planned for at least a couple of days ahead when tickets were booked in advance. Every day there were three shows, but on Sunday which was a weekly holiday, until Mr Bhutto changed it to Friday, shortly before he was removed, there was also a morning show. Some of the notable old movies were screened at that hour.

At the turn of the fifties there were four cinema houses in Saddar. There was Rex, which was the first theatre to be centrally air conditioned. Some of the finest English movies were screened there. Owned by one Mr Yousuf Mitha, Rex had the honour of being the venue of the first and so far the only international film festival. That was in the sixties. Film buffs and serious students of cinema saw such classics as Andrez Wajda's Polish classic *Kanal*, the memorable French movie *Hiroshima Mon Amour*, the brilliant Russian adaptation of *Hamlet* and Satyajit Ray's *Mahanagar*. One movie was shown in all the three shows on one particular day, but in the case of *Mahanagar*, when East Pakistanis living in Karachi thronged the movie house there were two extra shows after midnight. One Mr Mahmoud Fareedon had organized the film festival and had promised to hold one every year, but we never heard of him after the festival.

Rex was also the venue of a Czech film festival which astounded the movie-goers, with some of the most outstanding pieces of celluloid. *Carriage to Vienna* and *Closely Watched Trains*, which were part of the fare, were in the same league as the movies of Kurosowa and de Sica. Likewise we saw some of the masterpieces of East European cinema when a Polish film festival was held at Rex.

There were four more movie houses in Saddar in 1950. Regal, which didn't rank too high in the list of cinemas, and the two English theatres—Paradise and Capital. These two were owned by one Mr Mobed, a Parsi gentleman. While Paradise occasionally screened Urdu movies as well, Capitol was snobbish enough to show only English language films.

But perhaps the oldest of all cinema houses in Saddar was the open-air theatre, Mayfair. Since it had no roof over it, Mayfair was exposed to the vagaries of nature, which was why it was closed down by the end of the fifties.

The cinema houses to be built in the fifties included Odeon, near Regal cinema, and Rio on Elphinstone Street. The former showed Indian and Pakistani movies but Rio, which made its debut with the screening of Sophia Loren in *Atilla the Hun*, catered for the viewers of English movies. However, Rio didn't have the kind of reputation that Rex and Palace, or for that matter, Capitol and Paradise enjoyed. Often a strip of blue-film used to be attached to the main movie to draw extra crowd, which explains why one refrained from going there with one's family.

Two new cinema houses were built on Garden Road— Lyric and Bambino in the early sixties. They are still there, but in those days only English movies were released there. Such heavy-budgeted movies as *Cleopatra* and *Lawrence of*

Another view of Mohammedali Building: with a strip of shops below.

Arabia were first released in Pakistan in Bambino. Soon after the start of these two cinema houses, a mini cinema, Scala, was opened with the screening of a Russian classic. The management announced that only masterpieces of cinema would be released in Scala, but it seemed that they could not get enough of them. But the undoing of Scala was its faulty seating system, one could hardly see the screen, because the heads and necks of people sitting ahead of you blocked your view.

For the lovers of Russian Cinema, Voks Library run by the Soviet Embassy, used to hold shows of such Russian classics, *Ballad of a soldier, The Cranes are Flying* and *Peace to him who Enters* were among the masterpieces screened there. But going to Voks library, which was a forerunner of Friendship House, established in the seventies, was quite a hassle because the Intelligence guys grilled you the moment you left the place.

Voks Library was bang opposite one of the most beautiful buildings Saddar had. It was called the Bliss and Company Building. It was pulled down in the eighties when there was no legislation against the demolition of good old buildings in Karachi.

Saddar was in those days also the book lovers' paradise. Of the twelve to fifteen bookshops in Saddar, only two remain—Thomas & Thomas and Pak American bookshop. The first casualty was in the late forties, when the English Book House was sold by a Hindu bookseller who migrated to India. The new buyer converted it into a shoe shop. All he had to do was to change just one letter of this word thus the English Book House became the English Boot House.

Thomas & Thomas was the haunt of the students of English literature and Mr Nazeer, who was a partner, made it a point to give generous discounts to students. Not too far from Mr Nazeer's bookshop was a small kiosk, just below the Eastern Coffee House. One Haji Saheb ran the shop and he specialized in Bengali books and magazines. It was aptly referred to as Dacca Book Stall and, strangely enough, there was no board to announce the name of the bookshop. Haji Saheb, who was from what was then East Pakistan, was helped by one of his sons. One not so fine morning the son disappeared. He went to Lahore to become a film actor. Haji Saheb had a difficult time persuading the son to come back. The bookshop closed down when Haji Saheb quietly went away to Bangladesh in 1972.

A few steps away from Dacca Book Stall was another bookstall. It was next to the staircase of Eastern Coffee House. Again without any board, the bookshop specialized in paperbacks. In the same row as this bookstore, was Paramount Book Shop and it had books on wide variety of subjects. Books were not the only source of income for Salehbhai, the owner of Paramount, he also had the agency of *Newsweek* magazine. His brother Sulemanbhai, who owned the Paradise Subscription Agency near Masjid-e-Khizra was the agent for *Time, Life* and *Readers Digest.*

The man who made it really big was Hussainbhai, an Ismaili, who started with a small bookstall in the Capitol cinema lane. His Liberty Bookshop was crammed with books and didn't leave any space for him. The man really worked hard, and by the time he died in 1996, his company had become one of the largest importers of books, with retail outlets in three five-star hotels. His sons now run his business.

Among the vanishing bookshops was Greenwich, which had a section on books, and another on watches. There were quite a few bookshops which dealt exclusively with school and college books, and the leading one was Anthony Couthino & Company on what was then Clarke Street (now Shahrae Iraq,) close to St. Joseph's College. Opposite Anthony Couthino & Company was Book Centre, which had a wide range of comics and storybooks. But the owner, Malik Noorani, closed the outlet to specialize in law books. He is remembered not so much for his business in law books as for pioneering the publication of literary books in Karachi. In those days there was a strong feeling that Urdu books could only be published in Lahore, but Malik Noorani made Maktabaye Danyal his labour of love and was supported by such eminent literary figures as Faiz Ahmad Faiz, Syed Sibte Hasan, and Mushtaq Ahmad Yousufi. Maktabaye Danyal is still housed in the same premises—Victoria Chambers opposite Jabees Hotel.

If Thomas & Thomas was the haunt of students of English Literature, Kitab Mahal was one place where lovers of Urdu converged. Agha Zarkhusht who ran the bookshop was himself a writer and a venerable personality. There has been no bookshop in Karachi which specializes in books on Urdu literature and language ever since Kitab Mahal closed down.

Hameed Kashmiri, the noted short story writer turned playwright, ran a small bookstall on Elphinstone Street too, and in the evening the place became a rendezvous for fledgling writers.

Like Hussainbhai and Salehbhai of Liberty and Paramount, Shams Qureishi, the doyen of booksellers closed down his retail outlet—Mackwin & Company on Inverarity Road and concentrated on imports.

For second-hand books and magazines one visited Tit Bit Book Stall and Variety Book Stall, both near the Parsi Fire Temple. The other place where one could find second-hand books was the footpath near Thomas & Thomas.

Of all the ethnic groups that lived in Saddar, the Goans were the ones who dominated the locality. In the evenings they frequented the KGA Club near the Grammar School in smart clothes, and on Sundays they went to church. But like the Parsis, who formed another strong ethnic group in Saddar, they migrated in large numbers to North America and Australia. Now very few of them are still there. The flavour they lent to Saddar is, sadly, missing today.

One place which needs to be mentioned was the music school which was run by the Gramophone Company of Pakistan (later EMI) on the first floor of a small nondescript building on Dundas Street, that connected Victoria Road with Elphinstone Street. Then there was the Abbas School of Ballroom Dancing, which closed down in the sixties as ballroom dancing went out of vogue.

Surprisingly enough, there was just one garden in the whole of Saddar. Jahangir Park, near the Empress Market, remains the only breathing place for people who go to Saddar, but in the fifties and the sixties it was not the haunt of families, who preferred to go to Gandhi Gardens, the old name of Zoological gardens. The tall palm trees that one sees at Jahangir Park today were planted in the sixties when the place was given a facelift.

Among the endearing personalities of Saddar were the two brothers who owned Khan & Company, which specialized in shoes for males. They reminded one of the Gessler brothers, the two shoemakers in John Galsworthy's memorable short story *Quality*. The senior Mr Khan was a great admirer of the veteran Indian journalist, Frank

*A gharry in front
of Frere Hall:
fin de siècle.*

Moraes. He used to get *The Times of India,* which Moraes used to edit, every evening and the day the journalist left his job to join *Indian Express* as its editor, Mr Khan told his newspaper hawker to start delivering him *Indian Express* instead of the centurian *The Times of India.* The Khan Brothers were sticklers for good quality and were only too willing to replace their shoes if the customer found them faulty.

People like the Khans and Sethna are no more, and Saddar too has lost much of its importance, but there are still a good number of people who drift down memory lane. The Saddar of the fifties and the sixties is firmly etched in their memory.

Attiya Begum,
painted by
Fayzee Rahamin.

Chapter 13

AN EVER EXPANDING CANVAS

Marjorie Husain

Pakistan is a nation young in years but nurtured in the soil that cradled one of the first great civilizations of the world: The Indus Valley Civilization (*circa* BC 2300), with one of its most important capital cities, Moenjodaro, sited in Sindh.

Hundreds of carved seals made of steatite are considered by historians to be the earliest art pieces found in the subcontinent. Form Moenjodaro too, emerged the earliest major metal artwork of the subcontinent, a bronze figurine, four inches high, of a female in an exquisite dance pose. Located only forty miles from Karachi, Bhambore, once a flourishing port town known as Deebal, already boasted a long tradition of pottery and decorative arts when invaded by the young Arab warrior, Khalid Bin Walid in AD 711. Though these historic sites were lost to history for many years, their arts survived, emerging as motifs in diverse traditions throughout the subcontinent.

At the time of the partition of the subcontinent, art trends in Pakistan had been influenced by a diverse and intricate heritage of oriental and western traditions. Miniaturist, artists encouraged by the court of the Mughals, assimilated into their work elements from Persia, China, and Europe. From Calcutta emerged the New Bengal School of Art which adapted a Japanese method of watercolour painting to a Miniature School of Art ethos.

Pre-Partition art activity in Karachi was overshadowed by the city's reputation as a busy commercial sea-port. That there had been an art school in Karachi before 1947, we know from references left by the late Sughra Rababi

(1921-95). While a student of St. Joseph's Convent School, Sughra won top honours in an art competition organized by the All Sindh and Bombay Art Committee. The award led to her admission in a prestigious Karachi art institute, the Sarangati Art School, affiliated to Tagore's Shantiniketan University.

However, artists such as Ajmal Hussain, who arrived in Karachi in 1947, and Nagi who came from Delhi, found no established art traditions and so initiated their own. In Lahore, influenced by the New Bengal School, small scale soft watercolour paintings prevailed, propagated by teachers trained in the Calcutta School of Art.

A.R. Chughtai and Ustad Allah Bukhsh, both of whom had enjoyed considerable acclaim and patronage from the Indian princely states, abandoned subjects linked to Hindu mythology and introduced their own unique styles. Chughtai's romantic watercolour paintings depicted Pakistan's folk stories, or languid beauties assimilating detailed architectural elements from the Mughal era. He illustrated works of the great poets, and produced hundreds of exquisite etchings. Ustad Allah Bukhsh portrayed, in his painting, the robust customs and traditions of rural Punjab. Miniaturists Haji Shareef and Ustad Shujaullah reproduced the miniature paintings of a bygone era, in an effort to keep the art of miniature painting alive.

In Karachi, young painters from many parts of the subcontinent, eager for fresh stimuli, explored the exciting modern art movements of pre-war Europe. More than a decade was to pass before artists began to re-examine their own cultural traditions, and to assimilate art forms of the past in contemporary methods.

There was a shop in Zaibunissa (Elphinstone) Street which amongst other items, sold the accoutrements of art. Since this was the only art material outlet at that time, it was here the artists inevitably met.

Nagi's studio, in the Saddar area behind Paradise Cinema, became the focal point of artists in Karachi. There they gathered to talk, paint and make plans for the future. It was Nagi's influence that got them all together. The first Fine Arts Association was formed, and at weekends artists would go on excursions to Malir or Korangi to paint and sketch.

The Aiwan-i-Riffat was another cultural centre. The distinguished portrait painter, Fayzee Rahamin, and his wife

Attiya Begum, held Friday afternoon tea-parties for guests from all branches of the arts. Attiya, who had been the first young woman from India to go abroad for higher education, and Fayzee introduced to their circle, many unknown young talents. Artist Laila Shahzada exhibited her work for the first time ever at their residence.

In London, after graduation from the Royal Academy of Art, Fayzee had joined the studio of John Singer Sargeant the most admired portraitist of his day. Well versed in the classic western traditions as well as eastern art, Fayzee returned to his homeland with the aspiration of revitalizing the art of the subcontinent. Decorating the Imperial Secretariat, Delhi, in 1925, Fayzee blended aspects of Mughal miniature art into large panels. In 1947, at the behest of the Quaid-i-Azam, the artist and his wife left their home in Bombay to settle in Karachi.

Another prominent artist of the era was the portraitist Askari, who left his home in Lucknow to settle in Karachi where he painted numerous studies of the Quaid-i-Azam. Initially, there were no art galleries or regular exhibition centres in Karachi. When Zubeida Agha displayed a collection of abstract paintings in 1949, the venue was the YMCA. The first exhibition of its kind in Pakistan, Zubeida's work created controversy. Attiya Begum wrote letters to the press decrying the young artist's work as 'addled art'. Others spoke out in Zubeida's favour. Perhaps Attiya realized that the winds of change were beginning to blow. Nothing could stop contemporary art movements from taking root in the soil of Pakistan. Academists such as Fayzee were overshadowed by a new freedom of style.

One of the few landscape painters in Karachi in the early fifties, Mohammed Husain Hanjra, was a graduate of the Mayo School and a student of Ustad Allah Bukhsh. Hanjra became one of the first artists to be employed by a local

Red Flower,
Zubeida Agha, 1989.

Jamil Naqsh.

advertising agency. A new phenomenon in Karachi at that time, advertising agencies were to multiply and flourish, giving employment to numerous artists, including Bashir Mirza, Shahid Sajjad, Sardar, Jamil Naqsh, Maqsood Ali, Mansur Aye and many others.

In Lahore, Professor Shakir Ali became the founder of modern art in Pakistan, along with Bengali artist Zainul Abedin and Zubeida Agha. Art education was the *raison d'etre* of Anna Molka Ahmed who established a Fine Arts Department at the Punjab University. Her ambition was to train teachers from all the provinces of Pakistan, in order that art be taught throughout the country. These happenings affected events in Karachi, where artists from Lahore art establishments came to seek their living.

The 1950s saw a number of important art developments. A group of concerned people worked at fund raising in order to establish an art centre in Karachi, and in 1953 their ambitions were realized. The Karachi Art Council was established and the scope of cultural activities expanded. Art

Jamil Naqsh (first from left) and other artists at an exhibition.

classes were held and exhibitions mounted. In 1955, a painting by Jamil Naqsh caught the attention of a panel of judges, because of its disciplined, fine method of colouration. It was awarded a prize in a group display, perhaps the renowned artist's first ever. The media supported artists with considerable news space devoted to reviews of their work. In art circles the dramatic impact of Sadequain and Gulgee gave rise to excitement.

Sadequain painted his first mural in 1955. His work was seen by countless citizens at the Jinnah Hospital, the Karachi airport and the State Bank. The same year, his first public exhibition in Karachi was held at the residence of Mr Huseyn Shaheed Suhrawardy, then Foreign Minister of Pakistan. Later, during a stay near Gadani Beach where he had gone in search of solitude and peace, Sadequain had a revelation. He saw the moonlight reflected on

Sadequain.

*From the series **Cobwebs** by Sadequain.*

tall cacti plants. In his artist's vision these appeared transformed into turreted castles, towns and people raising their arms in supplication. Thus began the artist's renowned cacti series which lasted for a number of years. In 1960, Sadequain's painting *The Last Supper* earned him an award at the Beinnale de Paris and in 1961, in Pakistan, he was honoured with the President's Pride of Performance Award.

A prolific painter working in series, his work later became dominated by crows used as symbols of an effete and uncaring society. Sadequain used his art as a medium to express ironic social comments. The artist's ambition was to paint murals throughout Pakistan where they could be enjoyed by the masses. Sadequain's enormous murals are to be found in almost every city of Pakistan, the recurring theme depicting man's lifelong struggle and search for peace.

In his later years, Sadequain used calligraphy as an art form, starting a new train of thought. His influence on the development of local art was enormous. Coinciding with the mood of the times, calligraphy became the most popular art form in the country and remained so for over a decade. Sadequain's last work was a mural intended to cover the ceiling of Frere Hall, Karachi, in the hall now renamed the Sadequain Gallery. Sadly, it remained unfinished at the time of his death.

Opposite page: Ahmed Parvez

Gulgee (extreme left) and friends.

Trained as an engineer, Gulgee was much sought after as a portraitist, but preferred action painting, sweeping a full brush across a large canvas. Gulgee's abstracts developed into gestural calligraphy. He borrowed from Islamic cultural traditions such as mosaic and enamel work and embellished his work with precious and semi-precious stones, fragmented mirrors, gold and silver foil. Mosaic portraits in jade and lapi were admired by royalty and heads of state in many countries of the world, but it is in the divinely inspired abstract work that the essence of the artist can be sensed.

Shakir Ali, a man well versed with western and oriental art, founded his aesthetic philosophy on the analytical cubism movement, in which all forms were reduced to a cylinder, circle or cube. His art background encompassed London and Paris where he sought out the Cubist artist Andre L'Hote—and Yugoslavia. Shakir Ali was among a team of peace corps students who set out to rebuild the razed city of Lidice, destroyed with all its inhabitants as a reprisal act of the Nazis during the war. Deeply affected, Shakir Ali witnessed tiny green shoots pushing their way tenaciously through the scorched earth. He heard the trill of a bird, an image that emerged repeatedly in his work, and was convinced of the ultimate triumph of nature over man.

When Shakir returned to Karachi in 1953, he looked for work in the city but there was little scope for a man of his calibre. The only job available was that of a drawing master in a children's school with a pittance of a salary. Shakir Ali soon left for Lahore and the Mayo School of Art, which in 1960, was restructured as the National College of Arts. Shakir's tenure as principal of the school can be looked back on as a golden chapter in the history of Pakistan's art. With his profound understanding of modern art, Shakir Ali attracted a group of lively young artists who were to emerge as Pakistan's first generation of painters. Among them Ahmed Parvez and Ali Imam, were to have a considerable influence in Karachi, Parvez as a painter and Imam as an art dealer.

Pakistan's first conceptual artist, Rashid Arain, discovered a discarded cycle wheel in 1954. Throwing the object on a fire to melt the rubber, he extracted the misshapen metal relic and created a sculpture. Rashid Arain eventually gained a reputation in Europe as the 'voice' of third world artists, and for many years published a significant art journal, *The Third Text*.

As the capital city of the country, in the early years, foreign missions were situated in Karachi and many of the embassies were staffed with art enthusiasts. They sought out artists in their studios, and took an interest in their work. It became customary for foreign patrons to hold receptions in

*From the **Drift Moods***
series, by Laila Shahzada.

Rabia Zuberi with her colleagues at
The Karachi School of Art.

their homes to launch artists. Masood Kohari was then an up and coming young painter whose work was much appreciated. Bashir Mirza was another artist who, in 1963, held his first ever solo exhibition in the residence of the then Nigerian ambassador.

One of the few outstanding women painters of the period, Laila Shahzada, made news with an exhibition of paintings she called *Drift Moods*. A beautiful woman, Laila had fought against a male dominated art circle that labelled her as a painter of 'pretty pictures'. She came into her own, influenced by driftwood gathered on Clifton beach. These pieces, twisted into unnatural shapes by the churning waters of the ocean, the artist equated with the human condition, people forced into a set pattern by conventions and social obligations. With thick and rapid brush strokes, Laila painted twisted branches, vibrant with energy. The first artist to draw upon the Indus Valley Civilization for inspiration, Laila's series of paintings *Mohenjodaro*, rendered with visionary imagery, won her a gold medal in America, and the key of the city of New York.

Other women artists sprang into prominence. The Zuberi sisters, sculptor Rabia and painter Hajra, graduated from the Lucknow College of Art in 1963, and settled in Karachi. Finding the city lacked a regular art school, they began art classes in their home. The first batch of fifteen girls, which included Sumbal Nazir, filled the residence, and in the quiet days of the 1960s, often put up their easels on the street outside the Nazimabad house. In 1965, the Zuberis were joined by the talented Bengali artist, Mansur Rahi, from the Dhaka School of Art. In premises more suitable for a school, Mansur restructured the curriculum and became the first principal of the Karachi School of Art. From what had been a leisure time activity of an affluent society, the Karachi School of Art established in a working class area, changed attitudes towards art, training artists for professional careers as designers, studio artists and teachers.

To fill the growing demand, in 1966, a Central Institute of Arts and Crafts was established in the Arts Council premises, with sculptor-painter Ozzir Zuby as the first principal.

Composition by
Ahmed Parvez.

The Pakistan American Cultural Center became a popular venue for cultural programmes and art exhibitions.

From Lahore, Sheikh Ahmed distancing himself from his estranged wife, Anna Molka Ahmed, left his teaching post at the National College of Arts, and made his studio in Karachi. For many years he had been a teacher at the Central School of Arts, London, where, during the course of his career, he assisted Chughtai with language problems during the latter's study of engraving and etching. In Karachi, Sheikh Ahmed and a few chosen pupils worked on a series of book illustrations commissioned by American publishers. Sheikh Ahmed's most devoted student, Aftab Zaffar, years later became a noted teacher, artist and illustrator in his own right.

The early 1960s found artists Jamil Naqsh, Maqsood Ali, Shahid Sajjad, Naz Ikramullah, Mansur Aye and Bashir Mirza enriching art circles. Bengali artists settled in Karachi, fresh

Woman and Flower
by Bashir Mirza.

from the Dhaka School of Art. Mubinul Azim, Murtaza Bashir, Nurul Islam and Hamidur Rehman added colour to the art scene. Sardar had already developed the 'folk art' method of painting which became his signature style. Ahmed Parvez and Ali Imam returned from England to settle in Karachi, Parvez as a painter, Imam as principal of the Central Institute of Arts and Crafts. In 1968, Ali Imam was awarded the President's Pride of Performance, but Parvez was to wait another decade for official recognition.

The country entered a prosperous era. Multinational companies invested in Pakistan, impressive offices were built and chief executives began to look for paintings to adorn their walls.

The advent of Pakistan Television opened up new avenues of employment for trained artists. Art schools expanded. About the same time, Karachi's first commercial art gallery opened on Kutchery Road, funded by an art loving Englishman. The director, Bashir Mirza, named the gallery simply 'The Gallery', and ran it until 1969. The Gallery

Faiz Ahmed Faiz inaugurating Shahid Sajjad's exhibition.

WORKSHOP

Members of the workshop with Michael Ponce de Leon.

attracted an interesting motley audience of art enthusiasts and artists. A brilliant draughtsman, B.M. (as he is known) produced a set of drawings, *Portrait of Pakistan*, which were printed and enclosed in a chic, black and gold folder which sold by the hundreds to local and foreign buyers.

A landmark in art was the American sponsored three month long workshop in Karachi at the PACC. It was directed by the American printmaker Michael Ponce de Leon, who introduced a group of thirty selected artists from both wings of the country, to their initial printmaking experience. Ghulam Rasul, who went on to take a Master's in printmaking, Bashir Mirza, Ahmed Khan, Naz Ikramullah, Shahid Sajjad, Saeed Akhter and I were among the artists whose prints were acquired by the Smithsonian Institute, Washington, D.C.

After Bashir left for a two year tour of Europe, The Gallery continued to function under the auspices of Sultan Mahmood, one of the country's first collectors and advertisers. 1970 was the year that a significant art market first began in Karachi. Artists such as Colin David, Ahmed

Khan, Saeed Akhtar, and ceramist Mian Salahuddin, were among the artists from Lahore who exhibited their work in Karachi for the first time. In Karachi, Laila, Hamidur Rahman, Rabia and Hajra, Mansur Rahi, Parvez, Lubna Agha, Shakira Hadi, Ajmal, Kohari, Gulgee, Sadequain, Maqsood Ali, Mansur Aye, Jamil Naqsh, and senior painters Ozzir Zuby, Nagi, and Sardar, sold their paintings at exhibitions which germinated art collectors. Chughtai's brother, who managed the artist's affairs, regularly visited The Gallery, bringing the artist's work from Lahore.

Until that time, there had been virtually no art market, and little demand for art. The exquisite work of A.R. Chughtai sold for a few hundred rupees. Jamil Naqsh relates that in his 1960 exhibition of one hundred paintings at the Arts Council, only three paintings were purchased for the grand sum of Rs. 100 each. Even the Arts Council Committee, distinguished members of society, could not be prevailed upon to purchase art.

In the 1970s, the Karachi business community began to purchase works of art. Expatriates contributed to the interest in art and artists, but the main patrons were Pakistanis. The Karachi Auction Mart held several popular evening receptions in which invited guests, diplomats and artists participated. The *raison d'etre* of these events was painting auctions in which brisk bidding took place.

In 1971, Syed Ali Imam resigned as principal of the Central Institute of Arts and Crafts to begin a successful career as an art dealer. The Indus Gallery opened and Imam worked hard to guide and encourage a new breed of art collectors. He was the link between the artist, the media, and the buyer.

Women artists gained in prominence about this time. Lubna Agha influenced her peers and students, with abstractions focusing on large white lozenges of paint, streaked with scarlet. Nahid Raza began to display her work, as did Mussarat Mirza from Sukkur, Meher Afroz from the Lucknow College of Art, and Qudsia Nisar from the Punjab University Fine Arts Department. They proved that in the field of fine art in Pakistan women were more than a match for their male counterparts.

In 1974, A.R. Nagori, later to become Pakistan's first socio-political painter, established the Fine Art Department of Sindh University. He remained as head of the department until his retirement in 1996. Exciting art exhibitions took place in the 1970s. Artists tutored by Shakir Ali, others returning from abroad, and vibrant local talents created an active art milieu. Jamil Naqsh stopped exhibiting his work, yet his earlier paintings were displayed by private collectors. Maqsood Ali embarked on an outstanding series of works inspired by Bhitshah. Returning from Europe Bashir Mirza exhibited a series called *The Lonely Girl* and made art history. Kohari became involved with ceramics and created unusual and beautiful pieces.

The emergence of Islamabad as the new capital created hardly any ripples in the Karachi art market where local collectors were indulging seriously in art buying. Working in metal, Gulgee was

*From the **Woman** series, by Nahid Raza.*

Victims of the System, by A.R. Nagori.

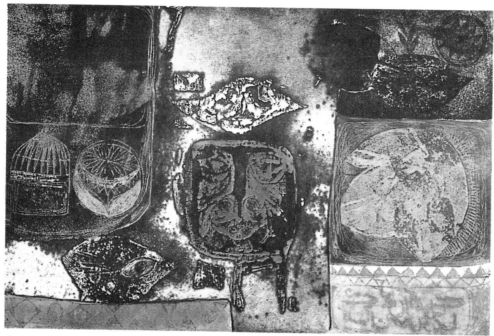

Green Song by
Shahid Sajjad

commissioned to create a bronze sculpture for a local bank, a delicately wrought map of intricate design. The art centre of Karachi was the Indus Gallery, where lavish receptions preceded art displays. There was a great deal of fun and entertainment. Ahmed Parvez, brilliant and eccentric, kept art circles buzzing with his antics. Sadequain travelled extensively and displayed his work in many countries. A group exhibition from Pakistan, held at the Commonwealth Institute, London, aroused considerable interest.

The decade of the 1970s saw the departure of notable Bengali artists to newly created Bangladesh. Zainul Abedin, Hamidur Rahman and Mobinul Azim left a void in the art world that was never filled. In 1972, government policies freed Wahab Jaffer from his business commitments to develop his talent as an artist and begin the collection that was eventually to make him one of the most important art collectors in the country. Artists in Karachi painted to the dictates of their own taste. Abstract, semi figurative, cubist and realistic art was prevalent. In the 1970s too, the Karachi School of Art produced an impressive flowering of artists. Riffat Alvi, Tariq Javed and Mashkoor Raza, who began to exhibit his colourful abstracts. Abdul Hayee, Zaheen Ahmed, and Ghalib Baqar reinforced the school's distinguished record of producing outstanding water colourists. Abdul Hayee began the tradition of 'on-spot' watercolour painting in Karachi and its environs, and was joined by a group of fellow artists and students, a tradition that continues to this day. A graduate of the Central Institute of Art, Shakeel Siddiqui mastered completely the *trompe-l'oeil* effect, amazing viewers at exhibitions of his work.

Meher Afroz held her first ever exhibition of mixed media prints in Karachi in 1974. She was accorded first prize in the graphics section of Pakistan's National Art Exhibition in 1977, and rekindled an interest in printmaking in Karachi. Najmi Sura exhibited her paintings for the first time ever in a group exhibition, combining traditional eastern elements into a classic style. Najmi's work, in which she enlarged miniature subjects and themes, were finely painted with rich detail and created an instant impact among art enthusiasts. Najmi, a student of Jamil Naqsh, commented that he had taught her three things; not to give interviews, not to exhibit her work, and not to copy Chughtai. In 1978, Ahmed Parvez was awarded the President's Pride of Performance medal—too little, too late. In 1979, he died of the effects of a stroke, still in his early fifties. A sadly troubled human being, his work, vibrant with colour and lyrical movement, belied his mental turbulence.

In the 1980s women dominated the art scene, and the feminist point of view began to appear in art. Nahid Raza was the first Pakistani woman to depict the problems of women in a male oriented society, while propagating the theory of women's powerful influence on the family and their greater flexibility.

A graduate of the Karachi School of Art, Hanif Shehzad exhibited a collection of still-life collages, put together from fragmented scraps of glossy paper. Shehzad was to become one of Karachi's noted watercolourists. The 1980s were, on the one hand, aesthetically oppressive, yet on the other showed a number of positive developments. A monumental sculpture in bronze was the result of two years work by Shahid Sajjad. Depicting the history of the Armoured Corps, the large, wall based relief, transformed a militant subject into a work of art.

In 1985, the Chawkandi Gallery opened in Clifton and rapidly became Karachi's trendiest art outlet. Two years later, the Rangoonwala Centre invited artist Riffat Alvi to become the director of the V.M. Gallery. Run by a trust, the non-profit making gallery offered younger artists, students, and unknown painters the opportunity to exhibit their work. Figurative painting was frowned upon during the military dictatorship, and calligraphy became a popular art trend. Traditionally, the status of the written word, integrated textually with pictorial representation, is a fine art form that goes back thousands of years. A number of artists showed renewed interest in the relationship between image and language, promoted by a need to examine their own cultural roots. Some artists adopted their styles to suit the art market. Among the genuine calligraphers, Shakeel Ismail, who graduated from the Central Institute of Art in 1983, produced interesting work. Antique metal objects were embossed with script. Shakeel went on to win a national award for his fine art pieces, but his standard of work was exceptional.

Printmaking came into its own and artists experimented with mono prints and etchings. It became a subject added to the curriculum of local art schools. Artists dealt with the trends in their various individual ways. Most quietly got on with their own work. The flamboyant artist Bashir Mirza laid down his brush for eleven years, refusing to paint until Martial Law was lifted. Then he went through a painting frenzy completing huge panelled portraits of his heroes. He experimented with acrylics for the first time and was soon making up for the lost years.

Professor Nagori, outraged by the wrongs he witnessed in Sindh, began to portray the plight of the people, using oils on small, brilliant hued canvases. Trained as a muralist, Nagori painted his cameos without thought of the art market, hence economics dictated the scale. In 1986, the Indus Gallery cocked a

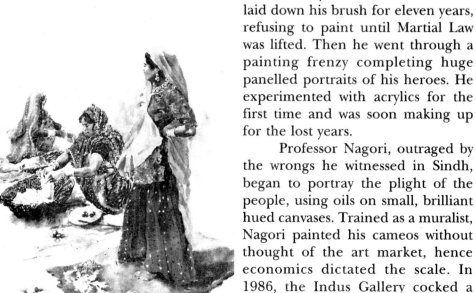

From the series on Thar by Athar Jamal.

292

snook at prevailing mores and exhibited his *Alphabet* series in which each letter initiated a socially conscious statement. The emotions of the artist exploded across canvas after canvas with turbulent strokes. Crimes against women and children, bonded labour, deforestation and the hypocrisy of those in high places were recorded and narrated on paintings that became aesthetic banners.

Tassadaq Sohail, living in London, visited Pakistan often and exhibited his miniature scale, Gothic fairytales in Karachi, eerily exciting work in which he ridiculed figures of authority. Sohail's work incorporated tiny figures of doom in surrealistic landscapes.

Ather Jamal exhibited watercolour portraits and studies, and rapidly became a favourite with local galleries and collectors. Wandering around Karachi's environs, Ather encapsulated the world of the *katchi abadies* and portrayed the nomadic people and their culture with empathy and dignity.

Military rule ended and a new decade began, but it was to herald a troubled, bloody time for Karachi. Political differences and ethnic violence became a fact of life in the troubled city. In spite of the constant strikes and fears, exhibitions continued and there was a formidable flowering of a new crop of artists. Nahid Raza opened an art centre, Studio Art in Clifton, which became a full fledged school of art. The Indus Valley School of Art and Architecture was established by a board of governors and founding member, Noor Jehan Bilgrami, became the principal.

Momart Gallery opened and introduced a vigorous young landscape painter, Chitra. The Kunj Gallery opened, for the first time offering visiting, exhibiting artists a studio to stay in. There was a lot of cross-cultural activity. Pakistani artists travelled abroad and foreign artists from Sri Lanka, China, and Nepal showed their work in Karachi. Riffat Alvi travelled to Zimbabwe and there studied a method of painting in which soil was incorporated as a medium. Her success led to a solo display of her work in the Commonwealth Institute, Leeds, and praise from the legendary British artist, Alan Davie. Further displays followed, including a three month exhibition at the Mermaid Theatre Gallery, London.

The interest in printmaking increased. Artists explored mono printmaking, a form of art that does not require

Composition by Qudsia Nisar.

expensive materials. Mohammed Kazim evolved his own method of embossed printmaking which earned him a national award and recognition in foreign countries. Artists Naiza Khan, Samina Mansuri, Mona Naqsh, Unver Shafi Khan, and Amin Gulgee exhibited outstanding work in local exhibitions. Young artists and veterans alike expressed socially conscious themes in their work. Students showed an astute awareness of the developments in their city in the subjects they chose for their thesis works. Exhibitions portrayed pain and outrage at the violence against mankind, and the environment.

Sponsored by the Goethe Institut, a workshop lasting three weeks gave six Pakistani artists working with one German artist the opportunity to express their ideas on *violence*. Later the work produced during the workshop was shown at an exhibition at the Karachi Arts Council.

Qudsia Nisar's veiled abstracts, Nahid's threatened women, Wahab Jaffer's androgynous faces of despair were ways in which these artists painted the world around them. Mehtab Amar Jamal began the *Croton* series in which she used the hardy, tenacious plant as an allegory for the suffering people of Karachi. Her sister Amber moved from figurative to abstract work, escaping to an aquatic world of inspiration.

In 1994, sculptors Durriya Kazi and David Aylesworth, worked with the students and teachers of the Karachi School of Art to create a mobile art display, a painted truck which was driven throughout Pakistan ending in Islamabad. The art caravan sought recognition for a genuine folk art, the gaudily decorated long distance truck. Two years later, David and Durriya joined forces with Iftikhar and Elizabeth Dadi to participate in the 'Containers '96 Display', in

Copenhagen, where the colourful folk aspect of their design won accolades from many countries.

Several important group displays took place in foreign countries, including Japan, the UK, where at Cartwright Hall, Bradford, an exhibition of work by women artists from Pakistan was shown, and America, where a group of fifty artists displayed their work at the Pacific Asia Museum.

A group of art collectors formed an association to preserve the work of Jamil Naqsh in a gallery dedicated to the artist. Known as the 'Friends of Jamil Naqsh', the group consisting of prominent citizens, persuaded the artist to exhibit his work after three decades of non-participation. His paintings, incredibly sensitive work, displayed in a series of one evening exhibitions, added lustre to the local art scene.

One of the earliest Karachi artists, Ajmal Hussain, celebrated his seventieth birthday with a retrospective exhibition at the Indus Gallery that spanned the years from the 1940s to the present time.

There are no signs yet of a National Museum of Art in Karachi, and no art movement has developed. Achievements are pursued by individuals as artists continue to paint according to their own inclinations, or the dictates of the art market. Art in Karachi has become an established fact of life. From a handful of artists, there are now many. Often they exhibit their work in international events. Schools catering to over one thousand art students flourish. Most of them are run by women. Karachi artists are extremely responsive to stimuli. They welcome the opportunity to join workshops and meet artists from other countries. Lacking the facilities found abroad, they rely on their own talents and determination to succeed in their challenging vocation. As time passes, Karachi artists endeavour to keep abreast of contemporary techniques and movements while maintaining on-going links with the past.

Liaquat Soldier and Akbar Chanchal in a comedy production staged in Karachi.

Chapter 14

COMEDY, TRAGEDY AND REALISM

Hameed Zaman

The history of theatre in Karachi started some time before the partition of the subcontinent, on the rickety platform of the nascent Parsi theatre. Like anywhere else, in pioneering work, theatre activity began with crude attempts, which with the passage of time transformed themselves into something greatly improved though not mature enough to be called sophisticated. The highs and lows in the graph depict a story of commercial, as well as artistic struggle in the face of social attitudes, perceptions of morality, taboos and creative possibilities. Theatre in Karachi has seen good and bad days. Its earlier phase was sustained by the Parsi theatre where lampooning and horseplay was the main fare.

Parsi theatre drew its inspiration from the growth and well being of the Bombay stage where financial prospects were much brighter. Talents were easily available and the number of audiences was steadily growing. Side by side, the foreign residents of Karachi had formed their own 'Little Theatres'. And the Parsi theatre which patronized the Gujerati language switched to Urdu because of its wide range of acceptance and easy communication.

The record of Urdu and Gujerati plays that were staged is preserved in the pages of the Zoroastrian Club's golden jubilee souvenir published in 1932. The information here is rather sketchy but, nevertheless, reliable. It is a pity that the Parsi community in Karachi has not shown much enthusiasm in conducting research on this remarkable chapter in its cultural history.

Karachi being an urban megapolis has little of an artistic past except, of course, in the presence of the Parsi theatre.

The city is so cut off from its hinterland that it can hardly claim to be an heir to Sindh's romantic folkore, music, and cultural heritage. The city has not fostered an indigenous culture, and during these fifty years, has not been able to crystallize its soul. Karachi is not yet complete and its characteristic ethos is still blurred. It has absorbed millions of refugees and is sheltering millions of fortune seekers who arrive here daily. Yet it has no patience for theatre which sprouts and grows in the fertile soil of sensibility, creativity, and intellectual maturity. And the stage which once flourished here, died an unnatural death. After Partition, a number of Parsis migrated to Bombay, leaving an obvious vacuum which no one dared to fill. But it took a very long time till the final curtain was drawn on the Parsi theatre.

According to the golden jubilee souvenir of the Zoroastrian Club, the first play of the Parsi Theatre was *Jugar* (gambling) which was written in Gujerati by a well known Parsi playwright, Bomanji K. Kebraji of Bombay. It was performed for three nights at the Mavolee Parsi Theatre, located on Bunder Road (now M.A. Jinnah Road). The theatre was owned by Navroji Dhanjibhai. The Club's next presentation was an Urdu play: *Bulbul-e-Bimar* in 1894 at the same theatre. To celebrate a Parsi festival, the club staged another Urdu play *Pak Daman* on 15 March 1903. Another Urdu play *Insaf-e-Nadir Shah* was staged in 1911.

It is apparent that the female parts were played by male actors as in the Shakespearean tradition. Those were the days when women folk dared not appear on the stage. In 1920, Karachi was lucky to have a hall. Katrak Hall was donated for public use by Khan Bahadar the late Sir Kavasji Hormusji Katrak. After Partition, the Hall was used by the Clifton players. However, much earlier in 1933 Homi Minwalla used the Hall for his play *Charley's Aunt*.

The plots of the plays were generally taken from *Dastans*, *Shahnama*, mythology, novels and European plays. They were mostly tear jerkers, sentimental farces, or simply based on absurd characters. The good characters were angels, while the bad ones, devils. The innocent suffered in some tragic way. Oppressed women expressed their feelings through many a touching song. The villain also had his songs which he sang with great gusto. If Greek drama made use of catharsis, so did Parsi theatre which kept the audience tense from beginning to end, watching the hero heading towards his destined doom.

Speaking of acting, it was rhetorical, melodramatic, and oversized. The high pitched dialogues, full of sound and fury, were sure signs of a thumping success. The comedy script had much local colour and exploited many allusions to current events and personalities. Thus the characters were more or less identifiable. The situations were couched in local happenings. It was a living theatre of the people, for the people. The response of the audience was immense. It enjoyed the fun and greeted the actors with warm applause.

The Parsi theatre, after many ups and downs, managed to survive till 1978, when under the auspices of the Zoroastrian Art Circle staged on an average, one play every two years. The Art Circle's last play was *Dhool Ma Phool* (Blossoms in the Dust), a three act play by Sarosh Irani, performed in 1972. In 1966, Sarosh Irani came up with a three-act play, a tragedy entitled *Bekar Balidan* (Futile Sacrifice). It was performed in aid of the relief fund for Pakistan war victims. The Zoroastrian Art Circle presented *Ek Naar trun Bimar*, an adaptation of an English comedy, *All for Mary*, in 1971. The Art Circle staged another comedy *Laay Mahri Mashook* (Hand over My Sweetheart). Another English play *The Seekers* was also adapted into Gujerati. Within a span of twenty years the Art Circle staged ten full length plays. Though dormant for so many years, the Zoroastrian Art Circle is sure to revive itself and breathe again. Sarosh Irani's last play *Dhaniyaia ne Dhakhara* was based on *The Wife's Whim*.

At the time of independence, Parsi theatre was alive but somehow it started to shrink and contained itself within the ambit of its ready made Parsi audience, thus losing its cosmopolitan character. It refused to come out of its shell to assist the nascent Urdu theatre when it was in the best position to do so.

English theatre was dominated by the British. They created their own 'Little Theatres', on the pattern of the one that existed in Simla, and were creating substandard versions of the English plays which swamped Drury Lane in London. The Clifton players and the British Council were active and presented plays like *The Lady's Not for Burning, Ring Round the Moon* and *Our Town*. *The Lady's Not For Burning* was staged by the British Council in Sarnagati

Building in Pakistan Chowk in their main hall through a makeshift arrangement. Two other plays were presented at the Theosophical Hall which had recently thrown itself open for such performances.

Urdu theatre in Karachi was struggling to be born and its activities were confined to some kind of variety shows, comprising one-act skits with dance and music items thrown in, for tempting the audience to stay on. It was a mixed bag which was neither here nor there. The handling was slipshod and there was more horseplay than performance. Not an unusual beginning in the annals of theatre, though in Karachi the situtation remained static without showing any promise for quite some time.

The only theatre auditorium which existed in Karachi in the early days was an evacuee property known as the Elite Theatre, once owned by a Hindu entrepreneur. It did not enjoy a high reputation and the so called plays, or variety shows to be more precise, could best be categorized as cheap and vulgar. It was against this background that some theatre enthusiasts got together and presented two plays which are still remembered. One was *Jhansi Ki Rani* and the other *Sohrab aur Rustam*. Some of the actors who were once associated with Agha Hashr Kashmiri, or were working with the well known Alfred Theatrical Company of Bombay, voluntarily appeared in these plays, including the late Abdur Rehman Kabuli, and the late Mughal Bashar. Both of them at that time were employed by Radio Pakistan.

These plays followed the pattern set by Agha Hashr, who was a brilliant literary personality of Lahore with a knack for direction and writing plays. Here dialogues used to be delivered at a high-pitched volume, because the use of microphones on the stage was as yet not known. The dialogues were written in versified prose, maintaining poetic cadence and rhymed scale. Curtains used to be painted elaborately to avoid over use of furniture and props on the stage. However, the only facility available, the Elite Theatre, was taken over by estate developers and the building was pulled down in 1953.

There were certain groups which were devoted exclusively to English plays, but their effort turned out to be futile as their impact was minimal on the local run of the mill theatre, first because of the language barrier and, second, because of class stratification. Here the twain did not meet and there was no love lost between them. The groups were status conscious, moving within prescribed social circles. Some of the plays which these so called elitist groups attempted included: *A Long Day's Journey Into Night, They Knew What They Wanted* and *Julius Caesar*. All these efforts lacked seriousness of purpose and were not intended to promote local theatre in any way.

The late Khwaja Moinuddin arrived in Karachi in 1950 and practically changed the theatre scene. He was a sort of catalyst who sought possibilities out of stagnation. A purposeful theatre was about to be born. His play *Naya Nishan* based on the annexation of Kashmir by India, drew sharp criticism from diplomatic circles and protests from India. That was the beginning of the new genre, and theatre became a vehicle for political and social expression, though it was still stylized and looked too theatrical on the stage. His second play *Zawal-e-Hyderabad* was again a success hitting India, which had already taken over the Muslim State of Hyderabad: Khwaja Sahib who belonged to Hyderabad was very bitter about this political *coup d'etat*. It was a very powerful play, though full of political slogans and with a slanted bias, but then the playwright was waging a war against political injustice. His *piece de resistance* was *Lal Qiley sey Laloo Khait Tak* which presented the dilemma of the immigrants and refugees who were struggling to adjust to their new predicaments.

The play became an instant success as Karachi was a refugee city and refugees were still pouring in. The theme was so near to their heart, as were the events, both local and contemporary. And their involvement was so direct. The play was drawing an audience of approximately ten thousand every day and had to be staged at the KMC Stadium. It ran for 140 nights without a break. Later it moved to Lahore and parts of Sindh. Still, the production was crude and unbalanced. Microphones were staging a comeback as the audience multiplied into thousands. The microphones had a disruptive presence on the stage. They hampered the view, beside forcing the actors to stay in their vicinity. This damaged the movement plan, placing and compositional structure.

Zia Mohyeddin, a well trained and tried actor from the London stage, came to Lahore because of personal reasons, read the script of *Lal Qila....* found it interesting and

Zia Mohyeddin, a colossus of theatre, who in the reading of prose and poetry in Urdu and English is unsurpassed in Pakistan.

accepted the offer from the Karachi Arts Council, which wanted to stage the play. And there was Alex Elmore, an orientalist who was also in the city. He had earlier designed the production of *Rukmani Devi* in India. And, of course, there was Mrs Sigrid Kahle, a Swedish lady married to a diplomat who was stationed at Karachi. She belonged to a family steeped in Orientalism. It was an opportunity for Mrs Kahle who wholeheartedly coordinated, supervized, and extended the fullest cooperation. She was willing to put the efforts of Khwaja Moinuddin to real use. Zia Mohyeddin and Alex Elmore (who later joined UNESCO) completed the production with a touch of professionalism. Mrs Kahle, herself a theatre enthusiast had earlier staged Sophocles's *Antigone*, herself playing the lead and worked with Alex Elmore. They all joined hands to make their new venture a huge success.

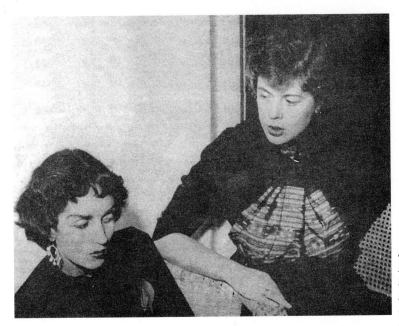

Sigrid Kahle and Hannelore Brunher, brought August Strindberg to Karachi in 1954.

However, the main hurdle again was the use of microphones which were to be discarded at any cost, but it required an intensive course of vocal training for the actors. They required sufficient time to train. The play was too unwieldy, its running time was more than four hours, which had to be edited and the script drastically curtailed. The conventional heavy stage settings were to be redesigned. It was to be the first professionally produced play to be mounted in Pakistan. The new version was a resounding success. It was a turning point, for Zia Mohyeddin with his training in a prestigious drama school and substantial experience of the professional theatre of London was attempting to put method into the prevailing madness and triumphed. The play also discovered some brilliant talents for the Karachi stage including S.M. Saleem, Ibrahim Nafees, Mohammad Yousuf, Subhani-ba-Yunus, Mahmood Ali, and others playing minor roles. They proved their worth as they matured.

In 1957 Khwaja Moinuddin formed a group of his own, under the title of the Drama Guild. Its first production was *Mirza Ghalib Bunder Road Per*, a hilarious assessment of the changing times and values, with a generation gap theme which was being discussed all over the world. Ghalib, a man of the nineteenth century, arrives in the middle of the twentieth in Karachi, a city which was going through a huge transition, coping and failing in the face of cultural chaos. Ghalib, with his literary finesse and old world values, is shocked to see this bewildering mess which a sea of change has brought, and is lost in the exploding situation. This encounter provided a lot of satirical and comic situations and became yet another hit. Most of the plots of Khwaja Sahib were woven around actualities and happenings of the day and managed to establish an instant rapport with the audience. His themes sprouted from the problems and lifestyles of the milieu, hence the intense involvement of the spectators.

In the meantime another veteran, a dedicated playwright, migrated to Pakistan. Ali Ahmed was associated with the UP branch of the Indian People's Theatre. On his arrvial in Lahore, he tried to establish a children's theatre but failed and decided to come to Karachi in 1955. He had his basic training in Calcutta and Bombay and was assocated with actors and directors like Khawaja Ahmed Abbass, Bimal Roy, Balraj Sahni, and Zia Sarhadi. In Karachi, Ali Ahmed founded an Avant Garde Arts Theatre (AGAT) in 1974, when he was still struggling to establish a People's Theatre in Pakistan. He had already forty theatre productions to his credit and had written more than twenty-five plays—ten originals and fifteen adaptations. In 1970, Ali Ahmed and some of his colleagues decided to form an Academy of Theatre Arts in Karachi. Thus, finally, NATAK (National Academy of Theatre Arts) was established.

Ali Ahmed in 1984, one of the landmarks in the theatre of the subcontinent.

Ali Ahmed was soon regarded and accepted as a progressive force with obvious leftist leanings. His themes were bold and revolutionary. He worked with symbolic sets and an uncluttered stage, using the simplest language of daily conversation. He did not indulge in the philosophy of dialectics, nor did he talk about Marxist postulates. Instead, he spoke in the language of the street and discussed problems faced by the denizens of the lower depths, highlighting the basic conflicts which existed in the woven fabric of the social order.

The other factor of his plays was the selection of locality where the play was to be staged—a new approach for Karachi audiences. It was the nearest thing to Street Theatre, though it was not quite that. He never used a big cast and tried to keep his premise clear and simple. The idea was to put the message across in the simplest possible terms. His significant plays and productions included *Zaat-e-Sharief; Subh Honey Tak, Sheshey Ka Admi, Quisa Jagtey Sotey Ka, Chaodhween Manzil* and *Safaid Posh*. His plays were frontal attacks on capitalist exploitation and satires on hypocrisy and sham.

After the death of Ali Ahmed, there were no crusaders in the field in Karachi, except for stray efforts by a few enthusiasts every now and then. Pursuing a quick buck, the society had little time for creative endeavours. Karachi has

Kamal Ahmed Rizvi and Rafi Khawar as Allan and Nanna, the Odd Couple of Pakistan Television.

not yet been able to establish a viable theatre foundation. With the advent of television it became much easier for theatre hands to put in less labour and earn substantial remuneration. Thus TV succeeded in attracting most of the talent, leaving theatrewallas high and dry. A casual survey revealed that there was no dearth of talent. They were too eager to show their worth, but somehow the consolidating factor was always missing and theatre leadership was lacking. Scarcity of funds could be another factor. It resulted in damaging the cause of theatre which almost fell into disarray, unhonoured and unsung.

In this hopeless situation Kamal Ahmed Rizvi, a one-man institution, remains the only shining star. He has already established his brilliant credentials as a playwright, actor, director and producer. In fact, he is a one-man phenomenon who manages all the departments of his projects. His TV serial *Alif Noon*, with his partner Rafi Khawar, catapulted him to the highest pinnacles of popularity. Every time this odd couple appeared on TV they brought the house down so to say and had become the darlings of the nation. Later Kamal Ahmed Rizvi wrote full-length plays for the stage. All his writings show undercurrents of social satire, a subtle exposure of social or official evil behaviour, patterns of exploitation or corruption. The audience laughed at their own follies, and on the sweet and sour attacks. His plays like *Khoy Hua Admi* is a satire on city life where a man is lost in the concrete jungle. Similarly his adaptation, *Lafangey Ki Diary* is a hard hitting play which had a corrective purpose. The treatment was polished and acting was up to the mark as he was using mostly TV actors, who maintained a balanced performance despite some hilarious patches. In that sense, I would say Urdu theatre

Khalid Ahmed and Sheema Kirmani, an essential part of the local theatre scene.

Rafi Peer, an extraordinary talent.

was coming of age though it was still working in fits and starts, for theatre had not yet acquired any permanent footing. It was still a matter of individual enterprise.

In Karachi, a husband and wife team, Khalid Ahmed and Sheema Kirmani, had made a mark through their deep involvement in theatre and dance. In a way, they are lucky to have the sponsorship of the Goethe Institut, which somehow or the other, took upon itself to patronize cultural activities in Pakistan, not only by encouraging and financing local talent but also at times by inviting German artists to Pakistan, and by holding seminars and workshops.

Khalid Ahmed and Sheema Kirmani presented an exciting play *Yahan Say Shehr Ko Dekho*. They were lucky that a celebrated Indian painter M.F. Hussain happened to be here and agreed to paint a special backdrop for the play, which when completed was both imaginative and evocative. It was done in very bold strokes in black and white interpreting the theme of daily killings in Karachi, so rampant in those days when existence had become a burden and life was so cheap. The play took the city by storm. It depicted the cruelty and horror of human life and questioned the very equation of human relationships. The Goethe Institut imported a huge odd-sized canvas for the backdrop and provided large tins of paint and other facilities to M.F. Hussain. The couple also appeared in Rafi Peer's well known play *Raz-o-Niaz* and staged a Greek tragedy *Antigone*.

That brings us to a famous personality of Pakistani theatre, Rafi Peer, a brilliant young man who was greatly impressed with the performances of Parsi theatre. His political association brought him into the folds of the

Muslim League, and as such he became involved in the Non-cooperation Movement. A warrant of arrest was issued in his name, and when he was to be arrested, he decided to leave for London for his law degree. There he came under the magic spell of London theatre. His new interest angered his family, and his allowance was first curtailed, then stopped. Finally, he decided to go to Germany and started working with the German theatre icon, Max Reinhard who was then the most renowned theatre personality of the era. After about a fifteen year stay and theatre involvement, he returned to Lahore where he worked and trained such actors as Prithivi Raj, Ashok Kumar, Om Prakash and Mubarak. He also wrote some dramas for All India Radio. Later in 1975, in collaboration with the well known Urdu short story writer, Chetan Anand, he made his first film *Nicha Nagar* which dealt with the theme of non-violence. The film bagged three Grand Prix awards at the 1948 Cannes Film Festival. After his death, his son Usman Peerzada, himself an actor of real merit, founded the Rafi Peer Theatre workshop in memory of his father.

While talking about Rafi Peer, whose impact was tremendous in terms of theatre production, all over the subcontinent, we have yet another theatre personality who is holding the fort, giving a boost to contemporary theatre in Pakistan, and is a constant factor in the current journey of growth. Madiha Gauhar who has been trained in London on a British Council scholarship, has given a new direction to Pakistani theatre and has brought it into the mainstream theatre of the sub-continent. She is the life and soul of Ajoka, an institute dedicated to the promotion of theatre in this country within its social context, taking up problems and issues on the platform for open discussion and debate, touching almost every subject under the sun, and creating awareness among the audience.

Ajoka being innovative and experimental has shown courage and boldness, and hence has always been under a cloud. Credit must however, be given to Ajoka for strengthening the concept of Street Theatre which has given a new direction and dimension by bringing theatre closer to the common man. The Goethe Institut in Karachi, and Tehrik-e-Niswan, took Street Theatre to the slums of Lyari which was hugely welcomed. It was a grass root theatre for the masses with no props. It was a highly motivated theatre which had a mission to fulfil. The short plays which it staged were socially relevant to the audience. A new spirit was infused in the people to stand up and fight for their own cause. It was dynamic and explosive theatre.

During the regime of the late General Ziaul Haq, discriminatory laws were passed against women. Tehrik-e-Niswan (founded in 1980) adopted Street Theatre as its own way of expression and protest. In December 1981, a play was performed for an all women audience in one of the depresssed neighbourhoods of Karachi. Over the years Street Theatre has become the mouthpiece of Tehrik-e-Niswan. It has already presented over a hundred short plays, dealing with the problems of women, which they face in the conservative society of ours. The best thing about the Tehrik is that a performance can be arranged at short notice. It is a problem oriented theatre, an alternative to formal education, meant primarliy for the illiterate audience.

The Alliance Francaise in Karachi played host to Ajoka when Madiha Gauhar brought a remarkable play *Ek Thi Nani* to honour one of the remarkable figures of Indian theatre and dance, Zohra Saigal who came to Pakistan to see her younger sister, Uzra Butt, after forty-seven years. Naturally, it was a sentimental journey and Ajoka made the best use of her presence and persuaded her to participate in the play, which was especially written for the sisters. In a way history was being made on the Alliance stage.

Both sisters belonged to Rampur in India. Zohra Saigal was the prima donna of the Uday Shankar Ballet and married her Hindu dance partner and stayed in Delhi, while Uzra Butt was a lead actress in The Prithvi Kapoor Theater till she got married and came to Pakistan. Both sisters appeared on the stage in *Ek Thi Nani* under the direction of Madiha Gauhar. The material was judiciously used by the playwright and director. Zohra (82) and Uzra

Uzra Butt, who witnessed numerous changes in the style and techniques employed in Theatre

(77), looked like characters from a children's story book. They appeared without any makeup and carried the play in hushed silence. Their histrionic prowess was simply overwhelming. Uzra found her elder sister marrying a Hindu and living in a permissive society in India, quite shocking, whereas Zohra wondered how her younger sister could survive in the conservative atmosphere of Pakistan and has folded her stage career for good for the sake of her husband. In between there was a granddaughter. The play was about her dilemma. An India-Pakistan cultural encounter was expressed through the creative example of good acting and a sound script.

In the same context I would like to mention here two experimental plays. The first is Sohail Malik's *Zabardastan*, the first musical in Urdu, and the second is Talat Hussain's *Said-e-Hawas*, staged in typical Agha Hashr style. Both were fairly successful in their mannerisms and style suggesting that Karachi audiences were not averse to experimentation.

Sohail Malik is essentially associated with English plays and created a stir when he produced *Zabardastan*. He took up a Broadway success *Fantasticks* and rendered it into Urdu (1992). Its revival at the Rex Auditorium ran for three weeks, a record in Karachi. It provided two hours of sumptuous entertainment combining, as it did, a simple story refreshingly told with a specially composed musical score. There were seven songs in Act I, and six in Act II. The Theatre Circle of Karachi headed by Sohail Malik, certainly deserves kudos for their experimental offering.

In 1991, Talat Hussain presented Agha Hashr's *Said-e-Hawas* as part of UNESCO's Theatre Workshop which he was conducting at the Karachi Arts Council. It was a difficult assignment for the trainee students, doing a period play with versified text and dialogues, which were to be delivered with rhythmic cadence, an accepted format and style in the late twenties. The play displayed the obvious influence of Parsi theatre, which in its turn borrowed from the Shakespearean stage as being played in London. Agha Hashr's plays have, by now, attained the status of classics. Set to folk music in the idiom of *Dadra* and *Thumri*, the play had all the ingredients to make it successful.

Yet another group led by Anjum Ayaz, a sculptor by profession, presented a dramatic version of Manto's two short stories. *Rahat Jan (Hatak)* and *Suraj* under the joint title of

Yasmin Ismail, one of the most talented and natural actresses who is equally at home in English and Urdu.

Aao Manto Karain. Yasmin Ismail, a sensitive actress, and Sajid Hasan a brilliant performer, both acquitted themselves well, while Akbar Subhani acted as the late Manto and maintained the continuity or, at times acted as chorus. Anjum's other presentation was *The Glass Menagerie* with an Urdu title: *Khaboon ke Kirchain.* It was well rehearsed and flawless.

It would be unfair if we did not acknowledge the role of some of the foreign cultural centres, which have extended all out support to some of the genuine and active creative groups to make their projects possible Such assistance was forthcoming right from the very beginning—from *Lal Qilay Say Lalokhait Tak,* and since then it's a story of continuous help and encouragement. For example the PACC, along with the British Council, are the oldest centres in Karachi and both have been helping, encouraging, and even financing such creative ventures.

In the recent past, the Goethe Institut sponsored *Yahan Sey Shehr Ko Dekho.* Its earlier presentation, Brecht's *Galileo,* was directed by Aslam Azhar. It was a great success and is well remembered by theatregoers. Recently, the Goethe Institut arranged a theatre workshop under the expert guidance of Jurgen Zielinski from Berlin, who was assisted by Reinlid Blaschke, also from Berlin, and as the end result presented *Raushni Key Darechey,* an Urdu adaptation of a German play, *Nathan der Werse* (Nathan the Wise) by Gotthold Ephraim Lessing (1729-81). The translation was done by Khalid Ahmed. The play was set in Jerusalem at the time of the Crusades in the twelfth century on the day of armistice which stops the war for a short while. It was a war of Christians against Muslims. In this historical situation religious intolerance, prejudices against those who held different views, power calculations and violence, dominated

311

daily life. Lessing has made intolerance and bigotry his theme. The cast included Sheema Kirmani, Khalid Ahmed, and Akbar Subhani.

The Goethe Institut also took the lead when it brought GRIPS, a world wide children theatre movement to Karachi, and made it really popular among children and adults. GRIPS, described by *Newsweek* as 'a mixture of gritty realism with a dash of utopia' sprouted from the Radical Students' Movement in Germany. It views children as political and social beings and tries to make sense out of a sometimes hostile world. A small child's fear of the dark is treated with the same seriousness as his or her fear of war. In this context of GRIPS, the contribution of Imran Aslam and Yasmin Ismail cannot be minimized, particularly in scripting and recasting the entire plays in terms of Pakistani situations. An old hand from the Dramatic Society of Government College Lahore, Imran Aslam was once part of Aaj Pa Theatre which later became Ajoka. He was also associated with Theatrewalley. GRIPS presented such plays as *Sazish Ki Wajah Say Khail Multavi, Choti Moti, Tota and S.M. Hamid, Langra Aam Kas Hota Hae, Unfit Ball Dunya Mere Hai.* All these plays dealt with subjects of social importance.

GRIPS has a philosophy of its own as expounded by its founder Vokert Ludwig, a noted socialist and Marxist, who challenged the theory of 'suspension of disbelief' and claimed that drama was not a form of catharsis as the Greeks interpreted it. And the argument was that if the audience goes through a process of catharsis, the motivation to act lapses. The audience must know that what they are watching is just a play, not reality. It is a process of alienation he is pleading. The audience must not immerse itself in the art form, and there must always be a kind of detachment between the audience and the play. Songs and discussions are deliberately introduced during the play to break the spell of identificaiton. In fact, we have seen such a tradition in the play of Agha Hashr Kashmiri, where progress of the plot is interrupted and a song or dance item is introduced. It is there even in our cinema, though unconsciously. It is accepted as a part of the plot.

The Alliance Francaise, too, has its honourable place in promoting our theatre, by offering and sponsoring some of the plays which were progressive in content and rich in their artistic worth. The play *Razia Sultan* under the direction of Imran Sherwanee was conceived against the traditional function of theatre, which amused and diverted the attention of the audience from the serious issues that were involved. *Razia Sultan* disturbed the audience by raising unsettled questions and attempting answers in order to find a final solution to human relationships.

The other play at the Alliance was *Sultan ka Faisala*, written by an Egyptian playwright, Tawfiq-e-Hakim and was translated by Asif Aslam Farrukhi. Set in the times of the slave kings of medieval Arabia, the play was about the dilemma of a king who faces the problem of legitimacy, because of his origin as a slave. The play highlights the supremacy of law over the sword. It was directed by Khalid Ahmed.

In terms of popularity, some foreign plays drew huge 'literate' crowds who were, in one way or the other, not foreign to these plays and eagerly awaited them on stage. They must have read the text already through various publications, or seen or heard them on the TV, or radio.

For example, Brecht is extremely popular in this subcontinent and repeat performances are held in Pakistan, India and Bangladesh. Becket's *Waiting for Godot* is yet another favourite with the audience here. Lorca's *Blood Wedding* (*Lahoo Suhag* in Urdu) proved a sensation in Lahore. The play was first staged in Madrid in 1930. Some portions of the play resembled *Mirza Sahiban* and matched life in Punjabi rural areas. *Khabon Ki Kirchain* an Urdu adaptation of *The Glass Menagerie* was staged at the PACC and drew huge crowds. Besides *Charley's Aunt* has been on the stage in Karachi in its Urdu version many times.

One may debate the efficacy of the visits of the foreign theatrical companies, but who can deny their educative value? They bring with them fresh techniques, new ideas and acting patterns and, above all, initiate dialogues on the international wavelength. In fact such visits gave birth to the English theatre in Karachi, an idiom which kept itself alive despite not so conducive an atmosphere.

To many, the theatre has a magic, to few it is still a wanton and wasteful pastime. However, the measure of success is still how many tickets it can sell or how many audiences are likely to buy tickets in the days to come, for all said and done, the theatre has always been, and will continue to be, a commercial venture.

A very encouraging phenomenon is the spontaneous growth of vernacular as well as Urdu popular theatre in Karachi. Unver Shahryar introduced *memani* dramas in the early seventies. These were played at the Adamji Auditorium and later at the Rex (Hashoo)Auditorium as well as other auditoriums in the city. These plays were largely slapstick comedies and were very popular among the traders and shopkeepers. The price of tickets was low, audiences were almost exclusively male and the humour therefore somewhat coarse. The early urdu plays in this genre were written by Furqan Hyder. The plays staged at present do not depend entirely on a script but the actors interact and exchange repartee with the audience. The disappearance of Rex auditorium and the general scarcity of theatres inthe city has dealt a blow to this popular theatre. The facilitation of this type of theatre would surely develop public taste for live theatre and nurture audiences for serious theatre.

Popular artistes Rita, Shazad Raza and Farooq Shazad in the 1995 stage play International Fakir *written and directed by Mehmood Usman Khan.*

The financial prospects of being in theatre are risky at best, and those who choose to contribute, may well have some of the religious fervour for the mystic roots of the theatre. The work is hard and the glamour perhaps overstated. The playwright, the actor, the director, and the

THE BRITISH COUNCIL

presents

EMLYN WILLIAMS

as *Charles Dickens*

The cover of a programme from an early British Council production.

set designer, all blend their efforts together only to conjure a reality of a moment.

Travelling troupes *of natak* or *nautanki*, casting the magic of their performance on the rural audience, enacting under shamianas or hardtop tents on the banks of the River Ravi, or the River Indus, the grassroot theatre which entertains fatigued and tired farmers far from the neon lights, has survived but in Karachi, it is only the urban theatre for the elite which really matters. It is studded with the big names of American, European and British playwrights, either in the form of adaptation or using text in the original. Parsi theatre is Karachi's past, *Is Shehr Ko Yahan Sey Dekho* is its present while *Dark Room* is its future; a mime theatre in

Newcomer Jugnu Salahuddin and the versatile Sania Saeed in a one-act play Balcony.

kabuki dress, written by Sarmad Sehbai and directed by Shoaib Hashmi, where avant garde and symbolism combine to take a step forward. Art form develops through a process of evaluation. Karachi is conscious of its growth in the medium of theatre, though it may be facing a lot of disappointment on many counts.

The presence of creative abundance is there, otherwise how could Karachi produce sixty-two plays within a period of ten years. Imran Aslam is a witness of that process of growth as he himself was associated with them in various capacities, as a playwright, actor, director, or producer. Various critics of newspapers in the country are witnessing this silent growth, experiencing Brecht and Beckett on one side and *Fantasticks* and *The Threepenny Opera*, on the other. In between grew *Rahat Jan* (*Hatak* by Manto) and *Lehaf* by Ismat Chughtai, one staged by Anjum Ayaz while the other was choreographed by Ms Mitha. A short story converted into a ballet.

The new generation of playwrights, actors, directors, and producers who do not carry the creative burden full time

Fahim Wyne and others star in one of the productions in English regularly put up in the city.

are to subsist through faith in this art form. Charles Dickens who himself was a great enthusiast and made his own cast 'nearly worked to death' wrote, 'It makes me wonder why one does things for nothing'. The answer to this enigma, perhaps is as complex as it is meaningless. Call it a compulsion, a madness of some sort, an inner urge which goes without rhyme and reason, or some heady excitement, the smell of the grease and paint, the throb and thrill highlighted by footlights, or simply the roar of the audience. Or, a commitment to a particular way of life to flourish, or perish, for the calling they have chosen to follow.

Karachi is full of such mad people who have cast their dice in favour of theatre. They are our only hope.

Cinema hoardings,
entertainment for the masses.

Chapter 15

A CLOSE-UP OF CINEMA, RADIO AND TELEVISION

Asif Noorani

The generation of the eighties, weaned on video cassettes and satellite channels, can hardly imagine the immense popularity which cinema enjoyed in Karachi, as it did elsewhere in the subcontinent. The golden period of cinema ran through the 'forties to the early 'eighties when it was dethroned, so to speak, by television.

Post-Partition Karachi inherited a large number of cinema houses—Majestic, Picture House, Plaza, Roxy (which was Rama before it was declared an evacuee property) Taj Mahal and Light House on Bunder Road and Regal and Mayfair, the open-air theatre (as cinemas were initially called), in Saddar. Then there were many others: Kumar, Nagina, Nigar (which was Prabhat until Partition) and Super, quite close to what is now M.A. Jinnah Road.

Many more show houses were built in not just the old localities but also the suburbs, particularly after Partition, boasted of a good number of cinema houses. Nazimabad, alone had four, and Liaquatabad two. It was a question of supply meeting demand. Today only one exists in these two localities. Many closed down in Saddar for instance, where Rex, the first to offer air-conditioning, Rio, Mayfair, Capital, Paradise, Regal and, quite recently, Odeon closed down. They yielded place to ugly and unimaginatively planned buildings, crammed with shops and offices.

Naz-o-Nishat, as the bus stop near the Seventh Day Adventist hospital was known, is still referred to by the same name, even though Naz Cinema, after a long legal battle, was demolished and the land is being used for building another non-descript shopping plaza. Ironically enough, it

*The demolition of
Naz Cinema,
end of an era.*

will continue to retain the name—Naz, in much the same way as Paradise and Rio markets do.

Gone are the days when friends and families used to plan a visit to a cinema a few days before the actual outing. There were separate counters for advance booking. Sundays used to have one extra show, and in the case of cinema houses, reserved for English movies, the Sunday morning shows usually offered an old hit for viewers who had missed them in their early screenings as also for those who were fond of repeat viewing.

The pop-corn munching generation, as the young men and women of the fifties and the sixties were called by their elders with some bit of disdain, made a beeline for restaurants after matinee shows to listen to their favourite songs on jukeboxes, while munching snacks. Children looked forward to being taken to such eateries as Pioneer Coffee House and Bundu Khan's famous *kabab-paratha* joint for dinner after the first show.

The front-benchers in the literal and the metaphoric sense were confined to the six annas or nine annas class. They were looked down upon (pun intended) by cine-goers sitting in the balcony and even those who went to the dress circle. Only Khayyam cinema had boxes, but the management saw to it that the tickets for those cubicles were sold only to families.

Cinemas also served as a rendezvous for callow romantics where they held hands in the dark. The only time I invited a young lady to a movie was at Khayyam Cinema. I was hoping that the company would be more exciting than the movie. Imagine my utter disappointment therefore, when the young lady came with a spoil-sport aunt, who approved of the rendezvous but made it a point to sit in between the two of us. Alas, my one chance of holding the young lady's hand was lost.

While talking of movies one cannot ignore the fact that Karachi gave the country some of the finest performers, both on and off stage. Among the actors were Waheed Murad, Mohammad Ali, Kamal, Shamim Ara, Nayyar Sultana and Lehri, to name just a few. Nadeem, who started his career as a playback singer in Karachi, made a name for himself in Dhaka , where his debut-making film *Chakori*, was produced. His second movie, like his first, proved to be a big box-office hit. On his return from East Pakistan Nadeem

Shabnam and Waheed Murad, matinee idols.

Deeba,
heartthrob
of millions.

tried to settle down in Karachi before moving to Lahore. Likewise, Shabnam and her composer husband Robin Ghosh, when they came to what was then West Pakistan, bought a house in Karachi initially.

Among the behind-the-screen performers who made their debut in Karachi and left the city reluctantly for greener pastures in Lahore, were director Pervez Malik, composers Sohail Rana and Khaleel Ahmad, singers Ahmad Rushdi and Mehdi Hasan, script writer Masroor Anwer, editor-director Iqbal Akhtar, cameraman Ayub and sound recordist C.G.C. Mandody. There were scores of others who started their careers in Karachi but after their first taste of success moved to the film capital of the country. Many film people who came from India, such as Nisar Bazmi, Nashad and Nakhshab made Karachi their home.

Even the burgeoning film industry in Lahore had to depend on Karachi for finance and three major distributors cum financiers—J.C. Anand, Nisar Murad and Mukhtar

Ahmad—had their main office. Anand's Eveready Pictures was the biggest film distribution house in Pakistan and his services to the country's film industry, particularly during its early stages, were second to none. Today his son, Satish Anand keeps the flag of Eveready Pictures flying. But unlike his father who concentrated only on movies, the younger Anand is also into television production. Nisar Murad and his only child Waheed Murad are no more and Mukhtar Ahmad's children gave up the film business long ago.

The first film studio to be built in Karachi was run by Deewan Sardarilal and the first movie to be produced in the city, *Mandi*, which featured old time singing star Khursheed was made in the studio. But as bad luck would have it the movie flopped miserably and the studio had to close down. A disheartened Deewan Sardarilal, who had the distinction of producing the first Pakistani movie, *Teri Yaad*, left for Bombay where his son has turned into a major film producer.

Eastern Film Studios, initially managed by A.G. Mirza and later by Saeed Haroon, was the first full fledged production studio. Many box-office hits were shot in this studio. Apart from Urdu and Sindhi films, the first Pushto film *Yusuf Khan-Sherbano* was also shot in this studio.

A smaller and not very well-equipped studio Modern Studios was built next door in the latter half of the sixties. Agha Khaleeli, a well known industrialist, set up the country's first colour film laboratory in Karachi too. All these institutions closed down. The studios dropped the shutter because for one thing there were more film making activities in Lahore, which was why the actors and the technicians who were in greater demand preferred to work there for they could hop from one studio to another and work in different shifts.

C.A. Rauf, veteran advertising man, set up International Studios in the industrial zone of Federal B Area in the seventies, but the studio caters only to advertising films and TV serials, made by independent producers.

Today, no feature film is produced in Karachi but one can see a revival of interest in movies. The more educated class may continue to watch television and get video films, but the less educated, lower middle class has returned to cinema houses. However, once in a while when a better film from Hollywood is imported, even the members of the upper class throng the cinemas, for a mini screen that a TV set offers is no substitute for the large screen in movie houses, where one is cut off from the outside world and where one is not likely to be disturbed by unannounced visitors or unexpected phone calls.

Like movies, radio's listenership has been revived to a certain extent with the launch of an FM station but it is not likely to recapture its lost glory. Again like cinema, the radio lost its coveted position to the new audio-visual medium in the late sixties, even though by that time, thanks to the availability of economically-priced transistorized radio sets, the radio had reached even the homes of the poor class.

During the fifties and the early sixties the radio station in Karachi, which was commissioned in 1948, had a great following. Much of the credit goes to Zulfiqar Ali Bokhari, the veteran broadcaster, who built up the station on solid grounds.

Such programmes as *Hamid Mian Ke Haan,* which had a record run, *Dekhta Chala Gaya* and *Muft Ka Jhagra* had a

Radio Pakistan.

A drama being recorded at the Radio Pakistan.

large body of loyal listeners, but no programme could equal the listenership of *Studio Number Nau*, which featured radio plays of a very high standard. At 9 p.m. on Sundays, the streets in Karachi wore a deserted look. I distinctly remember that while walking from one end of a street in Nazimabad to the other, one would not miss a single line from the play. Radio sets in every house were tuned to Karachi at that hour. Radio artists like Abdul Majid, S.M. Saleem, Arshe Munir, Mahmood Ali, Mohammad Yousuf, Humera Naim and, Sahab Qizilbash had a very large following among listeners.

Film music got a lot of support from the radio and the Karachi station's one hour programme *Aap Ki Farmaish* got so many requests for favourite numbers that at one stage they stopped announcing the names of the people writing to the programme producer for it was taking almost twenty-five per cent of the time.

Radio Ceylon was also very widely listened to and two of its programmes, *Binaca Geet Mala* which was broadcast on Sunday, and the programme of old hits *Aap Ke Anrodh Per*, were particularly very popular with film music enthusiasts. Compere Amin Sayani and announcer Gopal Sharma became household names.

There was more excitement and thrill in listening to the songs on the radio, because there was an element of inexpediency. As children, we used to take bets on which songs will make it to the top three positions in *Binaca Geet Mala* and if a particular song would be played in *Aap Ki Farmaish*—the one-hour programme on Sunday afternoons. The introduction of audio cassette players made one's favourite film songs much more accessible, but half the pleasure was lost for familiarity bred contempt. Before someone may say that gramophone records were there much before the audio cassettes gained currency, I might hasten to add that the discs and the record players were owned only by a minuscule minority. In a way, the cassettes robbed film music programmes of their popularity.

The first time Karachiites saw television was at the third Pakistan International Industrial Fair in the early sixties, when Philips had set up a small network.

Stars of Sitara aur Mehrunissa, *a popular TV serial.*

It was in 1967, two years after the TV stations in Lahore and Dhaka came on the air, that the Karachi station came into operation. In the early days, there were just a few hours of black-and-white transmission and Monday was the day-off as far as PTV was concerned. Such was the hold of television on Karachiites, that visiting friends and relatives was then largely restricted to Mondays. Some programmes such as the Haseena Moin serials and the American programmes had addictive viewers. I remember the parents of a bride and her groom had placed an advertisement in Dawn announcing that they had made arrangements for guests to watch the final episode of *The Fugitive* at the venue of the marriage. Someone who had gone to attend another wedding at the Beach Luxury Hotel told this writer that as many as six television sets were strategically placed in the 007 Hall of the hotel for the viewers to watch David Jansen eventually catch the one-armed man who had killed his wife.

Black-and-white sets were replaced by colour televisions in the late seveties and early eighties. Later in the decade television sets gained importance on another count: they became useful accessories to the video cassette players.

The onslaught of video cassettes could be gauged from the fact that almost every lane in residential areas sported a video renting parlour. A whole huge market of videoshops sprang up in Rainbow Centre, adjacent to Empress Market, where there are now shops specializing in video cassettes. If you wish to get a cassette of cricket matches you go to a specific shop and if you wish to buy videos of documentaries you go to another.

However, the invasion of satellite programme dish antennas have caused a big dent in the business of video cassettes. The introduction of cable TV is exposing our viewers to a number of foreign channels, but whenever there is a good Sindhi or Urdu serial from the two local channels, viewers switch over to them. Incidentally, Sindhi serials brought a touch of realism to PTV programmes and proof, if proof be needed, is that a couple of serials in the regional language became so successful that they were redone in Urdu and won wider applause all over the country, proving that Karachi Television has a treasure trove of talent.

The sunlit interior of the entrance hall of the once hugely popular Railway Hall Institute.

Chapter 16

A FIESTA OF ENTERTAINMENT

Anwer Mooraj

Entertainment in Karachi in the 'western' sense of the word, from the time the British hoisted the Union Jack until well after they pulled anchor in 1947 reflected in large measure the tastes and styles of the imperial power. At the outbreak of the first world war, when the sun had not yet set on the empire and Britannia still ruled the waves, Karachi was very much a British city.

> The English population of the Station was made up almost entirely of officials; either civil or military. There were only ten business houses in Karachi then. Social life was based on the life of society in England. Calling which was between the hours of 12 noon and 1 p.m. was *de rigueur* and strictly observed; unfortunate men having to wear frock coats and top hats. Ladies costumes consisted of voluminous skirts covering the feet with fold upon fold of garments underneath, and steel ribbed corsets enclosed and compressed their waists. All parties were strictly formal and for dinners, even in the hot weather, full evening tail suits, with stiff skirts, were worn.[1]

It is an interesting observation that out of the fifteen gentlemen who attended a meeting in Frere Hall on 25 May 1871 to discuss the possibility of starting a club in 'Kurrachee for the whole of Scinde' nine wore military uniforms, two were doctors and the other four civil servants.

It was possibly the Sind Club (when it was located in a bungalow on Elphinstone Street) to which the famous traveller and orientalist, Sir Richard Frances Burton, was referring when he wrote in 1876.

There is, I may tell you, a neat little club, but it lacks chambers. Karachi cannot yet boast of an hotel; nor will she before she belongs to the Panjab...[2]

While soirees were held on a regular basis at the homes of British officers, it wasn't until August 1873 that mention was first made of some sort of social activities in the prestigious Sind Club. A special meeting was called to decide whether the Club should hold a ball. The proposal put before the meeting was

> That a Ball be given by such Members of the Sind Club as wish to subscribe and that it be called the Sind Club Ball; such Ball to be held only if thirty shares be subscribed for by Members within the next seven days.[3]

The requisite number of subscribers was apparently forthcoming, and a fancy dress ball was held in Frere Hall. It wasn't until 15 October 1885 that the second Sind Club Ball was given. Ball number three took place in October 1888

> But it was not until 1892 that the Ball became an annual affair. From then onwards it was taken very seriously and several pages of the minute book were filled each year with the arrangements authorized for it, and the duties of the members who were appointed to superintend it, and to look after the comfort of the Club guests. All Officers of Regiments stationed in Sind and Quetta were invited, as was also the Agent to the Governor General at Quetta. Also all married couples belonging to the Gymkhana, except when the husband was a member of the Sind Club, received invitations...On all occasions full dress and decorations were worn.[4]

The quality of the food served was consistently good. Turbaned and uniformed native bearers, used to the shenanigans of the military and civil types, and trained to ignore the minor indiscretions of members who couldn't hold their liquor, were always in attendance.

A further advance in social life was the introduction in 1896 of band guest nights for men only. These were held every Saturday night and were apparently most popular, though in 1902 they were restricted to fortnightly events. The entry of ladies into the social life of the Club was still further encouraged in 1903 by the introduction of pre-dinner band evenings on the lawns of the Club. The band played on the lawn opposite the dining room and the other lawn was given up to tea parties.

> This institution served a very useful purpose for it enabled the 'burra Memsahibs' to entertain the younger men who had not yet reached the status of dinner invitation, and, what is more important, it gave the young men, who could not afford expensive dinner parties, the opportunity of returning hospitality and of entertaining their lady friends. Altogether the move was a most popular one, even among those members of the Club who were not invited to the tea parties; for they sat on the Billiard Room Chabootra enjoying their drinks, surveying the galaxy of beauty and fashion and unquestioningly delighting in the facetious remarks that passed among them. It was a fashion parade of Karachi's highest order, even to the extent of those who had been taken for a ride (and sometimes those who had not), changing from their dirty riding kit into immaculately clean breeches, top boots and intensely horsey riding coats.[5]

Social activities took place at two other clubs. One was the Karachi Boat Club, a tall timbered building overlooking the Chinna Creek, constructed in 1885, whose interesting feature is a combination of black woodwork and white plaster, and the other was the Karachi Gymkhana.

> Earlier known as the Ladies Club, it began as a small structure at the edge of the racecourse, but acquired a large Tudor-style building in 1886 when it moved to its present location on Scandal Point (now Club) Road.[6]

According to an ornamental plaque placed inside the entrance to the Gymkhana Lt. Col. G. B. Simpson was the first president. This was in 1886. W. W. Smart ICS, the second on the list, was elected president in 1923. The plaque is silent on the period in between the two dates.

The dance bands that performed regularly at these three clubs during the second world war, often attired in black tie and cummerband, played ballroom music in strict tempo and usually took their cue from their guru—Ken Mac of the Taj Mahal Hotel in Bombay.

While the British had their Lindy Hops and scavenger hunts, bridge parties and tennis courts, well-to-do Indian residents of Karachi, who had developed a taste for club life

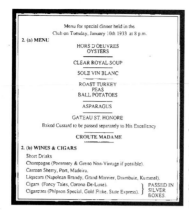

Menu for special dinner held in the
Club on Tuesday, January 10th 1933 at 8 p.m.

2. (a) MENU

HORS D'OEUVRES
OYSTERS

CLEAR ROYAL SOUP

SOLE VIN BLANC

ROAST TURKEY
PEAS
BALL POTATOES

ASPARAGUS

GATEAU ST. HONORE
Baked Custard to be passed separately to His Excellency

CROUTE MADAME

2. (b) WINES & CIGARS

Short Drinks
Champagne (Pommery & Greno Non-Vintage if possible).
Carmen Sherry, Port, Madeira.
Liqueurs (Napolean Brandy, Grand Marnier, Drambuie, Kummel).
Cigars (Fancy Tales, Corona-De-Luxe).   } PASSED IN
Cigarettes (Phipson Special, Gold Flake, State Express). } SILVER
                                                 BOXES.

*Dining at the Sind Club:
no expense was spared.*

but were still denied membership to the three established British clubs, decided it was time they had a place of their own. After considerable effort on the part of a handful of city elders, The Karachi Club was established in its present location on Dr Ziauddin Ahmed Road. Ballroom dances were a regular feature at the Club and a smooth wooden floor had been constructed for this purpose. On Sundays members could listen to concerts by a salon orchestra, as they sat on the shady lawn in rattan chairs and sipped their gin pahits.

By the year 1930 goods produced in the United Kingdom were very much in evidence in the few shops that existed. Pear's soap, Sanatogen wine, Cadbury's chocolate, Sloan's liniment, and Craven A cigarettes had become household words. Of the few cars that could be seen on the streets, the Austin and the Morris were the most prominent. And in the European restaurant at the railway station, the menu consisted of the inevitable clear soup, roast mutton with mint sauce, and fried potatoes, followed by the ubiquitous cream caramel, referred to by the native cook as *puteen*. Baked custard, a close cousin of the popular cream caramel, was apparently a standard item at the Sind Club. In a menu printed for a special occasion, it was 'passed separately to the Chief Guest' in preference to Gateau St.Honore!

> Some Indian cooks never graduated much beyond caramel custard, which was easy to make and convenient because there were always plenty of eggs and milk. However, it became so overworked it was nicknamed '365'—served every day of the year. Lady Hay recalls that they refused to have custard at home, since it was served in dak bungalows and railway stations *ad nauseum.*[7]

In the early 1950s, once the sea had swallowed a big red sun at evening, and revellers started getting ready for a night on the town, all roads led to the celebrated watering hole on the first floor of the Central Hotel known as The Casino. Nobody knew why the place had been given this particular nomenclature. There were no roulette tables or slot machines. In fact, no gambling ever took place on the

An advertisement, circa 1932, for De Reske cigarettes, exhorting the reader to 'Smoke Craven A for your throat's sake.'

"Tipside Down"

" Bother! I've lit my cigarette the wrong end!"

" Calm yourself, child. That's an 'ivory'-tipped De Reszke you've got hold of, and you can go on smoking it even if you have lit it 'tipside down.' You see, these new 'ivory' tips are quite unlike any other tips. They burn just like ordinary cigarette paper, without

taste and smell; so lighting up at the wrong end doesn't mean throwing away a first-rate cigarette like these. But next time see that you put the tip end in your mouth, and let your soft lips caress its gleaming ivory-like surface. Then you'll know the uttermost perfection of smoking comfort."

"IVORY"-TIPPED *or* PLAIN

DE RESZKE

Virginias

10 a shilling

Other De Reszke Cigarettes include *Americas*, 25 for 1/10, *Americas de Luxe* (Hand Made), 25 for 2/- ; and *Jeans* (Turkish), 25 for 3/2
You are invited to try any of these cigarettes as our guest in the De Reszke Salon, 110 Piccadilly, London, W.1 (J. Millhoff & Co. Ltd.)

premises. The Casino was essentially a restaurant where a guest was served an excellent meal on clean, crisp table cloths of the pink chequered design favoured in France, and all the alcoholic beverages he could consume. Great attention was paid to detail. Sparkling cutlery and expensive crockery which carried the Casino logo and freshly cut flowers were in evidence every day.

The place had an atmosphere which the dapper, balding manager, a white Russian emigre known as Arty, tried to perpetuate. Arty was rather like one of those Ruritanian counts that one read about. He occasionally sported a monocle, smoked Turkish cigarettes stuck in a long ivory holder, and was full of anecdotes about intrigues in high places. He had that look of splendid imperturbability which is the hallmark of the maitres d'hotel in the more fashionable eating establishments of Europe. But though the food was outstanding, the clientele that poured in night after night, dropping names, and flashing banknotes in an effort to secure a table, came chiefly for the booze and the music. There was no shortage of the former and the latter was provided by a pianist named Stefan Eros, and his Hungarian Serenaders. It was a band the likes of which the city had never seen or heard before, and was not likely to see or hear again.

Night after night as champagne corks popped and waiters tripped over inebriated revellers who had slid under their tables, Eros and his Serenaders recreated the romance of pre-war central Europe. This was the era of ballroom music, of accordions and violins, and Spanish steel guitars, of Mantovani, Geraldo, Cugat, and the Lecuona Cuban Boys. It was an era of romance and elegance and taste when dances were intimate and like the tango, sensual. One moment Eros took his guests on a musical tour of Vienna and Berlin in the finest tradition of Marek Weber, and the next the thump of conga drums, the swish of maraccas and the click of claves would transport them to the open air dance halls of Havana. On one occasion, a clutch of dancers had just finished negotiating a tricky Argentine tango when the Casino was invaded by a group of noisy American sailors in uniform. Eros suddenly unleashed a tornado of stomps and rags of King Oliver vintage that made the boys in white so happy that they bought everybody several rounds of drinks.

Most evenings the band packed up around two o'clock in the morning, but on weekends the musical instruments were finally put away when a rising sun decanted burgundy through the high windows, and bleary-eyed revellers were served a hearty breakfast, courtesy of Arty. But after a while the novelty wore off. And in spite of the Russian's efforts things began to slide. Eros didn't renew his contract and fights broke out frequently between inebriated guests, and at times, between the guests and the staff. The police were often called in to cart off the more exuberant of the riotously festive guests some of whom had started to wade deep in the underworld. The time had come for a change. The nightbirds wanted something better, something more exclusive and sophisticated.

The Palace Hotel which housed the popular Le Gourmet.

Karachi had come of age. The big spenders, fuelled by a boom in the textile and jute industries, suddenly descended on the city. They wanted action of the kind they had seen in the night clubs of Bombay and Calcutta. And this is just what Le Gourmet promised to do. Situated on the ground floor of the Palace Hotel, a solid structure with an old world charm which later belonged to the Ramchandani family, the Gourmet was the closest thing to a French restaurant the city had seen. The manager, Narinder Bakhshi, promptly set about introducing dishes like Chateaubriand and Chicken a la Kiev. Having a steak cooked on a stove at one's elbow was quite a novelty for the Karachi of the 1950s.

Panna, star attraction at the Gourmet

And as there was an unlimited supply of whisky, and the wine list contained the best that Bordeaux, Burgundy and the valley of the Loire had to offer, the more cosmopolitan guest knew the evening was going to be special.

The Gourmet had the usual ingredients which made for a successful night club—good food, a well stocked cellar, wonderful music and a congenial atmosphere. Everybody who was somebody wanted to be seen in the place. The Gourmet, however, introduced a new element—cabaret. Besides the usual assortment of heavily rouged Can Can girls, who threw their long gaitered legs into the air while the Italian orchestra played a selection from 'Orpheus in the Underworld', there were also sophisticated magic shows, experiments in levitation and solo performances by a sensational local classical dancer, Panna.

Dinshaw B. Avari owner of the Beach Luxury Hotel, located off Queens Road, was certainly aware of the competition. He had a wonderful orchestra led by a dashing young band leader, Julian Young. But this was just not enough. What he desperately needed was a singer to serenade the wayfarers who used to collect in the creek in the evening to cool off in the sea breeze, and down a bottle or two of Chianti. Tino, who hailed from sunny Italy, arrived in 1958 accompanied by his German girlfriend Marlene, and a large repertoire of Neapolitan folk songs. The duo took Karachi by storm. Within a few weeks the porch in the Beach Luxury Hotel, fringed by date and coconut palms, became the hottest spot in town. Way past the happy hour, after the tenor had wrung from the last Neapolitan serenade every drop of its emotional juices, the audience waited with bated breath as the orchestra struck the opening bars of the all time favourite from the grasslands of the Argentine—'Adios Pampa Mia'. It was the duo's *piece de resistance*, a truly shattering climax to an evening of great entertainment. The rhythmic buoyancy, the tension of the beat, the range of instrumental colour, and the increasingly intense and confident ecstasy with which the duo countered the crisp instrumental attack, made the tango truly compelling.

There was always a number of encores, for the audience just didn't think it had ever had enough. Marlene's crowd winner was a catchy Venezuelan number called 'Alma Llanera' which Lina Romay, singing with Xavier Cugat and his orchestra, had immortalized in the 1944 film *Bathing Beauty*. Marlene had a wonderful smoky voice and her sharp edged phrasing was most effective. Tino, not to be outdone, would then plunge into the ever popular 'Malaguena'. Emitting a fearsome flamethrower energy, he would stretch the long, sustained melody, hanging on to a single high note for a full two minutes before unfurling long lines of lyrics with spontaneous melody-spinning of great originality.

By the time Avari inaugurated his 007 nightclub in 1964, Tino and Marlene had already set sail for the Bay of Naples. But they left behind a void which has never really been filled. They were the last musical ambassadors of an age of elegance and good taste.

The management of the Inter Continental Hotel, anxious to cash in on the growing interest in night life, diverted some of the traffic to the Nasreen Room, a late night restaurant which appealed to the *nouveau riche*. But in spite of the band, good food, and a well stocked cellar, the place never had quite the ambiance of the Gourmet, or the exuberance of the Casino.

Meanwhile, as the booze flowed and the locals developed a preference for fading continental blondes, a number of seedy establishments cropped up in different parts of the city. The Excelsior, located off Elphinstone Street, was a pioneer of the sleazy joints where cabaret meant strip tease. Posters and advertisements regularly billed the performers as stars of the Folies Bergere, but the girls, slightly mawkish, occasionally maudlin, whimsically shaking their partially unclad bodies with exhausting twinkles, invariably turned out to be old campaigners from the bawdy nightclubs of Istanbul and Beirut. The client who had already tucked away a quart of the distilled essence of grain never knew the difference. Nor did he particularly care, as long as the girls were white, voluptuous and available.

There were other places that offered a different musical fare. A Filipino, Francisco, and his Serenaders appeared every night at the Marina Hotel after an initial stint at the Excelsior. A softly scampering muted guitar, seething with Hawaiian references, churned out gleaming classics like 'Sweet Leilani' and 'Sing me a song of the islands.' For a few rupees a guest got a long, cool drink made from fermented coconut water, and a glimpse of Francisco's daughter, Conchita, a grass skirt clinging to her slim waist, a lei of hibiscus around her neck, and a gardenia in her long black hair as she swayed to a hula. This was the only place in Karachi that played the kind of music that Felix Mendelssohn and Lani MacIntyre had popularized in Britain during the war years.

For lovers of Jazz and Swing who lived in the fast lane, the place to go to on Sunday mornings in 1950 and 1951 was the Marina Hotel opposite Electric House, where trumpeter Pat Blake held court. This was Jazz at its best. Blake was an artist in whom an organizational intelligence and an appetite for improvising were in creative balance. He hit notes as if sculpting in marble, and his rough, hard-driving style was the invigorating antithesis of classical grace. For sheer swing and energy his band swept the board.[8]

There were other smaller groups that gravitated around a pianist or a drummer who performed for a fee. One of the most notable of these, who was too implacably talented to just fade away, was F.X.Fernandes, a piano teacher by day and leader of a combo by night. One of the great catalysts of popular interest in strict tempo dance music, he was at his best when ploughing through a rumba. His piano was always full of storming base lines, explosive chords and slashing runs.

Those who just wanted a little background music, a drink and a plate of nuts without any sexual frills, frequented one of the many bars that could be found in Saddar. Mondi's in

Frere Street and the Ritz Bar opposite the Paradise Cinema in Clarke Street, with their swing doors, were the market leaders. But the Paris bar on Preedy Street, the U-Bar on Garden Road, the Empress Bar and Toddy shop near Empress Market, and the Hirjina Bar on Frere Street also had their loyal and regular customers, as did the Cecil Bar, the Marina Bar and Nusserwanji's. Almost every alcoholic beverage from rum and vodka, brandy and gin to the locally brewed toddy was available.

A number of eateries served excellent meals over the years, and the foreign tourist would be taken to places with exotic names like the Four Seasons (in the Metropole Hotel), the Chandni Lounge (in the Inter Continental Hotel) and Shezan. But the local gourmet in search of a good grill would invariably select Agha's Tavern in the North Western Hotel— one of the city's classiest licensed restaurants.

In Karachi around the time of Partition, native musical entertainment was limited to occasional presentations by Sindhi Hindu musicians and dancers, and to what was available in the bawdy houses in Napier Road within the confines of the red light area. With the establishment of Radio Pakistan in Karachi, the foundation of a distinct Pakistani tradition was laid. Radio Pakistan was, in fact, a kind of institutional fulcrum which tried not only to evolve a separate tradition by absorbing many of the folk cultures

A side view of the North-Western, one of the railway hotels, which served the finest cuisine that money could buy.

that existed in the country, but also by encouraging and nourishing a host of local singers and musicians, some of whom subsequently achieved fame and popularity.

When compiling a history of native style entertainment it is fashionable to start with the stars who carved out a name for themselves at home and abroad—singers like the late Nusrat Fateh Ali Khan, whose appeal lay in the personal, idiosyncratic spontaneous transformation of songs and the recognition of the subtle, expressive and unique qualities of the human voice. And the late Ghulam Farid Sabri whose lustrous baritone and pulsating vibrato won him many admirers. Both *qawwals* were in constant demand in Karachi at a variety of functions.

But no appreciation of the great musical fabric that unfolded in Karachi during the last fifty years would be complete without mentioning some of the pioneers, and there was a whole raft of older singers that the historian would cast in the 'classical' mould.[9]

A word of explanation is necessary at this stage. The music that a listener heard on Radio Pakistan at the time of partition and the music that he still hears today (which could be perhaps described as the result of 'stylistic cross pollenization') is essentially melodic. This is in sharp contrast to the European tradition where early melodic music changed into current harmonic music. Though efforts have been made to ensure that serious Pakistani music evolves a distinct and separate cultural identity, for the origins of the classic style one has to turn to the roots of the subcontinental tradition, which is not only one of the oldest in the world but also a major system of music. The music of India, according to the learned music historian, B.C. Deva

Is one of the most highly developed and sophisticated musical systems of human society. Particularly its micro-tonal pitch differences (sruti-s as they are called), its melodic schema (ragas) and the rhythmic subtleties of its tala are amongst the most cherished artistic contributions of India to world culture.[10]

Many female Pakistani singers distinguished themselves in either, or both the classical and light-classical tradition.[11]

An important area of musical entertainment which, while extremely popular in Karachi, also came to the notice of impressarios and promoters abroad, is the qawwali. Ghulam

Farid Sabri and Nusrat Fateh Ali Khan have already been mentioned. Both qawwals received considerable exposure in the west, where the hypnotic beat has an instant appeal. The former introduced the saxophone into his collection of instruments which produced a ripe, eloquent lyricism. He also enlarged his range of percussion by throwing in a pair of bongos which did not go down too well with the purists. And the latter, influenced by the highly articulate Englishman, Peter Gabriel, who introduced him to the modern disco beat which enlarged his palette of sound effects, ended up producing a more meditative trance-like music. One of his most trenchant recordings which became an instant hit in Pakistan and abroad and triggered a cult is *Mast Qalander.*

Before the arrival of these two musical giants of entertainment, a number of qawwals had transmitted their beautiful sounds over the ether. By far the most outstanding was Manzoor Ahmed Khan who later adopted the surname Niazi. He frequently sounded as if he was on a knife edge of strength and poignant vulnerability. He was greatly in demand at functions and his popularity spread like bushfire. Qawwals are usually classified according to their style: *sufiana* (devotional) and *awami* (popular). Certain qawwals such as Azeem Prem Ragi, Ghulam Fareed Sabri and his brother Ghulam Maqbool, Kalwa Banney, and Zaki Taji sang both

(From L to R) Amir Mohammed, Ghulam Ghaus, Masroor Ahmed, Manzoor Ahmed Khan Niazi, Mahmood Ahmed and Abdullah.

(From L to R) Farooq Ahmed Khan, Mohammed Ahmed Khan, Mahmood Ahmed Khan, Raees Ahmed Khan and Khaleeq Ahmed Khan.

types of qawwalis. Manzoor Hussain Niazi, Bahauddin, Naseer Khan, Jaffer Nizami, Farooq Mian, and Ghulam Khusro specialized in *sufiana*, wheras Baray and Chote Saleh Mohammad, Sami Azad, Roshan Sitara, Ata Mohammad and Ahmed Azad sang the popular or *awami* type of qawwalis.

Some connoisseurs of indigenous music spent endless hours listening to their favourite instrumental soloist. Instruments (*vadya*), according to B.C.Deva, are considered to be of four basic types

> *tata vadya* (stringed), *sushira vadya* (wind), *avanaddha vadya* (drums), and *ghana vadya* (bells, plates and rods). Among the *tata vadya* are the *veena*, the sitar the tamboora (plucked) the *sarangi*, the *dilruba* (bowed); the wind instruments are the flutes, the *shehnai*, the *naferi* and the *nagasvaram* (Indian oboes); the drums comprise the *tabla*, the *pakhawaj*, the *mraidang*, and so on; bells, rods, etc., are common though not generally used in concert music.[12]

The *sarangi nawaz* who performed for Radio Pakistan during the last fifty years were Baba-e-Moseeqi Ustad Bundoo Khan, Ustads Zahuri Khan, Nathoo Khan, Hamid Hussain, Wahid Hussain, Zahid Hussain, and Nawab Ali Khan. One heard also Ghulam Mohiyuddin, Noor Mohammad Khan, Faiz Khan, Hussain Bakhsh, Niazu Khan, Ibrahim Khan, Ghafoor Khan, Waheed Muradabadi, Khan Mehboob Khan and Sajid Noor Khan.

When one mentions the sitar the five names that immediately spring to mind are Sharif Khan Poonchwalla, Ustad Kabir Khan, Ustad Machchoo Khan, Ustad Imdad Hussain, and the irrepressible Ustad Raees Khan—the most important living sitar player in the country. There were also *beenkar* such as Ustad Habib Ali Khan and A. Rashid Khan, and Ustad Rafique Ghaznavi who was a virtuoso on the *vicheetra veena*. The *sarod* in the hands of Ustad Nazar Hussain became an instrument capable of producing the most divine metallic sound which was often spine tingling in its intensity. Lal Mohammad and Ustad Salamat Hussain produced some of the most soulful wails in recorded music when they played the flute, capturing a flowing and contemplative sound in the company of ideally flexible, responsive partners.

The banjo is normally associated with the southern and south-eastern United States. There was, however, a couple of banjo players in Karachi, Ustad Bilawal Belgium and Khaliq Dad who achieved a high degree of professionalism. Bilawal, who was a tough musician who had endured numerous hardships, apparently adopted the surname 'Belgium' after being told that in spite of being overrun by hostile forces in both world wars the country had survived with honour!

No orchestra is complete without the violin, generally regarded as a European instrument and an integral part of both the symphony orchestra as well as the chamber music ensemble, even though the bow, according to Curt Sachs, is first mentioned in Persia and China in the ninth century A.D. The inclusion of the violin in the Radio Pakistan orchestra is possibly due to the pre-Partition influence of the various orchestras that performed over All India Radio, whose music directors recognized the great brilliance of tone and the highly dramatic and virtuoso qualities of the instrument. The infinite variety of its technical capacities, ranging from all manner of bowing, to plucking and percussive effect were not lost on the Radio Pakistan violinists, though the use of pizzicato was rare. Quite a few violinists who were known for their excellent fingerwork exploited their skills to luxuriate in the contrasting textures of sensual pleasure and poignancy.[13]

The *avanaddha vadya* element in the classical music of the subcontinent is of supreme importance. As in New Orleans Jazz where musicians traded riffs as part of the call-and-response tradition, the tabla player engages in a similar *sawal-jawab* dialogue with a sitar or sarangi player. The celebrated Indian sitar virtuoso, Ravi Shankar, frequently engaged in light hearted *jogal bandi* with his highly

Amy Minwalla: a superb dancer who was greatly in demand.

Parveen Qasim: in the execution of the Kathak she was unsurpassed.

Raffi Anwar, Nahid Siddiqui, Sahira Shahjehan, and Nazir Ahmed, stars of the PIA Arts Academy and cultural ambassadors of Pakistan.

accomplished tabla player, Allah, Rakha to the amusement and enjoyment of an appreciative audience. Karachi had a round dozen of highly gifted *tabla nawaz* who performed in a variety of concerts and other musical functions.[14]

No description of native entertainment is complete without mentioning dance, of which Karachi has always reaped a rich harvest. One has to only mention the words 'classical dancing' in an enlightened group of older citizens and the names of Amy Minwalla, Panna, Parveen Qasim and Nahid Siddiqui leap up like a highland fling. Amy Minwalla has always been something of a legend in Karachi, and Parveen Qasim is the finest Kathak dancer this city has had the good fortune to watch. Ustad Shafiullah Khan, senior music teacher at the PACC, fondly recalls that occasion in 1961 at the Sikandar Hall in Dhaka when a fierce, three-way competition took place between Amy Minwalla, Parveen Qasim, and the actress-dancer Rani. Each girl gave everything she had in a programme calculated in both content and performance to leave an ineradicable impression on its audience. At the conclusion of the session a highly appreciative General Umrao Khan presented each girl with a shining guinea.

When cultural delegations were sent abroad by the Pakistan government, the dances that were chosen were usually those that were supposed to represent the folk cultures of the four provinces. A number of talented young men and women were trained at what used to be the PIA Arts Academy. Some of the folk dances like the khattak and the bhangra had an authentic touch, but direct borrowing from a variety of sources resulted in a wide range of kitsch.[15]

In 1964, R.K. Ramesh initiated the Ramesh Arts Circle— a cultural group which bivouacked off the streets of Karachi and entertained bystanders with a selection of songs and dances and the odd clowning routine. Ramesh performed with his three daughters and son. Today, his grandchildren are doing the same sort of thing, a thread of performance tradition having been passed down by some process of cultural osmosis.

A number of cultural groups like the Ramesh ensemble sprung up over the years, the most prominent of which was the Azad Art Circle, established by Qamar Azad and Anwer Baloch. After the death of the former, Anwer Baloch set up the Paradise Club which did quite well. A number of clubs subsequently mushroomed of which Mahmood Light Music, Bazm-e-Sangeet, the Jubilee Art Circle, Pak Modern Art, and the Rim Jhim Art Circle had their clientele. These

The fisherman's dance: a bit of kitsch for the tourist.

Vital and Rozina:
carrying on the
tradition.

musical groups also had their patrons, and provided performers a springboard for future engagements. Comedians such as Moin Akhtar and Aslam Chabela, dancers like Salomi and Reshma, singers such as Farida Tabassum and Parveen Akhter, and musicians of the calibre of Javed Alla Ditta and Ghulam Ali, in a sense, served their apprenticeship in these art circles and clubs. In this connection Nawaz Ghulam Hussain Qadir needs special mention. He was not only a distinctive compere who was associated with Radio Pakistan, but also the founder of the Qadri Art Circle through which a number of stage shows were organized and promoted.

At the time of the second world war there was an ethnic minority in Karachi of a fairly substantial size. This was the Anglo-Indian community which provided the middle management in the railways, customs, dockyards and police. Under the British the 'Anglos', as they were frequently referred to, enjoyed certain privileges. After Partition, however, they tried to come to grips with a changing political environment and discovered their status had been redefined. The more adventurous migrated to the United Kingdom and Australia. Those that remained tried to adjust, however unsuccessfully. Though the 'Anglos' practiced the Christian faith, and though many of them could have passed for Europeans, they found themselves occupying a relatively low rung on the social ladder and were discouraged from joining the three exclusive gentlemen's clubs, deeply steeped in tradition where British brahmins carried on the caste system which controlled membership and attendance.

Ian Stephens put it rather nicely in a passage written in the 1940s entitled 'The British Caste System', which appeared in Laura Sykes' eminently readable book about British mores and folkways in India. Though the observations refer essentially to British attitudes in Calcutta they were true of other parts of India as well. Stephens writes

> British society in India, over the decades, had evolved peculiar... snobberies of its own, borrowing (no doubt subconsciously) from the Hindu caste system, and creating distinctions undreamed of "at home". Civilians, in the covenanted Government services, especially the ICS, became in effect Brahmins, calmly conscious of superiority over all the others. And Army officers assumed a stand-offish Kshatriya mien. These two constituted the topmost British castes... Oddest probably, however, was the caste cleavage within the business community itself. You'd find it in most of the big cities, but specially evident in Calcutta. There, to be in 'commerce', gave vastly more status than 'trade'. The latter was thought degrading. It made a really low level Vaisya out of you... Luckily a newspaperman, anyway if on *The Statesman's* staff and a friendly sort, could wiggle through most of the indigenous British caste-structure without much annoying anyone...[16]

The 'Anglos' had their own meeting place located next to the race course in the cantonment area. This was the

The entrance to the
Railway Hall Institute.
Inset: A section of
the tiled roof.

Railway Hall Institute, named after A.G. Hall, director general of Pakistan Railways after partition, affectionately referred to as the Loco. On week days a member could enjoy a dish of curry and rice, washed down by a bottle of beer, supplied by the Murree Brewery for about eight rupees. And on Saturdays around eight in the evening, a stream of young men in slacks and shirts, their short sleeves tucked up an extra inch to reveal rippling biceps, their hair carefully combed and brilliantined, turned up with their young ladies at the Loco. They came by tram, bicycle, motor-cycle and *gharry*. And they certainly knew how to enjoy themselves. The bands that performed were made up of local boys who were as talented as they were

One of the original pillars
now covered by plaster

The crest of the pillar.

A section of the building seen through the arch in the portico.

Two bricks stored in the manager's office carry the legend 'BASEL MISSION TILE WORKS' and '1865'.

The enchanted garden where time seems to stand still.

The deserted ballroom with its wooden floor, which once quivered to the explosive rock 'n' roll beat

The swimming pool with its blue tiled floor, cool and inviting and inert as glass.

enthusiastic. They played all sorts of dance music, from hot jazz of Jelly Roll Morton vintage to the fiery Latin beat of the undisputed king of the Cuban son, Don Azpiazu. Romantic interludes were provided by budding young tenors who emulated the style of Bing Crosby, the high priest of the crooners.

No description of a night out at the Loco would be complete without mentioning the inevitable jam session. It

was in this department that the dancers excelled. The way
the young studs threw their partners over their shoulders,
under their arms and between their legs, working up a lather
of sweat, while a highly charged audience clapped in unison
to the hypnotic beat, whipping up a crescendo of applause
as the couples finally sank to their knees, exhausted but
exhilarated, was the high point of the evening's
entertainment. The Loco retained its appeal for a decade
after partition, but as it lost its ground root support it
gradually faded into the mists of memory.

Karachi's other significant Christian minority is the Goan
community, which traces its origin to a former Portuguese
colony on the west coast of India. Local Goans, whose
members are almost exclusively Roman Catholic, are loyal
and patriotic citizens of Pakistan who have always risen to
the call of duty. Profoundly religious they have been able to
keep up many of their traditions, and the local parish in
certain localities continues to form a focal point for
community activity. The more affluent members of this
community are widely travelled and many have made the
pilgrimage to the Vatican. But it is a rare Goan who, while
planning his international itinerary, has not wanted to or
thought about slipping in a fortnight's visit to the land of
his forefathers, for there are few places on earth that are
lovelier than the 63-mile long strip of coastline on the
Malabar coast of India, 235 miles south of Bombay.
Copywriters churning out travel folders have tried to outdo
one another when describing the place, but few writers have
captured the sights and sounds and flavours of Goa better
than Frank Simoes in his brief preface to Thomas Vaz's
portfolio of photographs on the land of his birth

> Goa's children have long sought to celebrate the many-splendid
> joys of their land in verse, word, song and image. Nature aids
> and abets. Virgin dawns reveal a land of lush green valleys and
> serendipitous beaches where your's are likely to be the only
> footprints, highlands of burnt amber, sparkling rivers, springs
> and fountains, groves of mango, casuarina, palm and endless
> horizons of emerald paddy, newly minted towns burnished with
> laughter and good fellowship: all one and at peace with a richly
> tapestried past, a cultural heritage that spans thousands of years
> and pays handsome tribute to the rich legacies of Dravidian,
> Hindu, Muslim and Portuguese empires.

*The Karachi Goan
Association Building
which hosted Gilbert
and Sullivan operas.*

Legions of conquerors have passed this way, yet there are no scars. The people are essentially happy and generous of spirit. The values of kinship and community are held sacred. The ancient blessings are still given, each dusk, parent to child, grandparent to parent, until the very oldest blesses the youngest by the charismatic laying on of hands. It is impossible to tell where a village ends and the fields begin because the symbiosis is whole and complete: man and his environment are in seamless communion. A small but singular miracle.[17]

The values of kinship and community are still cherished in Karachi, whether the Goan is at worship or at play. This is a community that has produced cardinals (like His Eminence the late Joseph Cordeiro), bishops, several priests and nuns. Karachi Goans have held high ranking and responsible posts in the Pakistan armed forces, government departments (like Cyril D'Cruz, chairman of the Peshawar Electricity Board), judiciary (such as Justice C.M.Lobo and

Justice H.T.Raymond), customs, railways (like Frank D'Souza, member of the Railway Board before partition), posts and telegraphs and the Karachi Port Trust. Of the gentlemen mentioned in this paragraph, the last four served as president of the Karachi Goan Association.

There is, however, one area in which the Goan community has always excelled—and that is in the field of music and dance. On 15 February 1886 when the first Penny Reading was held at the residence of one of its members, a highly responsive audience heard recitals and orchestral overtures which included Haydn's Second Symphony and Schubert's Sonata No.2. On 16 February 1887, the day the Golden Jubilee of the reign of Queen Victoria was celebrated, the foundation stone of the Portuguese Goa Association was laid amidst great pomp and ceremony. The building was finally completed at a cost of 14,013 rupees (which included the price of the land) and the opening ceremony which was held on 24 May 1888 was celebrated by holding a grand ball.

The building, however, though it contained a library proved to be grossly inadequate for the growing needs of the community. And so, on 22 February 1903 at a special general meeting it was decided to purchase a plot on Depot Lines and to construct, among other things, a spacious hall. Two years later on Easter Sunday, the opening ceremony of the new PGA hall was performed by R.P. Barrow, ICS, collector and district magistrate of Karachi. As expected there was considerable festivity and a fifty-piece orchestra, conducted by Arthur James Fernandes, enchanted the large gathering of the representatives of the city.

The imposing new hall, designed by Moses Somake, has a large upper storey which is used as a concert hall as well as a ballroom. In 1929 Cincinnatus F.D'Abreo, one of the most outstanding members of the Goan community, died. A marble bust erected in his memory still stands in the lounge.

1936 was in many ways an important year for the community. Not only was the name of the Association changed to the KGA (Karachi Goan Association), the year also marked its Golden Jubilee. What better way to celebrate this important anniversary than by staging one of the most delightful of the Gilbert and Sullivan Savoy Operas—*The Gondoliers*! A distinguished audience which included the governor of Sindh, Sir Launcelot Graham and Lady Graham, attended. In 1941, after nine months of gruelling practice, the members staged another Gilbert and Sullivan opera— *The Pirates of Penzance.* On opening night the governor of Sindh Sir Hugh Dow and Lady Dow attended along with the entire Sind cabinet. There was a standing ovation when the final curtain came down. Goan elders reflect with a certain pride that during the interval, Sir Hugh visited the cast in the green rooms, complimented the director on the gorgeous costumes and performance and remarked that the production would have brought envy to the Doyly Carte Opera Company.[18]

Though the Goans were quite expert in staging all manner of theatrical productions, it is in the field of western music and dance that they are unsurpassed. Like the Filipinos they appear to be born with some special gift for appreciating melody, harmony and rhythm, and for passing on this gift to the next generation.

The bands that performed in the KGA Hall through both world wars tackled every kind of music score that came down the publisher's pike. Couples danced to the Charleston, the Lindy Hop, the Lancers, the one-step, the paso-double, the Gay Gordons, the Valeta, and the Lambeth Walk. These were followed by bouts of boogie woogie and later, rock'n'roll. The hard core of dancers, however, preferred ballroom dancing (or what British bandleader Victor Sylvester referred to as 'strict tempo'). This was something the Goan musical groups played with equal facility.

Some of the bands that made a mark, and are fondly remembered by members of the older generation, are the Correas—(Alex and Micky with Tex O'Shea), Jitterbug Joe, The Keynotes (with Janu Vaz), and the Soares Brothers. The Correas were brimming with all the old pre-Bop virtues of relaxed, loping rhythms, conversational solos, accessible themes and lots of Blues. Jitterbug Joe had some awesome percussion. When he played Jazz one heard the idiom's pungent tonalities, switch-back rhythms and ensemble sounds. The Keynotes will be remembered for their swinging elegance, their superb vocal improvization, and the uninhibited simplicity with which they developed a flowing, even, inexorable rhythmic momentum. And the Soares Brothers had a little bit of everything: oblique, muted trumpet style, fragile alto sound and velvety baritone, sparky cross rhythms and a rich tapestry of percussion. With the coming of prohibition, and the ban on gambling in the late seventies, the character and nature of entertainment in Karachi, in the 'western' sense of the term, underwent a transformation. The serving of alcohol became a strictly clandestine affair in some clubs, but the bars all disappeared. So did the cabarets and strip joints. Regrettably the coffee houses, where long-haired intellectuals of various persuasions spent endless hours dawdling over a cup of espresso or cappucino, the worries of the world draped across their beanpole shoulders, are no more. Customers fondly remember Zelin's Coffee House, situated on the corner of Victoria Road and Bunder Road which was established at the time of the Korean War, and could be described as the market leader. The place was hugely successful. For a few annas, a customer was offered a steaming cup of coffee brewed from Brazilian coffee beans and an opportunity for a stimulating discussion. In the early fifties the philosophers Sartre and Hegel were still the high priests of the temple, and it was quite fashionable to be an existentialist or a dialectical materialist.

Meanwhile, a revolution in music and dance had taken place in the United States, Europe and parts of the far east. Ballroom dancing was limited to a few exclusive establishments and was gradually being suplemented by 'modern dancing' where couples are united by the vague consciousness of a shared activity. Nightclubs which featured orchestras and bands cut their overheads and replaced them with a disc jockey, a selection of cassettes and a sophisticated amplification system, or small groups which used a synthesizer, the inevitable accoustic guitars and percussion.

The idea soon took root in Karachi and discos proliferated in the city in the early eighties. They popped up in five star hotels and in a number of highly unlikely places. One of the more successful discos was *Juliana* in the Holiday Inn, with its neon flourescence and its glitzy revolving crystal ball which hung from the ceiling, dispensing light and casting a nervous vigilance over the merry makers. 'Juliana' also closed down as did many of the others.

What the future western entertainment scene will be only time can tell. Perhaps a new kind of disco will emerge with more impersonal equipment. Perhaps it will disappear altogether as the younger generation makes a renewed effort to discover its roots.

A student relaxes: suggesting a life of unruffled serenity.

Chapter 17

BEING YOUNG IN THE FIFTIES

Anwer Mooraj

As I sat on the deck of the cargo steamer that bright and sunny March morning in the early fifties, watching the hungry bows bite open another horizon I thought of the city that I was leaving behind, perhaps forever. And as the ship gyrated to the piston throb that was bringing me that much closer to Genoa and Antwerp, I knew that a chapter of my life was closing, permanently and irrevocably. Those days of carefree youth, of tuck shops and midnight feasts, of pranks and practical jokes, and schoolboy romances where one talked and wrote a great deal of high falutin, were finally over. Once I got to London I would be accosted by a world of budgets and targets, and people programmed for competition. That winter, after I had successfully toured the towering landscape of landladyland, which had painted on its portcullis 'bed and breakfast' and the birds had died or flown their green and silent attics, my city came back to me in bits and pieces, forming a mosaic of people and places and events...

How well I remember the Karachi of the fifties. Everything was so safe and peaceful. On the economic front the scheming trawlers had not yet started to plough the sea's upset meadow. And on the political front there was a great deal of rhetoric without any real achievement. Ethnic violence was unheard of, and public enemy number one was the bicycle thief, a close relative of the nocturnal burglar. The urban armed dacoit, mercifully, had not yet appeared on the horizon. What a contrast to the roaring nineties where first information reports at police stations are simply littered with details of armed robbers forcibly taking away cars and motor-cycles at gunpoint, or robbing householders while holding women and children hostage. In the fifties there was considerable respect for the law. Stopping at the red light was absolutely mandatory, and offenders were duly punished. Examples of policemen offering an errant motorist a highly irregular, but less expensive option in settling a traffic violation fine, were extremely rare, and in the instances where it did occur the policeman was instantly dismissed.

The middle management of the Karachi police was occupied by a number of Anglo-Pakistanis who looked quite resplendent in their smart khaki shirts and shorts, caps, gloves, and boots. They rode powerful four-stroke Norton or BSA motor-cycles that were a match for the eight-cylinder sports cars that the scions of two powerful local families used when they raced all over town, and their very presence inspired a sense of awe and respect for the law. The police was, after all, very particular about the speed limit in the fifties. The most lionized officer of his generation was an inspector of English stock who went by the name of Edward Thaddeus. He had a rich, fruity voice and a pendulous lugubrious dignity. On Sundays when the bell above the neighborhood chapel tolled six o'clock with dismal finality, he and the members of his large family dutifully attended the evening service. The rest of the week he held open house at his modest residence near the race course. People from all walks of life turned up at these drinking sessions. Regular guests who had all the trappings of middle class respectability ensured that the Thaddeus cellar remained well stocked, for they knew that an honest policeman could not possibly entertain in the style that he did on his small salary. I have a vivid recollection of one of those sessions. This started innocently enough, with a new entrant to the club displaying a stifling intellectual smugness over a statement made by one of the senior citizens. This was eroded by the time he had gotten through his fourth peg. And it eventually disappeared altogether when he found himself fiercely attacking the very proposition he was so vigorously defending at the beginning. A few rounds of *risque* stories followed, embellished by remarks from those purveyors of gossip who fed off the carcass of other people's reputations and eventually, around eleven o'clock, one of the guests announced what was evidently a most implacable intention to be sick...

*The good old tram: infrequent,
innocuous and inexpensive.*

There weren't many cars in the city in 1950. One did see lots of *gharries* and tongas. But for the student who seemed never to be in any kind of hurry, and for whom events contrived to suggest a life of unruffled serenity, there was always the good old bicycle. This ever-reliable two-wheeler took me literally everywhere—to school, to the *sherbet* stalls of Bohri Bazaar, the dances at the Loco, the cinema, the *nihari* shops on Burns Road, the Kothari parade at Clifton, maths tuition in Saddar, the Manhattan soda fountain where the ice cream carried exotic names like Green Goddess, Purple Prince, and Hangman's Blood, Irani restaurants that served delicious trotters,

*Four friends at the
Kothari Parade: the city
was safe and peaceful.*

Napier Road, to gawk at the dancing girls, the Karachi Club Annexe for the early morning swim across the Chinna Creek, the zoo, roof-top jiving sessions on Victoria Road, Nishtar Park with its air of rude eloquence, and Cincinnatus Town where young guitar-wielding Goan men still serenaded their sweethearts under balconies while a tide of green lapped up to the window boxes.

There was a popular picnic spot that the bicycle couldn't reach unless, of course, it had an amphibian attachment. The place was called Sandspit. To get to this stretch of beach we had to take a tram which trundled along its metal veins from Empress Market to Keamari, from where we hopped into a bunderboat. Picnics with the boys and girls from the Grammar School took place during the day. We swam, flirted, played volleyball, or just sat on the beach munching sandwiches and got roasted in the summer sun. It was great fun. But the next three days were sheer agony, once the skin started to peel. It was almost impossible to cover the upper part of our body which smarted at the slightest touch. After a few such heroic experiences one of the Grammarians suggested a moonlight picnic in the harbour. I remember that outing as if it took place yesterday. It was the beginning of the monsoon. The breeze was cool and agreeably damp. There were fifteen of us in the bunderboat and one of the boys had taken the precaution of bringing along his guitar. We glided past an oil tanker moored in the flat-calm of the harbour and headed for the twinkling lights which signified that ships were anchored in the distance. A full round moon was given speed by flying scarves of white cloud and cut a jagged silver path on the sea. Starting with *Lovely Hula Hands*, we went through the whole gamut of Hawaiian songs. Then came the cowboy melodies and songs from the shows, and it wasn't until the first rays of the sun lit up the eastern sky, that we headed back to the wharf.

Of all the thoroughfares through which I pedalled my Hercules bicycle, the one which had the most distractions also happened to be the main artery of Saddar. In 1951, Elphinstone Street was the centre of the universe. Traffic moved both ways and cyclists often rode six abreast. As it was their firm conviction that stopping at the zebra crossing applied strictly to motorists, cyclists frequently knocked down with great panache pedestrians who came in their way. Ghulam Mohammad & Sons was the closest thing Karachi had to a department store. And if one wanted cold cuts or Swiss liqueur chocolates, the English Cold Storage was the place to visit. This store sold also smelly Danish and Dutch cheeses that often made an uninitiated customer sniff his armpits, or inspect the soles of his shoes the moment he entered the shop. If one had a leaky pen which produced a stripe in one's shirt, not intended by the fabric manufacturer, he took it to the Fountain Pen Corner where the Gaya Brothers ran a nursing home for the tired and exhausted Parker or Waterman veterans, and regularly performed surgery on the less expensive Blackbird whose torso had been damaged in a fall.

Young men who couldn't make a mark with members of the opposite sex at the twice-weekly Gymkhana dances, because they displayed a special talent for stepping on their partners toes in the tango, flocked to the Abbas School of Ballroom Dancing, where it was rumoured in six weeks a complete yahoo could be turned into one of the Four Horsemen of the Apocalypse. When word got around that a new Mozart violin concerto had made an appearance in the city, the western classical music buff headed for Haydn & Co. where records were neatly arranged in racks. And if one wanted a first class Chinese meal, there was no place like the ABC Restaurant, started during the second world war

The English Cold Storage: all that remains is the sign over the entrance.

Turab Photo Studio: capturing a fifty year passing show of personalities.

The ABC Chinese Restaurant: a survivor from the Second World War, named after America, Britain and China.

and named after America, Britain and China. For under five rupees one was served a plate of egg fried rice and sweet and sour chicken, while a stern Chang-kai-Shek looked down from a portrait on the wall. Though cigarettes were sold at every street corner, the connoisseur of Havana cigars knew he could always rely on Rodrigues & Co., tobacconists to the elite, to produce a box of 'Cohibas' or 'Romeo y Julietas.' On one occasion, when my father sent me to pick up a carton of Navy Cut, I came across a survivor from the Battle of the Somme. He bought a Burma cheroot, lit the reefer with the exasperating deliberation of his age, and described what it was like in the rain soaked trenches with shells exploding all around and lighting up the sky with a special incandescence.

An area that I frequented was the second-hand furniture shops in Sommerset Street and Frere Street, two of the most important arteries of Little Portugal. One of these establishments, Philip & Co., appeared to have an inexhaustible supply of gramophone records which had been left behind by the Hindus fleeing to India. Many happy hours were spent every week rummaging through the dusty stacks. The best recordings carried the bright orange-red HMV label, where for a month's pocket money Wilhelm Furtwängler and the Berlin Philharmonic Orchestra performed in my drawing room and introduced me to the nine immortal symphonies of Beethoven. Parlaphone and Odeon played host to the celebrated Italian tenors who gave the world the Neapolitan serenades of Cordillo, Di Capua and De Curtis. Another locality where one could pick up ten-inch and twelve-inch gramophone records, in fairly good condition, was the cluster of second-hand furniture shops in Arambagh. It was here that I discovered a small treasure trove of memorabilia on Ireland, and came across Irish ballads sung by John McCormack, Joseph Locke, and Richard Crooks. I had always been interested in Ireland and these records were to provide endless hours of listening pleasure in the years to come. One afternoon I met two Edwardian ladies dated by their wardrobe who belonged to an album world of Bible, lace and gramophone. They were collectors of Chinoiserie and Victoriana and enjoyed sifting through the sepia tints of history. One of them presented me a book on the emerald isle which, regrettably, is no more in my library. I have forgotten the title and even the

*Sweetmeats for the sweet
tooth: a survivor from the
early forties.*

name of the author. But in the preface there was a poem by Moira O'Neill which stuck in my memory and evoked in me a strong desire to visit County Tyrone and Donegal, and those places in the south with magical names like Limerick, Killarney, Galway and Connemara

Wathers o'Moyle, I hear ye callin'
Clearer for half o' the world between,
Antrim hills an' the wet rain fallin',
Whiles ye are nearer than snow-tops keen:
Dreams o' the night an' a night wind callin' -
What is the half of the world between?

I have yet to meet a schoolboy who doesn't like watching films. Back in the early fifties when there was no television or video cassette recorders, movie theatres provided great entertainment. The cinemas that screened English language films were the Paradise, Capitol, Palace, Plaza, and Mayfair. The last named was an open air cinema located opposite the Marina Hotel. It was rather like being in a garden. One sat on tall, high-backed rattan cane chairs, which rested on the dew-stained grass, and watched Alan Ladd make the

Khori Garden: a haven for collectors of second-hand books in search of a bargain.

Chopsy Building: this honeycomb was pulled down in the name of progress.

North-West Frontier safe for Christianity and the British Empire. It was at the Mayfair that I tasted for the first time, since my father had migrated from India, those hot and highly spiced beef *botis* wrapped in small loaves of white bread. This was the most delicious thing I had eaten since 1947 when I wolfed down that plate of Bombay Roast at the Deccan Queen restaurant at Poona railway station.

In 1950 there was a major cinematic event which took the city by storm. Samuel Goldwyn's *Samson and Delilah* had its premiere at the Paradise cinema. The film ran for a very long time and there was hardly a member of Karachi society who had not seen it. The cheapest seats down in the stalls cost six annas. And for a rupee and eight annas, one sat in relative comfort on sofas in the balcony. A special wide screen had been fixed for the event and hundreds of movie-goers sat transfixed as they watched Victor Mature decimate an entire army with the jawbone of an ass. The battle scene, fierce and clumsy, wasn't choreographed in the sweeping Hollywood style that cast war in the safe past tense. The slaying of the Philistines had a freshly minted terror and the scene remained with me for years afterwards.

These are some of the vignettes that take me back to the Karachi of the early fifties—a city that was safe and peaceful and where nobody ever seemed to be in any kind of hurry. People were also very tolerant, especially in the coffee houses where it was fashionable to hold left-wing views and to express anti-establishment sentiments. What a pity those lazy, carefree days are gone forever, like picture postcards, yellowed with age, stored in a half-forgotten trunk, never to be opened again.

The Jinnah Terminal

Chapter 18

BEING YOUNG IN THE NINETIES

Ayela Khuhro

I walk suavely into the darkened room. The smell of perfume and hashish fill the air. Techno music is blaring and 'Be my babeh' scream the mundane lyrics. The room is filled with young women…and men. The women are dressed to kill! Versace handbags, well fitted trousers and the latest creations from overpriced Pakistani designers. The men are chugging whiskies and vodkas like there is no tomorrow, which there may very well not be. The age group of the guests ranges from seventeen to thirty two, and conversations are loud and obvious, ranging from ratting about lousy school teachers to business deals and the highest paying bank jobs in town. My Karachi is like this. Appearance is all. What appears to be, is. There is no subtlety, complexity, layers of meaning, or if there is, nobody can be bothered to probe or explore. It's a get rich in a second society. No questions asked. Just show it off while it lasts.

I had returned to Karachi for a winter vacation after a year abroad in university and nothing had changed. The famous Karachi December promised to be action packed as always, despite the poor law and order situation, and constant political turbulence. December is always the season for festivity in Karachi. No messy monsoon rains, no power failures that occur over the summer and, most importantly, the weather is cool.

Before long I was spotted by my hostess, an old acquaintance from school. She had obviously greeted too many guests that evening, so I forgave her for staring at my forehead during our conversation. Her breathless speech to me was quite typical and representative of many Karachiites. 'Darling—how nice to see you again. I am so glad you could come. Oh! I love your pants. By the way, you must meet my fiancé. (in a whisper) Not only is he good-looking, but he is rich too. You are such a fool for going to college *yaar*! By the time you come back all these rich young men will be married! Oh! the Sindh Club waiters have arrived. Excuse me, I have to run...'

And so she did much to my relief! I began to walk around and socialize. From the corner of my eye I detect a rich eligible young man puking in the bushes. Perhaps the ailing roses will benefit. Fortunately I run into a bunch of old friends and begin to relax. They fill me in on everything that I had missed while I was away and then tell me about the coming attractions. Winter time, of course, is the mating season and dozens of people will be married. Billa's wedding was the talk of the town. It would be complete with two *mehndis* and a performance by Nusrat Fateh Ali Khan. He is determined to upstage his cousin's wedding party that had taken place a few months earlier. He has invited a thousand guests and will display a green eyed wife with a fair complexion.

A costume birthday bash.

Karachiites argue that they cannot be blamed for blowing parties and weddings out of proportion. After alcohol was banned in the seventies, the night club scene went down the drain. To make matters worse, the city violence hampers the youth from engaging in harmless activities, such as going to the cinema. Hanging out on the street is difficult too, as cops are often considered worse enemies than robbers. Young men and women can be hassled by cops for driving around or eating *nihari* (a meat and curry delicacy) on Burns Road. *Nikah namahs* (legal documents confirming marriage) and bribes are demanded, or else the alleged criminals can be locked up and the woman's reputation ruined. A friendly acquaintance called Sle Zee tells me of such an encounter that he and his friends recently had with the cops. Sle Zee had to pay the cops ten thousand rupees in bribes. My conversation with Sle Zee is interrupted by Spring Chickee. 'Have you been invited to the French Beach next Friday? It will be great. You should have seen the fat lobsters that we ate the last time,' she said excitedly. 'You have been out of the country for too long. Don't you know that private beaches are all the rage! ......Nowadays only losers go to Hawkes Bay and Sandspit. The weather is perfect as wwee......good grief...what is that ruckus yaar...oh my God...its DD's gunmen...'

'It's a fight...Oh no not again...'

'Who the hell invited this riff raff?'

'Run for cover???'

The ladies were all quickly ushered into the panicky hostess's drawing room. A fight had occurred as some angry young man had not been allowed to enter the party. His security guards had taken offense and manhandled the bouncer. After that, all hell broke loose!

'Get out my sight you eunuch....'

'I will kill you. —'

'Get out...of my house each and every one of you thugs...'
I sneaked out of the back door and went home.

Not all Karachi bashes end in such a manner, although many of them do. A nasty closure like this to a harmless social occasion is yet another example of how weaponry and power is abused by brash young men. There has been a huge influx of arms and ammunition into Karachi. Most of it left over from the Afghan war or manufactured in the northern regions of the country. It now means that every young punk on the street has the ability to access an AK47, and they do so with the ease that young people in other countries buy a Pepsi or a CD. BBC television recently named Karachi one of the most dangerous cities in the world and that is a very accurate description.

The lawlessness and insecurity of Karachi is something which I have experienced first hand some years ago when I was still at school. Then as now, dacoities were a daily occurrence in Karachi as were kidnappings for ransom. We read a new horror story every day. But somehow until it hits you personally you never think it is for real. With the atmosphere deteriorating daily my mother decided to take practical steps and acquired a pistol. She left it lying in her drawer and forgot about it until one day my grandmother urged her to do a bit of practice. That day she actually took out the pistol and fired a few shots at a tin can and a cocount, learning for the first time that the gun should be held with both hands and how it should be aimed etc., all patiently explained by my father. It was good fun as far as we could see. That night, in the early hours, the dacoits struck at our house. They scaled the walls and came in through a kitchen window. Then they came straight upstairs and tried to go into the bedrooms. They banged with a gun on my parents' door and demanded that they open. My father realized that something was very wrong but he knew that there were other family members in the house and some of their bedroom doors were not locked so he should head off the trouble if he could. He opened the door slightly and demanded to know who the intruders were. They started pushing and demanded that the door should be opened. My mother asked who they were and my father said 'robbers'. While my father was still talking to them, trying to stall them my mother quickly took her pistol and went behind my father. She saw the vicious looking man with his head above my father's. Almost instinctively she aimed her pistol, as she had learnt, with both hands, at the man's forehead above my father's head and fired. The bullet went straight into his head and he fell back. My father shut the door and we heard the pounding of feet on the stairs. When my parents went down about ten minutes later they found the dead body of the dacoit at the bottom of the stairs and all his companions gone. The whole episode was horrifying and unbelievable. My brother took lots of

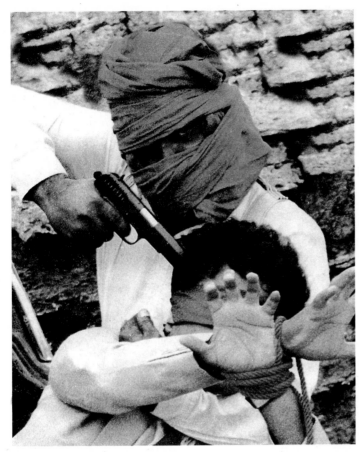

The ugly face of violence.

photographs of the dead dacoit till the police came and took the body away. My grandmother had his pockets searched and we found my grandfather's medals in them, which presumably he thought were made of gold! The children in the house were thrilled but my mother went through a trauma and could not sleep properly for months afterwards.

For many years we have lived under the constant threat of violence that can break out at any time. Most parents worry like mad about their teen-age kids from the moment they step out of the house until they return. Karachi gives Thomas Hobbes's 'survival of the fittest' theory a whole new twist, with a dash of Omar Khayyam. 'Eat, drink and be merry for tomorrow you may die!' Life goes on despite the terrible situation—and the parties go on with a vengeance!

At this point it is appropriate and convenient to emphasize that Pakistan's literacy rate is 'officially' only thirty per cent and that this includes people who only know how to write their names. A poor standard of education, forgery of examination results and poor teaching in public schools and colleges are often blamed for this. The tutors at these schools are given 'chicken feed' as salaries, due to which some of them bunk classes even more regularly than students, who are thoroughly distracted by politics, joining student unions and often taking up gun toting. So educational advancement is being replaced by power and politics.

But all this is a far cry from the serene and calm life sipping lemonade on the Sindh Club Chabootra (covered porch), and chatting with old friends from school. You are surrounded by manicured lawns, and pretty prize winning pansies, and chrysanthemums in immaculate borders. Perspiring individuals are running about with tennis rackets and swimming gear in their hands. Ladies in cotton saris are playing intense games of bridge. In the Sindh Club setting, I feel totally removed from the maniacal Karachi of the 1990s and seem to have been planted back into the British Colonial era. Waiters are bustling about in crisp white uniforms and serving their sahibs afternoon tea. Sleepy flies are buzzing about completely oblivious to human realities and signs that scream, 'Women not permitted beyond this area'. It is only when you drive out of these secluded grounds and notice a heroin addict lying on the sidewalk, that the harsh realities of life in Karachi are slapped into your face once again. Once more, the bad traffic starts to give you an anxiety attack, and the pollution gives you a chaotic throat. Multicoloured buses run on main roads that are by no means autobahns. Passengers stick out of these jam packed buses from all angles, the roofs, the windows, and the doors. A motorcyclist with a veiled wife, and an infant overtake us and almost get hit by the bus. The traffic signal turns red and the cars stop reluctantly. Beggars take their cue and start demanding a minimum of five rupees from the distressed drivers. They throw out rehearsed lines like day before yesterday's leftover lunch. 'Give us your money and you will be blessed with a fat baby and a healthy spouse.' Newspaper boys run around in the heat with sun-bleached hair flashing the headlines of The Daily Disaster that shrieks, 'Prime Minister dismissed by President—Will the ex-cricket captain take over?' A young boy selling flowers pushes him aside and claims that his roses are the sweetest smelling in town. The traffic is getting impatient, the honking of vehicles creates an unbearable din. At this cathartic moment, my oblivious friend exclaims, 'Next time we should go boating to the Marina Club!' The only way to retain a level of sanity in Karachi is by developing an immune system against the blatantly disturbing surroundings.

To my eyes Karachi is the most maddening mass of confusion that exists. The epitome of a crazy cultural fusion of East and West, the city that has been described by a journalist friend as 'the most stylish and swinging town of the subcontinent.' I counter argue that India was perhaps a more happening place than the conservative Islamic Republic of Pakistan. She replied dryly, 'Bombay is polluted and over populated...Karachi is the place to be'. Karachi may be cleaner and less congested than Bombay but it is not a resort by any means. The streets are positively

A crazy cultural fusion of east and west.

nightmarish, covered with potholes, bumps, and overflowing gutters. Many parts of Karachi, such as Landhi and Lyari, have poor sanitation, hardly any clean water, a minimum of facilities, although the people in these areas appear to be oblivious and immune to the problems that surround them. Karachi's civic services appear to be deteriorating rapidly. Piles of garbage lie uncollected on streets for days. Toxic fumes fill the air and people faint from the high levels of carbon mono-oxide in the atmosphere during the six o' clock rush hour.

Sometimes Karachi brings out my most passionate and nostalgic emotions, while at other times it forces me to reveal intense feelings of contempt and hatred. For example, eating *chaat* at Boating Basin has been an activity that people of Karachi have enjoyed for many years. While munching on this scary concoction of chickpeas in liquid spice, onions and potatoes, the world seems rather blissful. One laughs at the funny names of the shops that display a fascination with multiculturalism. A French ice-cream shop, a Big Apple burger joint, and the most popular, Little

Boating Basin, which comes alive at night.

American fast food restaurant, are all there. At times like these one forgets the violence and danger and that Boating Basin, located amidst the ritzy main Clifton Road and the residential area of Bath Island, has seen worse days. Two years ago, armed thugs invaded this peaceful part of town and wreaked havoc. Rockets exploded at the very spot where we ate our unhygienic cuisine. Sniper firing took place for hours. Many escaped death though some unfortunate people were not as lucky.

Satellite television is very much the in thing. Many argue that it is corrupting young poeple. MTV is an evil influence and the western media is satanic. However, the masses of Karachi are ignoring these accusations as they are quite fed up of two measly channels belonging to Pakistan television. Dish antennas peep out from every second roof-top, from the bungalows of up-town residential areas, to the shanty towns created from rural migration, to the deadliest and most frequently curfewed parts of the city. Zee TV, an up beat, channel featuring music videos from Indian films, game and chat shows, and Karaoke, has tremendous mass appeal. Now, with the help of Zee TV and some voluptuous Indian actresses like Madhuri Dixit, one can pick up the latest dance moves to perform at the next wedding.

What with the popularization of radio and satellite television and the deterioration of the law and order situation, the cinema is neglected. The last time I went to watch a film at Nishat Cinema, I had a disgusting experience. An obese fellow was chewing something methodically and leering at my group of friends. Before long, he opened his mouth, spat out betel juice that came flying out like a dart, staining a side of the wall and a part of my friend's Kashmiri shawl! We were appalled! Retaining one's culture is well and good, especially whilst watching an action packed Sharon Stone film, but *paan* is a traditional nightmare.

Weddings are a form of entertainment that 99.9 per cent of the Karachi population seems to enjoy. I belong to the 0.1 per cent category which does not enjoy weddings, simply because small talk and decking up to be on display is not my thing. Weddings provide an outlet for young men and women to meet, eventually marry, procreate, and add to the (unofficial) 16.5 million population of Karachi. Karachi waalas enjoy getting their children married off with tremendous pomp and splendour. Of course, the pre wedding celebration goes on for days, weeks and sometimes for months. Friends of the bride and groom practice dances to perform for the guests on the final day of the *mehndi* filled with song, dance and traditions. Religious festivals take place to bless the bride and groom. Brides are usually dressed in ornate and expensive outfits and their spouses in a western style suit, or the traditional shalwar kameez. Even if the family of the potential bride or groom are not financially sound enough to have a showy wedding for their offsprings, some sort of festivity must take place. Some people have been known to take large loans of money or not marry at all, since the wedding ritual has turned so terribly expensive in recent years.

Weddings supply a rich seam of anecdotal stories. I shall begin with the wedding fiasco of Ghulam Seth. An acquaintance of the family for many years, Ghulam Seth is an earnest chap with a comparatively low income. He took a large loan of money from some relatives which he had a hard time paying off, to maintain his honour and dignity. On his *mehndi*, his friends decided to tease him by hiring a

The wedding scene, getting into the swing.

transvestite to perform dances for the audience's peculiar sense of enjoyment. I must emphasize that the transvestite business is a thriving one. It is rumored that transvestites kidnap young boys, castrate them and add them to their community. However, this information is not proven. These transvestites live in a harmonious community together and are often hired to provide entertainment and comic relief at weddings, amongst certain classes of society. While some individuals pass off the entertainment they provide as frivolous and enjoyable, others find it both repulsive and demeaning, towards the performer and the audience. Ghulam Seth's *mehndi* kicked off with the arrival of the lone transvestite. He was clad in black and had an obvious breast implant. Unfortunately, his facial hair showed through an attempted clean shave, the five o' clock shadow not matching the fuschia lipstick at all. The audience began to hoot and cheer. Mehbooba (the transvestite) wiggled his curvaceous hips, pouted and winked for a while. Soon the music began to play and Mehbooba began to dance to a popular song from an Indian film. He swooned and shook, singing out in a high pitched bird-like shriek, *choli ke pechi*

Transvestites are sometimes called to entertain guests at wedding parties.

kya hai- choli me dill hai mera. Suddenly, Mehbooba made a bee line for Ghulam Seth and dramatically attempted to park himself on the terrified bridegroom's lap. The audience was tickled pink! However, the bridegroom's father who quite clearly lacked a sense of humour was livid. 'You boys are a bunch of lunatics...I am a respectable man— you have humiliated me.' The festivity came to an abrupt end. Later in the evening I overheard the bridegroom's friends complain, 'The *hijra* (transvestite) has been sent away and now all we have is Ghulam Seth's off beat drummers making a racket and some of his whiny relatives singing lousy songs....So where is the booze ?' Ghulam Seth is now happily married with kids—finally.

Sometimes a groom will have decided to be too traditional for his own good. For example, there was a yuppie US return who was trying to rediscover his cultural heritage. The reception was to be held at a five star hotel. The groom asked the manager of the hotel for permission to enter the gateway of the reception hall on a well decorated horse. The confused manager passed him off as a lovesick loony and agreed. Unfortunately, for the bridegroom, the hotel custodians had been extra meticulous in waxing the marbled floors that day. When the bridegroom entered before the eyes of five hundred guests and his excited wife, the horse slipped on the wax. Swooooosh Bang Thump Thump!!!! Both the horse and the bridegroom fell down on the freshly waxed marble floor. Some guests let out loud guffaws while others yelped in fear. Some feared for the groom while others feared for the horse. Luckily no one was hurt, except the bridegroom's ego.

A less catastrophic wedding comedy occurred at the famous fiasco of Inky and Bhindy. It was a high powered matrimonial alliance of two famous families. A unification of the industrial and agricultural realms of society by means of two individuals—Inky and Bhindy. Jet setting guests arrived from all over the globe. Black Label whiskey flowed. Sana and Safinaz (famous Pakistani designers) created the bridal garb. The local jewellers made plenty of business by supplying a mammoth chunk of the dowry. Jumbo prawns and imported caviar were served as finger food. It was a Dionysian affair by all means. And Inky the bridegroom decided to add a finishing touch to his perfect wedding party with a little dash of heritage. A regal red carpet was laid where the bride and groom would approach each other and walk to the stage. Inky appeared on a beautifully adorned camel. The audience was hushed in silence. He looked as handsome as ever in a crisp white shalwar kameez and a turban parked on his head. Unfortunately, the camel had eaten far too much that day. He was terribly defiant and Inky needed to coax it to walk along the red carpet and lead him to his wife-to-be. The camel trudged along wearily with the groom atop. The audience clapped. The bride blushed and beamed. And the camel got a sudden attack of diarrhea on the red carpet. The groom did not notice, stopped the camel and decided to dismount, promptly stepping into the camel's fecal matter. At that point, I kissed social etiquette goodbye and laughed quite loudly. Some joined me in my laughter and others not.

Karachi is like a giant fruit machine, all noise, jangles, lights flashing, a seeming chaotic disorder. It sort of works, and in amongst all the striving and effort and energy which people have to expend just to survive, somebody occasionally wins the jackpot. It is a game of fluke and luck, often shadowed by tragedies as the ceaseless conspiracies and plots play themselves out on the darker side of Karachi. Let us hope more compassion and responsibility enters Karachi's turbulent life as we go uncertainly towards the millenium.

The Civic Centre.

Chapter 19

KARACHI: PROSPECTS FOR THE FUTURE

S. Akbar Zaidi

Making predictions is a hazardous job, especially when they are about social, economic and political processes. A large number of books lie in the dustbin of history for predicting events into the future, based on what their authors perceived to be sound judgements at that time. There were those social scientists, now best forgotten, who wrote in the 1950s and 1960s, that Southeast Asian countries (including Japan) would never grow out of their poverty due to their cultural constraints, and would not be able to stand on their own feet always requiring aid from the west in order just to survive. There were those, some of whom were considered very eminent, who suggested in the 1960s, that Pakistan would emerge as one of the very few countries which would join the ranks of the prosperous, developed, countries. In 1950, when the Greater Karachi Plan was being prepared for the city, the Swedish firm given the contract estimated that Karachi's population would grow to around three million by the year 2000. Instead, Karachi's population crossed the three million mark thirty-one years earlier, in 1969, and now the estimate for 2000, is not three million, but fifteen million. Making predictions and looking into the crystal ball of social phenomena is indeed, a hazardous proposal, and the prospects of being wrong are very great.

Not only is the task of looking into the future made difficult as it is, but much of what we think we will see in the future, depends critically upon the times in which we exist. Who would have thought that Pakistan would be what it is today a few months prior to the fall of Zulfikar Ali Bhutto, before 5 July 1977. The military takeover by General Ziaul

Haq brought about a major disarticulation from the processes which were underway in the past and changed Pakistan permanently, just as much as did the General's death on 17 August 1988. The events following his death would probably not have emerged the way they did had he lived on, and have taken a trend and direction which few could have predicted.

To write about Karachi just looking into the next three years going into the millennium, is itself a difficult task, and to look much further into the next century, full of pitfalls. The last ten years of Karachi's history have made it into one of the most politicized, violent, volatile, ethnically divided and alienated cities, not just of Pakistan, but of the entire region.

However, this is neither 1990 or 1996, but the presumed dawn of a new beginning following the elections of 1997. There seems to be a mood of conciliation and renewed hope, not just in the city of Karachi, but also across much of Pakistan. This is the mood by which much of the writing on Pakistan is currently being influenced. Maybe this mood is just an illusion, and the bubble will burst before the year is over. What happens then, we are afraid to predict, not because we might be proven wrong yet again, but perhaps for once, we may just be proven right.

This chapter tries to understand and link the past with the present, and then based on these assumptions, suggests steps that must be taken to avoid many of the mistakes of the past. It makes no predictions, but tries to extend what one sees as logical extensions of a process. It makes assumptions based on a particular reading and understanding of how the city and its people have developed, and how they are likely to proceed. The main argument made in the chapter is that, the future of Karachi, for better or for worse, lies in the way politics is conducted in the city, and how the social and economic demands and needs of the people are addressed. Clearly, the link between political parties, government institutions and the development process, is central to any future developments.

The population of Karachi in 1729 was 250. A little over a century later when it was conquered by the British in 1839, it had grown to around 14,000. Much of the city's growth for the next century was due to the prominence given to it by the British, and due to the linkages made with the rest of the country. The development of the railways was probably the most important factor which resulted in the growth of Karachi. It was the closest port to Britain once the Suez Canal had been opened in 1869, and as early as 1886, was exporting more wheat than Bombay. The development of the canal colonies, of the barrages on the Indus and its distributaries, resulted in large tracts of barren land coming under cultivation. As agricultural production increased, and as trade (if that is the right word) with Imperial Britain expanded, so did the importance of this port and this city. Moreover, because of its location and importance to Britain, due to administrative changes brought about following the separation of Sindh from Bombay Presidency in 1936, Karachi, as Sindh's capital, also gained significant importance and began to develop as a modern, cosmopolitan city.

Independence changed Karachi permanently, disrupting and straining the link which had existed with the past. The impact of independence and migration, which was felt unevenly across the Indian subcontinent was, perhaps, nothing less than of catastrophic proportions for the indigenous people of Karachi. Prior to 1947, Karachi housed 450,000 inhabitants, where more than fifty per cent of the population was Sindhi and Hindus formed an overwhelming majority of the city. By the time the first census of the city following independence was held in 1951, the population of Karachi had risen to 1.137 million, of which 815,000 (as much as 72 per cent) were migrants from India. Of the 230,000 Hindus who lived in the city prior to Partition, 170,000 (74 per cent) had left the city. Now the main language spoken by the (new) residents of Karachi was Urdu, spoken by more than fifty per cent, while the city's population was now almost exclusively Muslim. Such catastrophic disruptions and sudden transformations are not common in modern times, with perhaps the recent history of Africa being an exception, a region with which there are many more parallels which apply to Karachi, given the recent violence and carnage. In a matter of a few years, a totally alien culture and language, with a history which was imported from many thousands of miles away, began to dominate a city, a province and for about three decades, the entire country.

While Karachi was the capital and since it was the only port, it attracted commerce and industry and developed a large service sector. There were many reasons why industrialists and traders wanted to invest and be located in Karachi, and why large amounts of capital was attracted to the city. The early years of economic development in Pakistan were the years of licence-raj and bureaucracy-inspired economic growth, and hence the need for proximity to government. Business was attracted to Karachi because it needed to be in constant contact with government and bureaucracy. Also, the city was the largest market for the few consumer goods that existed at that time, and as Pakistan was a country highly dependent on trade, to be near the port had cost advantages which no other city offered. Karachi, therefore, had all the appropriate natural and man made features which made it the centre of growth for the economy of Pakistan for at least the first three decades following independence.

The shifting of the country's capital to Islamabad and the development of agriculture in the Punjab following the Green Revolution in the 1960s, transformed the country and the city of Karachi, once again. Karachi, while still the largest city and economically and socially far more developed than the rest of the country, lost its relatively privileged position, with the ascendancy of the Punjab, particularly, central Punjab. It was this relative loss of dominance, and the perception that it was being discriminated against over the 1970s and 1980s, which resulted in the separate political articulation of the identity of the Urdu speakers of Karachi.

The emergence of the MQM as the representative of the *petit bourgeois* and lower middle class migrant from India has its genesis in the failure of the expectations of this group. These people had migrated from India essentially due to economic reasons and the desire to better themselves economically was paramount. In the early years following independence, the State played a dominating role over the economy mainly because the private sector was not well developed. These residents of Karachi, as elsewhere in Pakistan, felt that all their needs were to be fulfilled by the State. However, a young State was not able to fulfil all these expectations, and the result was frustration and a sense of alienation. In the case of Karachi, the numerous Plans that had been designed and implemented ended in failure (see chapter 6), adding to a sense of further unfulfilled expectations.

The migrants of Karachi who had been welcomed to a new city, province, and country, also began to resent the presence of the large number of Pakistanis who had migrated to Karachi from different parts of the country in the industrialization drive of the 1960s. The Urdu speaking residents of Karachi felt threatened by their presence and felt that these people would take over the jobs which they, the new locals, believed were theirs. From discontent to agitation, the 'struggle' over the perceived rights of the new settlers in Karachi, became a violent and armed conflict, first against other communities living in the city, and later against the State itself. It was this stand against the mainstream political groups and institutions of the Pakistani State which gave rise to the distancing of a large section of the people of Karachi from the rest of the country.

Many of the problems that exist in Karachi today and are likely to persist into the future, rest on the evolution of political trends established over the last violent decade. Karachi seems to have lost much of its history prior to the ignominious rise of ethnic violence and the future, in many ways, depends upon the evolution of the political process of the actors in the province and the country with those in the city. Before we examine prospects for the future, let us briefly put Karachi in the proper perspective of contemporary Pakistan.

Karachi is the largest metropolitan city of Pakistan. It is the industrial, commercial and trade centre of the country and has a well developed economy which continues to show growth rates in excess of six per cent per annum. Today, Karachi houses around 8.8 per cent of Pakistan's total population and 24 per cent of the urban population. The population growth rate is estimated to be around 5.6 per cent per annum of which three per cent is Karachi's natural growth and between 2–3 per cent due to migration. Karachi provides one-quarter of the country's federal revenues and 23.2 per cent of GDP. Not surprisingly, since it is the industrial and financial capital of the country, more than half of the country's bank deposits lie in banks in Karachi and almost three-quarters of all issued capital is raised in the city. In addition, 32.9 per cent of the national value added in manufacturing 26.4 per cent in trade, 61.6 per cent in banking and insurance and 37.7 per cent in services, is generated by the city.

Karachi has a high per capita income—$ 900 in May 1993—almost two-and-a-half times Pakistan's GDP per capita. Estimates show that more than 30 per cent of income accrues to the relatively affluent households in the city—those who earn as much as ten times the country's GDP per capita. Other indicators also clearly show Karachi's dominance in the economic and social sphere: the male literacy rate for Karachi is 20 per cent higher than Pakistan's overall male urban literacy rate, while the female literacy rate is almost twice as high as for the rest of the urbanized country. Although only 8 per cent of Pakistan's population lives in Karachi, it owns about 35 per cent of all television sets in the country and almost half of the cars including those from the rest of the province registered in Pakistan, are registered in Karachi.

Almost all economic and social indicators show that Karachi is still way ahead in terms of development compared to the rest of the country, despite the fact that other areas, notably central Punjab, have benefited due to changes in Pakistan's economic, social and political fabric. Nevertheless, the richest and largest settlement in the country, which supplies a large amount of revenue to the exchequer, has been confronted with serious problems which have hampered further development and progress. While the collapse and failure of government institutions has been all pervasive, Karachi's fate and problems may have been compounded by the uniqueness of the city's political developments. Violence and carnage dominated Karachi's landscape for much of the 1960s and exacerbated the 'normal' and typical problems associated with that of a large and fast growing metropolis.

The future prospects for Karachi depend critically upon how economic and social development takes place in the city. This is dependent upon who is to bring about that development, and how it is to take place. If, for example, the sense of alienation of the people here is based upon the feeling that they are not in a position to make decisions about their own city, i.e., that there is no effective city government to bring about change, then unless there is a change in how local government functions in this country, many problems will persist. If Karachi's population is going to approximately double over the next seventeen years, and reach around twenty million by 2015, the sense of control by the people and the representative of the city is perhaps critical.

While the failure of institutions to address the problems of housing and provision of basic services to the people of Karachi and the low income group and the poor in particular, can be explained by the way planning takes place and the way institutions are structured, the political alienation of the citizens of Karachi and of the poor, specifically, has led to the failure of institutions to deliver even basic services. While politics is the key to the problems and to the solution of better city level administration and government, individual and community level responses have tried to address immediate concerns for at least a section of the urban poor. Just as the private and informal sector has emerged in a big way as a response to governmental failure, so have a large number of community based, non-governmental organizations or NGOs, become active and have tried to improve housing and living conditions in Karachi.

Informal groups have developed at a community level to address specific problems in the delivery of services or in the provision of infrastructure. From the construction of open drains or the laying of underground sewers, to street paving and collecting garbage, groups have emerged to address specific issues and have then disbanded. Some groups have taken on longer-term projects and have set up schools and health clinics. Apart from community based groups, which are more focused towards an issue and prefer to work in one particular area as small as a 'mohalla' or neighbourhood, there are larger NGOs which usually work in more than one settlement and have a broader development outlook. Some welfare oriented NGOs have also emerged in recent years and have been successful in providing a wide range of services to the poor.

Development oriented NGOs are those which have merged in recent years as a response to the failure, inability and unwillingness of institutions of the state, to address the issues of citizens, particularly, the poor. Rather than simply carry out capital works as the state does, such NGOs involve and encourage communities to take hold of their own lives by organizing and filling the void created by the absence of the state. 'Participation' is no longer seen as simply involving poorer groups in implementation but far more as formulating what should be done, how it should be done and how limited resources should be used. The Organi Pilot Project is such an organization in Karachi which has had a far reaching impact on the lives of the poor in one large area of Karachi.

Despite the huge success of projects like the Orangi Pilot Project and smaller groups which have significantly altered the lives of many thousands of the poor in Karachi, NGOs are not the sole solution to address the problems of the low income groups in Karachi. NGOs cannot replace government at a city level; they can play a useful role either working with government or can then be effective in areas where government has failed to deliver services. Nor can government be replaced by the private sector through an indiscriminate process of privatizing state-owned and state-run concerns. While it is clear that government and its institutions have been a failure in the context of Karachi, the knee-jerk response of privatization or other options is inappropriate. What is required is reform of government itself, at the national, provincial and local level.

While one can list a number of reforms and changes needed in the structure of local city level government, these

The Orangi Pilot Project, which significantly altered the lives of thousands.

well-meaning suggestions will be merely that, unless there is a political demand for such forms of institutions, a political will to carry them through, and a politicized public and their representatives to actually administer, control and oversee such institutions. The desire to overhaul the local bodies system in Karachi will be lost on the ears of those who control politics, unless political forces put pressure of institutions of the state to accede to those suggestions. Reform itself is a seriously political matter dependent upon the dialectics of different political forces. With these political prerequisites, we address some of the concerns in local government that are critical for an improvement in the delivery of urban basic services.

There is little denying the fact that there is a need for a huge overhaul of the local bodies system to make it representative, responsible, viable and functionable. What is required is a powerful, autonomous tier of government in all municipalities in Pakistan, but particularly in the larger metropolitan areas, like Karachi. Unless local government is given the power to function as an effective tier of governance, it is unlikely that it will address any of the issues which affect the lives of the people. A self-contained and independent tier of government, is the first pre-requisite for better governance at the local level.

Local government, specially city government for a city the size of Karachi must be remodelled as a new administrative style is required for it to be at all effective. It should have the power to plan and implement development, not merely look after projects planned by a totally independent body in which local elected government plays no role. If finances are a constraint to the development programme of local government, then the city government should have the power to raise resources. The current distribution of functions between an unelected technocratic development agency like KDA (Karachi Development Authority), and an implementing agency which is supposed to maintain projects and plans developed by KDA, the KMC (Karachi Metropolitan Corporation), would need to be done away with. KDA would need to be subsumed under the KMC (or an elected city government) so that different agencies can work under one umbrella, rather than at cross-purposes as is the state at present. If city government is to be an effective medium of governance, it must also be party to the

The Karachi Municipal Corporation Building.

maintenance of law and order in the city; currently, the numerous agencies of the federal and provincial government at work in a city like Karachi, undermine all semblance of authority and control, and precisely for this reason, power over law and order is held by agencies which are not city-specific.

While the suggestions for local bodies and for reform of local government is necessary across Pakistan, the specific situation of Karachi warrants specific additional measures.

All the problems that local bodies and local government face throughout Pakistan, are compounded in the case of

Karachi. Whatever reform may be envisaged for local government in Pakistan in the future, whether of a constitutional, financial or administrative nature, for Karachi, political issues will have to be at the forefront, and must be a pre-requisite for any attempt at improving structure and performance.

However one sees the future of Karachi, it is dependent upon what happens in the rest of the country as well. For instance, considering that Karachi dominates Pakistan's economy, the fortunes of both are closely linked; if the overall economy suffers, so will Karachi's (and vice versa), affecting all who live here, adding to more of the problems which already exist. Politically too, Karachi has played a central role (not always positive though), in how the country is run and functions. For these reasons and because of the sheer strength of its numbers, Karachi is unique in the context of Pakistan, yet suffers from most of the problems which affect the rest of the country as well. The urgent need and desire for change in the institutions of government at all levels, but specially at a local level, affect all administrative units in the country. In order to bring about this change, Karachi's position as an outlier will have to change, and greater integration with the overall mainstream political process will be made necessary.

For many of the reasons outlined in this and other chapters in this book, Karachi has been on the periphery of many developments which have taken place in the country. In some cases, the city has led the way and set new trends; in others, it has disassociated itself from what has been happening elsewhere in Pakistan, preferring not to participate. With the recent signs of the maturity of political parties within the city, and with more economic development and growth taking place, there are signs which suggest that, perhaps, the relative isolation of Karachi is nearing an end. Indeed, if this is the case, such trends must be welcomed and appreciated, for the future of Pakistan and that of Karachi, is inextricably bound together. The prospects for the future, not just of Karachi, but of Pakistan as well, depend critically on the assimilation of the former with the latter. Greater integration, but with more autonomy, decentralization, and local level control, is the key for a more prosperous future for Karachi and for Pakistan as a whole.

NOTES AND REFERENCES

Chapter 1

1 Eggermont, P.H.L., *Alexander's Campaigns in Sind and Baluchistan and the siege of the Brahmin town of Harmatela*, Leuven University Press, 1975.
2 Ibid., p. 43.
3 Ibid., p. 45.
4 Ibid., pp. 46-7.
5 Ibid.
6 Baloch, N.A., 'Antiquity of Karachi', *Pakistan Journal of History and Culture*, January-June 1993, vol XIV No. 1, pp. 9-10.
7 *Al Umadat al Mahriya fi Zabt al Ulum al Bahriya* (Arabic) Damascus 1970 quoted by Baloch op. cit., p. 8.
8 Sidi Ali Capudan, *Mu'hit*, quoted in Baillie, A., *Kurrachee, Past, Present and Future*, p. 20.
9 Quoted in Eggermont, op. cit., p. 42.
10 Tibbets, G.R., *Arab Navigation in the Indian Ocean before the coming of the Portuguese*, London 1971, p. 449, quoted by Baloch, op. cit.
11 Baloch, op. cit.
12 Mentioned by Arif Hasan in 'Another Time, Another Place' article in *Herald*, Karachi, August 1986.
13 Mayne, P., *Saints of Sind*, John Murray, London 1956, p. 1.
14 Lieutenant John Porter, 'Remarks on the Bloachee Brodia and Arabian Coasts', quoted in Baillie, op. cit., p. 21.
15 Ibid., p. 21.
16 The *Chachanama* gives an account of the Arab conquest of Sindh. Daibal, Debal or Diul (as in Diul Sinde) appears to be a generic name for the major part of Sindh.
17 *Medieval Routes to India*, Lahore, 1977.
18 Ibid., p. 23.
19 Crowe, Nathan, *An Account of the Country of Scinde*. Selections from the Records of the Commissioner in Sind.
20 Masson, Charles, *Narrative of various journeys in Balochistan, Afghanistan and the Panjab*, London, 1842, pp. 470-1.
21 Ibid.

22 Quoted in A.H. Siddiqui, *Karachi, The Pearl of Arabian Sea*, Karachi, 1996, p. 17. The two gates are obviously a reference to the two gates of the town, Mithadar (sweet water gate) and Kharadar (salt water gate) which faced the green belt and wells and the sea respectively.

23 *Karachi, The Pearl of Arabian Sea*, Karachi, 1996, p. 17.

24 Huttenback, R.A., *British Relations with Sind, 1799-1843*, University of California Press, 1962, p. 3.

25 Law, Edward, *A Political Diary, 1828-30*, London, 1881, vol. II p. 92.

26 Lord Auckland to Sir Richard Jenkins, 21 May 1939, quoted in Huttenback, op. cit., pp. 58-9.

27 Huttenback, op. cit., pp. 59-60.

28 Ibid., p. 58.

29 Ibid., p. 51.

Chapter 2

1 W.P. Andrew, *The Indus and its Provinces, their political and commercial importance*, London, 1857, p. 2.

2 Keith Young, *Scinde in the Forties*, (edit. A.F. Scott) London, 1912, p. 7.

3 Ibid., p. 9.

4 Ibid., p. 13.

5 Ibid., pp. 23-4.

6 Ellenborough, quoted in H. Khuhro, *The Making of Modern Sind*, Karachi, 1978, p. 12.

7 Keith Young, op. cit., pp. 8-9.

8 Dalhousie to Frere, 6 Dec. 1853, Frere Papers (British Library).

9 Khuhro, H., op. cit, p. 219.

10 Brow, op. cit., p. 3.

11 Ibid., p. 4.

12 R.H. Davies, Report quoted in Khuhro, op. cit., p. 220.

13 Lambrick, H.T., *John Jacob of Jacobabad*, London, 1960, p. 296.

14 Frere to Lord Falkland, Governor of Bombay, no. 459 of 1853, quoted in Khuhro, op. cit., p. 224.

15 loc.cit.

16 Ibid., p. 225.

17 Burton, R.F., *Sind Revisited*, vol. II, p. 307.

18 Khuhro, H., op. cit., p. 211.

19 *Gazetteer of the Province of Sind*, B vol. I, Karachi, 1926, p. 47.

20 loc.cit.

21 Khuhro, H., op. cit., p. 284.

22 Ibid., p. 52.

23 Baillie, A.F., *Kurrachee, Past, Present and Future*, Oxford University Press, Karachi, 1975, p. 108.

24 Gazetteer op. cit., p. 48.

25 Ibid., p. 59.

Chapter 3

1 E. Thompson and G.T. Garrat, *The Rise and Fulfilment of British Rule in India*, Allahabad, 1962.
2 Lawrence, Lady Rosamund, *Indian Embers*, pp. 362-3.
3 Ibid., p. 363.
4 Ibid., pp. 364-6.
5 Feldman, H., *Karachi Through A Hundred Years*, p. 144.
6 Ibid., p. 145.
7 Lawrence, Lady Rosamund, op. cit., p. 384.
8 Ibid., p. 353.
9 Nanda, B.R., *Gandhi Pan-Islamism, Imperialism and Nationalism*, Bombay, p. 306.
10 Ibid., p. 272.
11 Lawrence, Lady R., op. cit. pp. 205-06.
12 *Daily Gazette*, Karachi, 16 Jan. 1933.
13 *Jamshed Nusserwanji, A Memorial*, The Jamshed Memorial Volume Committee, Karachi, 1954, p. 84.
14 Khuhro, H., *Documents on the Separation of Sind from the Bombay Presidency*, Islamabad, 1982, vol. I, p. xvii.
15 Khuhro, H., *Mohammed Ayub Khuhro, A Life of Courage in Politics*, (unpublished Mss. p. 151).
16 Quoted in Jones, A.K., *Muslim Politics and the Growth of the Muslim League in Sind, 1935-1941*, Ph.D dissertation, Duke University, USA.

Chapter 4

1 Chaudhri Mohammed Ali, *The Emergence of Pakistan*, p. 198.
2 Ibid., p. 199.
3 Resolution of the Council of Sind Muslim League, 2 February 1948, Khuhro Papers.
4 Ibid.
5 Khuhro, H., *Mohammed Ayub Khuhro, A Life of Courage in Politics*, Chapter 18.
6 Constituent Assembly Debates, 22 May 1948, quoted in H. Khuhro, ibid.

Chapter 5

1 Napier, Priscilla *Raven Castle: Charles Napier in India 1844-51*, London, Michael Russell, 1991.
2 Baillie, Alexander F., *Kurrachee: Past, Present, and Future* (1890) Karachi. Reprinted by Oxford University Press, 1975.
3 *History of Karachi Port*, compiled by Azimusshan Haider. Published by Secretariat Karachi Port Trust, 1980.
4 Khuhro, Hamida, *The Making of Modern Sindh: British Policy and Social Change in the Nineteenth Century*, Karachi. Published by Indus Publications 1978.
5 Khuhro, Hamida, 'Introduction' to the *Memoirs of Seth Naomul*

Hotchand, Karachi. Reprinted by Oxford University Press, 1982.

6   Karachi, *Who's Who and Why,* 1932.

7   Khuhro, 'Introduction' to *Memoirs of Seth Naomul Hotchand,* Karachi. Reprinted by Oxford University Press, 1982.

8   Khuhro, Hamida, *The Making Of Modern Sindh: British Policy and Social Change In The Nineteenth Century,* Karachi, Indus Publications, 1982.

9   Khuhro, Hamida, *The Making of Modern Sindh: British Policy and Social Change in The Nineteenth Century,* Karachi, Indus Publications, 1978.

10 Karachi, *Who's Who And Why,* 1932.

11 Gupta, Nagendranath, 'Dayaram Gidumal': a leaflet, possibly an obituary with date, publication and source not stated.

12 Gupta, op. cit.

13 Karachi, *Who's Who And Why,* 1932.

14 Karachi, *Who's Who And Why,* 1932.

15 Feldman, Herbert, *Karachi Through a Hundred Years 1860-1960,* Published by Karachi, Oxford University Press, 1960.

16 Feldman, Herbert, *Karachi Through a Hundred Years 1860-1960,* Karachi, Oxford University Press, Pakistan 1960.

17 Shafi, Alhaj Mian Ahmad, *Haji Sir Abdoola Haroon: A Biography,* published by Begum Daulat Anwar Hidayatullah (Undated).

18 Shafi, Alhaj Mian Ahmad, *Haji Sir Abdoola Haroon: A Biography.* Appendix III: 'Separation of Sindh: A Financial Enquiry'. Published by Begum Daulat Anwar Hidayatullah, Karachi.

19 Shafi, Alhaj Mian Ahmad, *Haji Sir Abdoola Haroon: A Biography.* Published by Begum Daulat Anwar Hidayatullah, Karachi, date not given.

20 Lari, Suhail, *A History of Sindh,* Karachi, Oxford University Press, 1994.

21 Jalal, Ayesha, *The Sole Spokesman: Jinnah, The Muslim League and the Demand for Pakistan* Cambridge, Cambridge University Press, 1985.

22 Wolpert, Stanley, *Jinnah of Pakistan,* New York, Oxford University Press, 1989.

23 Jalal, Ayesha, *The Sole Spokesman: Jinnah, The Muslim League and the Demand for Pakistan,* Cambridge, Cambridge University Press, 1985.

24 Jalal, Ayesha, *The Sole Spokesman: Jinnah, The Muslim League and the Demand for Pakistan,* Cambridge, Cambridge University Press, 1985.

25 Shamsie, Muneeza: An interview with Ayesha Jalal: *Dawn* Friday Magazine, 21 October, 1994.

26 Wolpert, Stanley, *Jinnah of Pakistan,* Oxford University Press, New York, 1989.

27 Alavi, Hatim A., *The President,* Jamshed Memorial Volume. Publisher and date not stated.

28 Jamshed Memorial Volume, publisher and date not stated.

29 Alavi, Hatim A., *The President,* Jamshed Memorial Volume.

30 Pirzada, D.A., *Hatim A. Alavi: A Pillar of the Pakistan Movement,* Karachi, Mehran Publishers, 1994.

31 Pirzada, D.A., *Hatim A. Alavi: A Pillar of the Pakistan Movement,* Karachi, Mehran Publishers, 1994.

32 Khuhro, Hamida, 'G.M. Syed: A Man of Vision'. Undated

33 Khuhro, Hamida 'G.M. Syed: A Man of Vision'. Undated.

34 Shamsie, Muneeza, 'A Life Devoted to Human Welfare', published in *Dawn* Magazine, Friday 11 June 1982.

35 Shamsie, Muneeza, 'Dr Akhtar Hameed Khan: the guiding light', *Dawn* Tuesday Review, March 7-13, 1995.

36 Khan, Akhtar Hameed, *Orangi Pilot Project: Reminiscences and Reflections,* Karachi, Oxford University Press, 1996.

37 All the information which follows is culled from *Abdus Sattar Edhi—an Autobiography: A Mirror To The Blind* as narrated to Tahmina Durrani. Published by National Bureau of Publications, Islamabad, 1996.

38 *Abdus Sattar Edhi—an Autobiography: A Mirror to the Blind* as narrated to Tahmina Durrani, National Bureau of Publications, Islamabad, 1996.

Chapter 6

1 Bengali, Kaiser; (1988), 'The Economy of Karachi; Growth and Structural Change' Applied Economics Research Centre, University of Karachi.

2 Federal Bureau of Statistics, Statistics Division, Government of Pakistan, 'Survey of Small and Household Manufacturing Industries, 1983-4.'

3 Karachi Port Trust, Karachi.

4 Khan, Akhtar Hameed, 'The Miracle of Orangi Credit Trust', Economic and Business Review, *Dawn*, 18-24 March 1995.

5 Lewis, Stephen R., (1969), *Economic Policy and Industrial Growth in Pakistan*. George Allen and Union Ltd., London.

6 Memon, Mohammad Yacoob, 'Growth and Development of Capital Market in Pakistan,' *Dawn* Supplement, 31 October 1995.

7 Papanek, Gustav, F., (1970), 'The Location of Industry'. *The Pakistan Development Review*, vol. X, no. 3, Autumn.

8 Port Qasim Authority, Karachi.

9 Sindh Bureau of Statistics, Development Statistics, 1994.

10 State Bank of Pakistan, Annual Report 1995-6.

Chapter 9

1 *Census of Pakistan 1951; Pakistan; Report and Tables Vol.1* by E.H. Slade. Karachi, Manager of Govt. Publications. Chapter 5, Statement 5-B.

2 Ibid., Table 2, Section 2 and 3.

3 Ibid., Table 9-A. Also see Tariq Rahman, *Language and Politics in Pakistan*. Karachi, Oxford University Press, 1996, pp. 110-13.

4 Hamza Alavi, 'Politics of Ethnicity in India and Pakistan'... *Pakistan Progressive* 9: 1 (Summer 1987).

5 For the riots see Richard Lambert, 'Hindu-Muslim Riots'. Unpublished Ph.D. Dissertation, University of Pennsylvania, 1951. For Urdu literature see Mumtaz Shirin (ed) *Miyar* (Lahore: Naya Idara, 1963) and *Zulmat-e-Neem Roaz* compiled by Asif Aslam Farrukhi (Karachi: Nafeees Academy, 1990). For Hindi works see, Ramesh Mathar and M. Kulasretha, *Writings on India's Partition*—Calcutta:

Simant Publication, 1976). For literature in English see Tariq Rahman, 'Critical Prejudices to Aspects of Partition Literature: Universal Versus Ethnocentric Values', *The Toronto South Asian Review* 11: 1 (Summer 1992), 69-78.

6 Linda and Khalid Shah, *Refugee: A Novel,* New York. Thomas Y. Crowell Coy, 1974.

7 Ibid., p. 240.

8 Ibid., p. 241.

9 M.A. Seljouk, *Corpses* (London: Gerald Duckworth Ltd., 1966), p. 91.

10 Ibid., p. 42.

11 Adam Zameenzad, *The 13th House,* London. Fourth Estate, 1987; Mirza A. Raquib Beg, *A Blossom in the Dust,* Karachi. Privately published, 1992.

12 Tariq Rahman, *A History of Pakistan Literature in English* Lahore Vanguard Press Ltd, 1991, 144-6.

13 A. Zameendad, p. 3.

14 Ibid., p. 153.

15 Ibid., p. 202.

16 M.R. Beg, op. cit, p. 149.

17 Ibid., p. 221. Ibid., p. 134.

18 Anwer Mooraj, *Sand, Cacti and People* Karachi. Greengrove Press, 1960; *Harbour Lights,* Karachi, Mumtaz Publishing House, 1992; *Wild Strawberries and Other Articles,* Karachi, Royal Book Company, 1992.

19 A. Mooraj (1960), p. 20.

20 *Wild Strawberries,* p. 21.

21 Ibid., p. 22.

22 Khalid Hasan, *Scorecard* (Lahore: Wajidalis, 1984).

23 Omar Kureshi, Karachi. Jaykay Publications 1955, p. 20.

24 A. Mooraj, *Harbour Lights,* op. cit, p. 47.

25 Omar Kureishi, op. cit, p. ii.

26 Tariq Rahman, *A History of Pakistani Literature in English,* Karachi, Oxford University Press, 1996.

27 *First Voices: Six Poets From Pakistan* (ed) Shahid Hosain. (Karachi. Oxford University Press, 1965); *The New Harmony* (ed) Syed Ali Ashraf (Karachi: Dept of English, University of Karachi, 1970); *Pieces of Eight: Eight Poets from Pakistan,* Introduced by Yunus Said. Karachi, Oxford University Press. 1971; *Wordfall: Three Pakistani Poets* (ed) Kaleem Omar, Karachi. Oxford University Press. 1975.

28 Nasir Ahmad Farooqi, *Faces of Love and of Death.* Lahore. Privately Published, 1961, p. 27. Also see *Snakes and Ladders.* Lahore. Watan Publications, 1968.

29 Masroor, *Shadows of Time.* Delhi. Chanakya Publications, 1987.

30 Kamal K. Jabbar, *Selling Oranges in a Banana Republic: Prose and Poetry* Karachi: Royal Book Company, 1996, p. 6.

31 Diana Storr, *Solar Dust.* Lahore. Plus Publication, 1990, p. 46.

32 Hanif Kureishi, 'The Rainbow Sign'. In *My Beautiful Laundrette* London. Faber and Faber, 1986, p. 16.

33 Ibid., p. 22.

34 Ejaz Rahim, *Cactus in My Throat,* (Islamabad: Leo Books, 1996), p. 19.

35 Parveen Pasha, *Shades of Silence (Poems),* Lahore. Sang-e-Meel, 1996, p. 37.

36 Arif Viqar, *Karachi: Poems* Karachi. Alhamra Publications, 1983, p. 38.
37 Omar Tarin, *The Anvil of Dreams*, Islamabad: Leo Books, 1994 p. 33.

Chapter 10

1 Shahid Javed Burki, *State and Society in Pakistan 1971-7*, London. The MacMillan Press 1980 p. 11.
2 Shahid Javed Burki, *State and Society in Pakistan 1971-7*, London. The MacMillan Press, 1980 p. 12.
3 Shahid Javed Burki, *Pakistan and Nation in the Making*, Oxford University Press, 1986, pp. 44-5.
4 Muhammad Sadiq, Twentieth Century Urdu Literature, Karachi, Royal Book Co., Karachi (1983) p. 321.
5 Zamir Niazi, *The Press in Chains*, Karachi Press Club, p. 19.

Chapter 11

1 Sindhi Language Authority, Hyderabad Sindh, 1993.
2 G. Clerk, Governor of Bombay quoted in H. Khuhro, *Making of Modern Sind*, p. 240.
3 G. Stack, ibid., p. 243-244.

Chapter 16

1 *The Sind Club 1971-1991* by J. Humphrey and Azhar Karim, p. 12.
2 *Sind Revisited* by Richard F. Burton, p. 43.
3 *The Sind Club 1871-1991* by J. Humphrey and Azhar Karim, p. 49.
4 Ibid., p. 50.
5 Ibid., p. 53.
6 *Karachi during the Raj* by Yasmeen Lari and Mihail S. Lari, p. 176.
7 *The Raj At Table* by David Burton, p. 176.
8 The other members of the band were Don Gonsalves (tenor sax) Dennis Frisley (alto sax) Marselin Goveas (alto sax) Mack Mohan (drums) Dick D'Costa (double bass) and Rodney Mendonca (piano).
9 Such a list must include Ustad Habibuddin Khan, Ustad Qudratullah Khan, Ashiq Ali Khan, Ustad Ramzan Khan, Ustad Hameed Ali Khan, Ustad Manzoor Ali Khan, Ustad Umaid Ali Khan, Ustad Ghulam Rasool, Fateh Ali Abdullah, Zafar Ali Khan, Ustad Amin Ahmed Khan and Salim—Azeem Prem Ragi's son. Listeners who found the *pucca gana* too heavy and preferred something lighter turned to the lilting melodies of other singers like S.B. John, Zawar Hussain, Ahmed Rushdi (who was much in demand as a playback singer in Pakistani films) Taj Multani, Iqbal Ali, Kalim Sarwar, M. Kaleem and Habib Wali Mohammad.
10 *Indian Music* by B.C. Deva, p. 3.
11 According to Ustad Safiullah Khan and Faqir Mohammad, of the music teachers at the Pakistan American Cultural Center, mention must be made of Malika Pukhraj, Khursheed Ambalewali, Jeeran

Koosoorawali, Champabai, Nighat Seema, Rashida Begum, Kajjan Begum, Ishrat Jehan, Kaukab Jehan, Nasima Shaheen, Asma Ahmad, Naheed Akhtar, Mehnaz and Pervez Dastur. There were quite a few who made a name for themselves on television such as Tina Sani, Afshan Ahmad, Madhu Almas, Deborah Daniel, Nazeer Begum, Nighat Akbar, Fatema Jafri, Runa Laila, Shahnaz Begum and Nazia Hasan.

12 *Indian Music* by D.C. Deva, p. 3.

13 The most prominent violinists were Mohammad Shareef, Sardar Hussain Hashim, Mukhtar Hussain, Ashraf Hussain, Zakir Hussain, Maqsood Hussain, Zafar Hussain and Mazhar Hussain.

14 Fakir Mohammad believes that the list of *tabla nawaz* should include Ustad Ballay Khan, Ustad Allahditta Khan, Ustad Khursheed Ali Khan, Wajid Ali Khan, Afzal Hussain, Abdur Rashid, Bashir Khan, Ustad Abid Hussain, Dilawar Hussain, Ustad Ghulam Hussain, Jiray Khan and Nemat Khan.

15 A number of male and female dancers performed a variety of dances as the occasion demanded, which was an indication of their versatility. Some, however, specialized in a particular style. Local dance instructors are accustomed to referring to *Kathak* as 'classical' to distinguish this north Indian dance from other styles which are conveniently lumped together as 'folk' and 'south Indian'. The dancers who specialized in *Kathak* are Parveen Qasim, Nahid Siddiqui (and her pupil Nighat Chaudhry) and Ananda Devi. There were those who fitted into the 'classical' mould like Amy Minwalla, Panna, Saloni Solomon, Meena and Ishrat Chaudhry. There were others who performed in cabaret and did a vulgarized version of the *Kathak* to titillate the jaded appetites of an all-male audience such as Munawar and Kishwar, Shakila, Jamila and Farida Anjum. A Bengali dancer named Shelley specialized in Manipuri, and Sheema Kirmani is probably the only known expert in Odissi, a distinct east Indian style. Among the male dancers one must mention Mahraj Ghulam Hussain Kathak, Rafi Anwar who introduced *Bharat Natyam* (along with Madam Azurie), Mohammad Yakub Memon and Ghanshyam Dada who along with Nilima Ghanshyam was a major figure in the south Indian style.

16 *Calcutta Through British Eyes 1690-1990*, chosen and edited by Laura Sykes, p. 36.

17 *Goa, Images and Impressions* by Thomas Vaz, Introduction

18 Richard D'Oyly Carte (1844-1990,) English Impressario and producer of light operas who brought together the librettist Gilbert and the composer Sullivan for 'Trial by Jury' 1875. D'Oyly Carte's exclusive ownership of them ended with the expiry of Sullivan's copyright in 1950.

NOTES ON THE CONTRIBUTORS

Hamida Khuhro

Dr Hamida Khuhro was educated at the Universities of Karachi, Cambridge, Oxford and London. She is a historian and has taught at the universities of Karachi and Oxford and lastly Sindh University where she was Professor of History. She left the university to concentrate on writing and political work. She has published a number of books including Making of Modern Sindh, *and has edited the popular* Sindh Through The Centuries. *She has written a number of other books as well as numerous articles in learned journals.*

Muneeza Shamsie

Muneeza Shamsie was educated in England and has lived in Karachi for most of her life. She contributes regular freelance articles, interviews and book reviews to Dawn, She *and* Newsline *and is the editor of* A Dragonfly in the Sun: Pakistani Writing in English, *an anthology of poetry, fiction and drama, published by Oxford University Press (1997) to commemorate 50 years of Pakistan. In 1989 she was delegated to the 1989 International Seminar on English in South Asia at Islamabad. She is a founder member of a Karachi hospital, The Kidney Centre. Between 1975-82 she worked with the Association of Children with Emotional and Learning Problems (ACELP) to teach music and mime to mentally handicapped children. She is married and has two daughters.*

Shahida Wizarat

Dr Shahida Wizarat did her M.A. in economics from Vanderbilt university, Nashville, Tennessee, USA, and her Ph.D. in economics from the University of East Anglia, Norwich, England. She is a professor at the Applied Economics Research Centre (AERC) at the University of Karachi. Her research papers mainly in the area of development economics and industrial economics have been published in journals of international repute, both in Pakistan and abroad.

Arif Hasan

Arif Hasan, born in 1943, is an architect in private practice in Karachi and has taught architecture and planning since 1970 in Pakistan and abroad. He has written a number of books on housing and urban issues, mainly on Karachi, and has been a consultant to various international agencies on environment and conservation related issues. He is the principal consultant to the well-known Orangi Pilot Project since 1982 and in 1990 received the UN Year of the Shelterless Memorial Award. He is also the chairman of the Urban Resource Centre in Karachi and is a member of the Master Jury of the Aga Khan Award for Architecture.

Noman Ahmed

Noman Ahmed studied architecture at the department of architecture and planning, Dawood College of Engineering and Technology, Karachi and graduated in 1989 obtaining the Faculty's Gold Medal and Mehdi Ali Mirza Award for Academic Excellence. He received a masters degree in city planning from the Middle East Technical university, Ankara, Turkey in 1992. He has undertaken several research projects and self-motivated studies related to architecture and urban development and has various published papers, reports and monographs to his credit. He is a regular contributor to the leading newspapers of Pakistan, and editor of the Architecture and Planning Journal *which is published by the Department of Architecture and Planning, DCET, Karachi.*

Tariq Rahman

Dr Tariq Rahman did his M.A. and Ph.D. from the University of Sheffield, and his M.Litt in Linguistics from the University of Strathclyde, Glasgow. He has also completed a course on language and the mind at the University of Cambridge. In 1995-6 Dr. Rahman was a Senior Fulbright Scholar in the USA. He has held professorships at two universities and is now at the Quaid-i-Azam University, Islamabad. He is highly published, having more than fifty research articles in international journals and seven books to his credit. His latest book Language and Politics in Pakistan *(Oxford University Press, 1996) has been highly acclaimed by reviewers.*

Muhammad Ali Siddiqui

Dr Muhammad Ali Siddiqui, born in 1938, is a well-known Urdu critic and journalist. At present director of the Quaid-i-Azam Academy, a research body under the federal ministry of culture, he taught the course of Literary and Cultural Heritage of Pakistan at the Pakistan Study Centre, University of Karachi. He is a member of the AICL (Association of International Critics, Paris), affiliated to UNESCO. He has authored and edited ten books—seven of them works of criticism and translations, and three on the Quaid-i-Azam. He has also been writing a literary column in Dawn, *under the pen name of 'Ariel' for more than thirty years. He was twice awarded the Best Writer Award in 1976 and 1979 by the Pakistan Writers' Guild.*

Asif Noorani

Born in Bombay in 1942, Asif Noorani has been writing for national newspapers since he was in his late teens. At twenty-one he started editing Eastern Films, *the country's most widely circulated English language film magazine. Later, he headed the advertising department of a multinational. Now editor of* Star Weekend *he reviewes books and plays, and writes travelogues and pieces on cultural subjects, mainly music.*

Marjorie Husain

The well-known art critic Marjorie Husain has been a prominent figure in Pakistan's art circles for over two decades. Promoting local art and culture both in the country and abroad, she has arranged art exhibitions of Pakistani artists in foreign countries, written a history of art in the subcontinent for the Pacific Asia Museum, Pasadena, USA and given numerous lectures here and in western countries. She is a contributor to Dawn Review.

S. Akbar Zaidi

S. Akbar Zaidi was born and raised in Karachi, and lives in Karachi out of choice, and says that he would not like to live anywhere else. He is a social scientist and has studied at the University of Cambridge and at the London School of Economics. He was an Associate Professor/Senior Research Economist at the Applied Economics Research Centre, University of Karachi, where he worked for almost fifteen years. He has published two books on different aspects of Pakistan's economy and society, and has dozens of publications in international journals. S. Akbar Zaidi currently works as an independent researcher, and is working on his third book, a textbook for students of Pakistan's economy, to be published by Oxford University Press.

Hameed Zaman

Hameed Zaman started his career in Radio Pakistan in 1954, after obtaining his master's degree from Lucknow, India. He was a programme producer and also a broadcaster. In 1964 he joined Morning News *and subsequently became editor of* The Mirror *after the publisher, Mrs. Zaibunissa Hameedullah, left for Ireland. He was also the editor of* The Third World *for a period. For a while he freelanced for the* The Muslim *and joined the staff of* The News *in 1995. His speciality is themes which centre on theatre, art, literature and poetry.*

Anwer Mooraj

Anwer Mooraj was educated in India and England and is a graduate of the London School of Economics and Political Science. He started his journalistic career in Dawn *in the 1960s as an assistant editor, was the founding editor of* The Herald *in 1970 and served as chief executive of the* Gulf News, Dubai *from 1982 to 1985. He is widely travelled and is the author of three books,* Sand, Cacti & People *(1965),* Wild Strawberries *and* Harbour Lights *(1992). A management expert he is currently executive director of PACC (Pakistan American Cultural Center), and contributes articles to newspapers and journals.*

Ayela Khuhro

Ayela Khuhro did her O levels from the Lyceum in Karachi where she edited the school magazine and was group leader for environmental issues. At present she is doing her BA at the College of Wooster in the USA where her main subjects are history and classics.

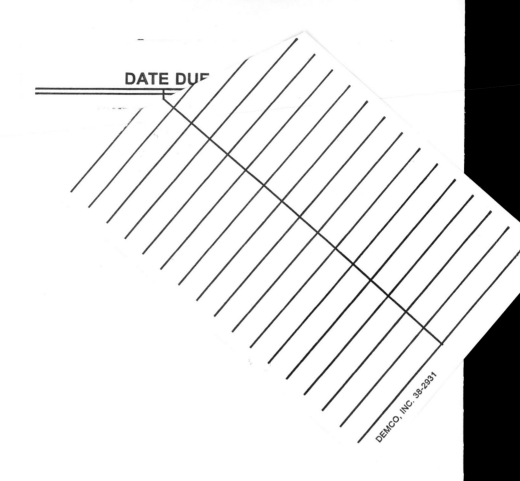

DATE DUE

DEMCO, INC. 38-2931